Moral Courage in Organizations

Moral Courage in Organizations

Doing the Right Thing at Work

Editors

Debra R. Comer and Gina Vega

Routledge
Taylor & Francis Group

LONDON AND NEW YORK

First published 2011 by M.E. Sharpe

Published 2015 by Routledge
2 Park Square, Milton Park, Abingdon, Oxon OX14 4RN
711 Third Avenue, New York, NY 10017, USA

Routledge is an imprint of the Taylor & Francis Group, an informa business

Library of Congress Cataloging-in-Publication Data

Moral courage in organizations : doing the right thing at work / Debra R. Comer and
Gina Vega, editors
    p. cm.
Includes bibliographical references and index.
ISBN 978-0-7656-2409-3 (hbk. : alk. paper)
1. Business ethics. 2. Courage. 3. Organizational behavior—Moral and ethical aspects.
4. Work—Moral and ethical aspects. 5. Employees—Conduct of life. I. Comer, Debra R.,
1960– II. Vega, Gina.

HF5387.M645 2011
174′.4—dc22   2010027705

ISBN 13: 9780765624109 (pbk)
ISBN 13: 9780765624093 (hbk)

CV 08.19.2019 1838

Dedication

DRC: In memory of my beloved father and mother, Dr. Nathan and Rita Comer, who showed me the importance of moral courage.

GV: In memory of Pat Primeaux, SM—my "rabbi," dear friend, mentor, and inspiration.

I am most pleased when I hear the stories of those of you who have fought the good fight and in the end, usually after much personal sacrifice and hardship, are vindicated.

The fight for justice against corruption is never easy. It never has been and never will be. It exacts a toll on our self, our families, our friends, and especially our children. In the end, I believe, as in my case, the price we pay is well worth holding on to our dignity. You are an example to others, and it is my belief that many of those who have yielded to temptation secretly admire your courage and envy your honesty.

—Frank Serpico

Contents

Foreword

Moses L. Pava

This volume on "moral courage" is a joy to read and study. Debra Comer and Gina Vega have collected, organized, and edited a group of essays written by several prominent contributors on an important and timely topic that is often overlooked in discussions on business ethics.

As teachers of business ethics, we spend a great deal of time deliberating about the right course of action to pursue in a given set of circumstances, as if, magically, once we have the "correct" answer, the solution will implement itself. But business managers tend to compensate employees who take outsized risks in pursuit of maximizing profits, not those who demonstrate strength of moral character. We therefore need to spend more of our time contemplating how and why it is that some people seem to get it right (at least sometimes) and others take the path of least resistance or the one that leads to the most organizational rewards.

We often encourage students to engage in lively theoretical discussions about what is right and what is wrong, but we almost never talk about what truly motivates us as investors, employees, consumers, managers, and human beings. Talk of emotions is bracketed out of the dialogue. Business schools simplify the complexities of human behavior in order to make it easier for us to model, control, and predict economic behavior. Students who study our textbooks may take them seriously, read them literally (even if we don't), and assume that such simplifications provide an accurate picture of how people "really" behave in business. When I ask my accounting students about corporate social responsibility, for example, they tell me that corporate social responsibility is merely rhetoric designed to fool environmentalists, consumer advocates, and other do-gooders. And, if you believe the explicit messages of finance and accounting textbooks and have internalized their implicit messages, the students are right.

Reading this book provides a different, more positive perspective for academics, managers, and students to consider. It describes a world where people can act for the greater good, at least on occasion, and under the right set of circumstances. Human behavior is understood as complex, uncertain, and multilayered. People are not like the stick figures of economic textbooks who always promote their own interests, nor is it assumed that they will always do the right thing, once they know what it is they are supposed to do. This book encourages us to do the right thing, but it reminds us that there is often a huge gap between knowledge and action. Moral action is often costly to the decision maker, and this volume puts this insight front and center.

Moral courage, like moral imagination, is one of those big, provocative ideas that ask us to rethink our old theories and comfortable ideas. As a society, it seems that we have always understood the importance of courage in dealing with physical threats and obstacles. From the earliest grades in school, we are taught to honor military heroes and astronauts. Football stars and racecar drivers are our children's and our own contemporary heroes. More people watched Super Bowl XLIV, played in February 2010, than any other television program in history. We stand in awe at the daring behavior of our soldiers and athletes. We wonder how it is that they act with such seeming calm and poise in the face of real danger and risks to their physical survival.

This book on moral courage in organizations challenges some of our most closely held beliefs. Who is to be held in our highest esteem? Is it a whistleblower who risks his or her job to protect the rest of us from tobacco companies that hide scientific findings linking cigarette smoking to disease, or a baseball player who doesn't flinch in the face of a hundred-mile-an-hour fastball? In the end, the whistleblower is often viewed with suspicion and sometimes even with contempt. We wonder, "Why did he or she wait until *now* to come forward? What are the whistleblower's *real* motives?" The fate of the courageous baseball player, by contrast, is usually fame and fortune (at least, while he can still hit).

Moral courage is the fuel that helps us to do the right thing, even when it is painful and when there will be no accolades awaiting us at the end of the day. Moral courage is an evocative concept that has generated many interesting questions, as the chapters of this book make plain. It is one of those interesting ideas that generate other interesting ideas. At the same time, it is not so open-ended as to elude scientific scrutiny and systematic study. The authors of this volume operationalize the concept ably and examine it with both imagination and rigor.

It is not always easy to summon moral courage. In the face of personal loss, we begin to ask all kinds of questions: How do I know my action will make a difference? Is there any guarantee that if I do the right thing, others will join with me? Why should I do something, when our own leaders seem apathetic and lost? And, how do I even know that I'm right in the first place? To help promote moral courage, we need role models and stories, in addition to systematic thinking. This volume provides many examples of those role models and helps us to begin to answer some of these questions. The chapters in this book whet our appetite for continued study, encourage us to examine our own behavior, and help us to begin to bridge the gap between our aspirations and our actions.

This book is dedicated, in part, to the memory of Patrick Primeaux, a premier teacher of business ethics and a longtime chair of the Theology Department at St. John's University in New York City. For this reason it is truly a special pleasure and privilege that I have the opportunity to write this foreword. Pat, one of my closest friends for many years, dedicated his career to serving others and bringing others into the circle of his love. In my own case, he encouraged me to write and speak not only with my intellect, but with my heart as well. He had a profound influence on how I teach and think about business ethics. I know he had such influence on many other colleagues and hundreds of students over the years. I remember the time he visited me in Massachusetts and reached my house before I got there. My father let Pat into the house, and in the thirty-minute gap between his arrival and mine, he and my father had already become fast friends.

In the last year of Pat's life, he and I talked many times on the telephone. Although Pat knew he was dying, *he* would often cheer *me* up with his wisdom, sense of humor, and compassion. When others might have been desperate and bitter, he was calm and assured and concerned for his friends. Similarly, Pat put others' needs before his own when he was well. He was a person of deep and abiding faith who always spoke truth to power, taking risks for what he believed was right. Where does such strength come from? How does one develop and nurture one's own moral courage and pass it on to others? Pat gives us hope, encouragement, and tangible proof that even if we don't yet have all the answers to these questions, it is possible for us to rise above our own egos and our own interests and to do the right thing.

Acknowledgments

We, together and individually, would like to acknowledge everyone who played a part in making this book happen.

First, we pay tribute to a few people at M.E. Sharpe, Inc., especially Harry Briggs, our executive editor, for believing in our book from the start and guiding us without hovering; and Elizabeth Granda, whose uncommon facility with detail (in a culture that denigrates this vital ability) and unfailing follow-through are rivaled only by her pleasantness. Additionally, we thank Ana Erlić, our Production Editor; and Susan Burke, our Copy Editor.

We thank Moses Pava, for his heartfelt foreword; and our fellow contributors—Rick Bagozzi, Susan Baker, David Callahan, Mary Gentile, Al Gini, Roland Kidwell, Steve Kohn, Jeff MacDonald, Bernie Matt, Dan McCarthy, Dennis Moberg, Leslie Sekerka, Nasrin Shahinpoor, Judy Spain, and Judith White—without whose ideas and efforts this book would not have been possible.

Special Acknowledgments from Debbie Comer

I acknowledge the Zarb School of Business and Hofstra University, for supporting my work on this book. I received a summer research grant in 2008 to develop the book proposal, as well as a reduced course load in the fall of 2009 and a sabbatical in the spring of 2010 to provide time for writing and editing. I am grateful to Gina Vega, for agreeing to join me in this project; to Susan Baker, for believing that perfection should be pursued, even though it won't be achieved; and to Janet Lenaghan, for asking about (and listening to reports on) my progress. I thank my husband, Jim, for his love, advice, and support—and for always caring more about doing the right thing than about what other people think; and our precious sons, Rudy and Jake, for learning to wait patiently whenever they heard, "I'm in the middle of a thought!"—and, most of all, for their immeasurable love.

Special Acknowledgments from Gina Vega

I acknowledge the Bertolon School of Business, for giving me a course release to work on some of the more challenging elements of producing this book; and my husband, Robert, for his encouragement, patience, listening to my lengthy ramblings, and his proofreading and copyediting of my work.

Introduction

Why Moral Courage Matters in Organizations

Debra R. Comer and Gina Vega

Something's Missing from Ethics Instruction

In spite of stepped-up attention to ethics training and education since the scandals of the 1990s, more than half of the employees surveyed by the Ethics Resource Center witnessed misconduct in their private-sector, nonprofit, and government workplaces within the past year.[1] Conflicts of interest, abusive or intimidating behavior, and lying topped the list of most frequently observed forms of misconduct; financial fraud was not far behind.[2] Why is ethics instruction not working?

The Status Quo

Much of the education and training in ethics tries to develop individuals' ability to identify and to become sensitive to the variety of ethical issues in the workplace,[3] and to use moral philosophical frameworks to reason critically about them.[4] The premise, or at least the hope,[5] of a typical course in business or professional ethics or a standard organizational ethics training program seems to be that advising students or employees to pay attention to ethical considerations and to harness the ideas of moral philosophers will help ensure that they display morally stellar behavior. Of course, it is worthwhile to be mindful of the ethical implications of our own and others' actions and to be able to apply the ideas of Aristotle, Kant, Mills, and other great thinkers to make sense of ethical questions in organizations. But because *knowing* the right thing to do is not the same as *doing* the right thing, it is also important to focus on the factors contributing to the discrepancy between moral reasoning and moral behavior in the workplace.

Moral Courage: The Missing Ingredient

Two factors contribute to this knowing-acting gap: (1) moral motivation, the desire to put moral considerations above other concerns; and (2) moral courage.[6] Suppose that Lil and Bill face the same ethical situation at their workplace and that both know what the morally correct path is. Lil has low moral motivation and is therefore indifferent about pursuing the principled path, but Bill has high moral motivation and wants to take it.[7] Nevertheless, he may reject the moral path if it involves personal hardship or even mere inconvenience.[8] Indeed, in order for moral behavior to match moral judgment, moral motivation is necessary but insufficient. A person also needs *moral courage*, "the resolve to act on moral convictions even when it is not comfortable or self-serving to do so."[9] Moral courage is what "compels or allows an individual to do what he or she believes is right, despite fear of social or economic consequences."[10] Just as acts of moral courage are exceptional,[11] the topic of moral courage receives scant, if any, attention in most ethics classes.

It would be futile to try to change the values and principles of immoral individuals, who, bereft of moral motivation, have no interest in behaving honorably.[12] At the same time, those who *do* want to behave with integrity are shortchanged by ethics classes that underestimate or even ignore how the realities of the workplace can sometimes dissuade them from following their sound moral reasoning and good intentions. "Organizations can . . . make moral behavior much more difficult,"[13] but this book is designed to equip decent people—that is, those who have solid values, know what is right, and want to take the high road—with the knowledge and skills to act with moral courage. Enhancing the moral courage of those who want to do the right thing is the sensible way to foster more ethical behavior in the workplace.

A defining criterion of moral courage is the actor's recognition that abiding by values and principles is likely to lead to some personally unpleasant consequences.[14] Consider three classic stories—"The Emperor's New Clothes,"[15] "The Balek Scales,"[16] and *Horton Hears a Who*.[17] The child who points out the unclad emperor does not display moral courage. The adult townspeople's collective insecurity makes them easy marks for the swindling pseudo-weavers, who claim that only the wise can see their special fabric.[18] But the child, too innocent to be fooled, merely speaks the truth. In contrast, Franz Brücher, the preteen protagonist who discovers that the Baleks' rigged scale has cheated his peasant family and their neighbors for generations, does act with moral courage. Franz is aware of the perilous repercussions of blowing the whistle on the landed gentry, but outrageous injustice compels him to take action. Horton, the auditorily advantaged elephant, also displays moral courage. Horton vows to protect the microscopic residents of Who-ville. Because the other animals cannot hear the Whos' small voices, they question Horton's sanity and taunt, assault, and even attempt to imprison him. Through all of this, Horton steadfastly shelters his new friends until he can prove their existence.

Moral Courage in Organizations

A 2009 newspaper article reported that graduates of some business schools have pledged to behave ethically.[19] But promises of good behavior can be difficult to keep—especially by those who do not prepare for the traps that can derail sterling intentions. It is important to recognize that organizations do not always welcome their members' principled actions and may, instead, present obstacles to right action.[20] Organizational pressures can compromise our moral behavior,[21] and we may be more vulnerable to these pressures than we would (like to) think.[22]

To rise above these pressures, we need to understand and foster moral courage. The chapters in this book contain the observations, insights, and recommendations of people who have explored the impact of organizational context on ethical behavior in the workplace and the ways in which members of organizations can deal with situational factors that conspire against their behaving according to their ethical principles.

Overview of the Book

The chapters that follow focus on the organizational challenges we will (continue to) encounter as we struggle to do the right thing and present tools and ideas that we can apply to our organizational careers and personal lives. The book has four sections, followed by a final integrative section.

Part I. The Organizational Pressures That Make Moral Courage Necessary

The chapters of Part I make the case that moral courage matters because the workplace so often threatens to compromise our principles. In chapter 1, Al Gini draws eclectically from contemporary social science to portray the organizational elements that compete with our sense of right and wrong—and urges us to consider other people's needs and not just our own. In chapter 2, David Callahan responds to Debra R. Comer's questions about the implications of "the cheating culture" on moral courage in organizations by discussing the societal conditions that cause us to abandon our principles, as well as the changes that could bring about more ethical behavior. We close Part I by presenting, in chapter 3, our concept of the Personal Ethical Threshold (PET), the point at which each one of us succumbs to organizational pressures. We describe the processes by which we come to yield to these pressures—even when we would rather do the right thing.

Part II. The Faces of Moral Courage

Part II offers examples of individuals who have acted with moral courage, that is, those who have adhered to their values and principles in spite of unpleasant personal consequences—and those who have not. Gina Vega's chapter 4 explores some of this century's scandals, scams, and misguided beliefs to highlight how giving in to temptation instead of honoring one's values has contributed to current economic and social failures. The other chapters in this section illustrate moral courage in varied organizational situations. Stephen M. Kohn, in chapter 5, looks at employee whistleblowers who often pay a steep personal price for challenging unethical behavior in their own organizations to try to protect others from harm. In chapter 6, G. Jeffrey MacDonald considers the relationship between religious or spiritual faith and moral courage, asking whether individuals who feel a calling are more likely to follow their convictions in the workplace. The remaining two chapters of Part II feature individuals who run organizations that require them to act with moral courage. Roland E. Kidwell introduces us in chapter 7 to Wyoming-based social entrepreneurs, who have traded in the typical self-oriented goal of amassing personal wealth to start and sustain businesses that improve the lives of others in their communities. In chapter 8, Judith White discusses the moral courage of NGO leaders who risk their lives in their quest to secure human rights and democracy in Burma.

Part III. The Skills and Information That Enable Moral Courage

Part III addresses the skills and information needed to enact moral courage. Mary C. Gentile's chapter 9 discusses how preparation and practice can give employees the proficiency and confidence to behave in accordance with their values. In chapter 10, Leslie E. Sekerka, Justin D. McCarthy, and Richard P. Bagozzi draw from the experiences of military officers to identify the component competencies of moral courage and then recommend ways to develop these competencies. Judy Spain's chapter 11 concludes this section of the book by clarifying the legal rights and remedies that help to protect employees who act with moral courage.

Part IV. Changing Organizations with Moral Courage

Part IV focuses on changing organizations from the top down to promote moral courage and exercising moral courage to change organizations from the bottom up. Chapter 12, by Bernard F. Matt and Nasrin Shahinpoor, examines the contributions of conscientious dissenters who call attention to organizational misbehavior and recommends what organizations can do to make dissent an everyday part of their culture. Debra R. Comer and Susan D. Baker's chapter 13 explores how individuals can form a morally courageous coalition and provides advice for those seeking to effect bottom-up change to make their organizations more ethical. In chapter 14, Dennis J. Moberg describes the organizational conditions that managers can cultivate to support their employees' expressions of courage.

Finally, in chapter 15, we review and integrate the ideas of the previous chapters to leave you with a set of guidelines for acting with moral courage in organizations.

Of Courage and Coffee Beans

Some years ago, one of us received via e-mail a charming parable,[23] which she has adapted for use with her students. An abbreviated version follows:

> A woman asks her adult grandson to follow her into the kitchen, where she fills three pots with water and boils the water in each. In the first pot of boiling water she places carrots, in the second she places eggs, and in the third she places ground coffee beans. After several minutes, she turns off the heat. She removes the carrots from the first pot and places them in a bowl, scoops the eggs out of the second and places them in another bowl, and ladles the coffee into a third bowl.
>
> The woman emphasizes to her grandson that each of these three substances has encountered boiling water, but has reacted differently. She asks him, "How do *you* respond to adversity? Are you the carrot that initially seems sturdy, but wilts and loses its strength? Are you the egg, becoming embittered after your formerly fluid interior hardens? Or are you like the ground coffee beans, which change the very condition that brings the pain? The boiling water releases their fragrance and flavor. If you are like the ground coffee beans, then, as you confront difficulties, you improve as you enrich the situation around you."

The display of moral courage engenders a happy outcome in *Horton Hears a Who*: after Horton demonstrates that there are Whos in Who-ville, his erstwhile enemies decide to join him in safeguarding his new friends.[24] In contrast, Franz's morally courageous act in "The Balek Scales" has horrific consequences: his little sister is killed during a raid by the police; he and his remaining family members must leave their village; and the Baleks continue to use their fraudulent scale.

In *To Kill a Mockingbird*, fictional small-town attorney Atticus Finch explains (moral) courage to his young children: "It's when you know you're licked before you begin but you begin anyway and you see it through no matter what. You rarely win but sometimes you do."[25] We admire these noble sentiments, but would not ask (nor would we want) you, our reader, to martyr yourself or even to waste your efforts. Instead, we offer this book to help you to understand and practice moral courage in ways that will enable you to realize your ethical goals. It is our hope that the chapters in this volume will inspire and guide you to respond in ground-coffee-bean style to workplace pressures that threaten to compromise your values and principles. When we act with moral courage, we do the right thing for ourselves and our organizations.

Notes

1. Ethics Resource Center, 2008a, 2008b, 2008c. We thank Susan D. Baker for bringing these survey results to our attention.

2. Ibid.

3. Gautschi and Jones, 1998; Morris, 2001; Williams and Dewett, 2005.

4. Brady, 1999; Fort and Zollers, 1999; Meisel and Fearon, 2006; Morris, 2001; Sims, 2002.

5. Marino (2004, B5) would call this premise a "fantasy."

6. Rest, 1994.

7. Aquino and Reed, 2002; Blasi, 1984.

8. Batson and Thompson, 2001.

9. Roussouw, 2002, 414.

10. Peterson and Seligman, 2004, p. 216; see also Kidder, 2005; Mahoney, 1998; Miller, 2000; and Solomon, 1999.

11. Ozick, 1992.

12. As Schonsheck quipped, "[I]f I had indeed figured out how to transform bad people into good people, I would be in a much more lucrative profession" (2009, 48).

13. Roussouw, 2002, 415.

14. According to Kidder (2005), moral courage involves an awareness of and willingness to endure these negative outcomes for the sake of one's principles.

15. Andersen, 1837/1959.

16. Böll, 1972.

17. Geisel, 1954.

18. The townspeople, who contradicted their perceptions in order to conform to the majority, remind us of many of the participants in the experiments of Asch (1955, 1956).

19. Wayne, 2009.

20. Mahoney, 1998; Moberg, 2006.

21. Comer and Vega, 2005, 2006, 2008.

22. Nordgren, van Harreveld, and van der Pligt, 2009; also see Sayette et al., 2008. Indeed, Andreoli and Lefkowitz (2009) found a relationship between encountering such pressures and behaving unethically.

23. Although this story has been attributed to Mary Sullivan, most online references state that its authorship is unknown.

24. "After all, a person's a person. No matter how small" (Geisel, 1954).

25. Lee, 1960, 128.

References

Andersen, H.C. 1837/1959. *The emperor's new clothes*, trans. and illus. E. Blegvad. New York: Harcourt.

Andreoli, N., and Lefkowitz, J. 2009. Individual and organizational antecedents of misconduct in organizations. *Journal of Business Ethics* 85(3), 309–332.

Aquino, K., and Reed, A. 2002. The self-importance of moral identity. *Journal of Personality and Social Psychology* 83(6), 1423–1440.

Asch, S.E. 1955. Opinions and social pressure. *Scientific American* 193(5), 31–35.

———. 1956. Studies of independence and conformity: I. A minority of one against a unanimous majority. *Psychological Monographs: General and Applied* 70(9), 1–36.

Batson, C.D., and Thompson, E.R. 2001. Why don't people act morally? Motivational considerations. *Current Directions in Psychological Science* 10(2), 54–57.

Blasi, A. 1984. Moral identity: Its role in moral functioning. In *Morality, moral behavior, and moral development,* ed. W. Kurtines, and J.L. Gewirtz, 128–139. New York: John Wiley & Sons.

Böll, H. 1972. The Balek scales. In *Classic short fiction: An international collection,* ed. J.K. Bowen and R. Van Der Beets, 398–405. New York: Bobbs-Merrill.

Brady, F.N. 1999. A systematic approach to teaching ethics in business. *Journal of Business Ethics* 19(3), 309–318.

Comer, D.R., and Vega, G. 2005. An experiential exercise that introduces the concept of the Personal Ethical Threshold to develop moral courage. *Journal of Business Ethics Education* 2(2), 171–198.

———. 2006. Unsavory problems at Tasty's: An experiential exercise about whistle-blowing. *Journal of Management Education* 30(1), 251–269.

———. 2008. Using the PET assessment instrument to help students identify factors that could impede their moral behavior. *Journal of Business Ethics* 77(2), 129–145.

Ethics Resource Center. 2008a. *National Business Ethics Survey®: An inside view of private sector ethics.* Arlington, VA: Ethics Resource Center.

———. 2008b. *National Government Ethics Survey®: An inside view of public sector ethics.* Arlington, VA: Ethics Resource Center.

———. 2008c. *National Nonprofit Ethics Survey®: An inside view of nonprofit sector ethics.* Arlington, VA: Ethics Resource Center.

Fort, T.L., and Zollers, F.E. 1999. Teaching business ethics: Theory and practice. *Teaching Business Ethics* 2(3), 273–290.

Gautschi, F.H., III, and Jones, T.M. 1998. Enhancing the ability of business students to recognize ethical issues: An empirical assessment of the effectiveness of a course in business ethics. *Journal of Business Ethics* 17(2), 205–216.

Geisel, T.S. 1954. *Horton hears a Who!* New York: Random House.

Kidder, R.M. 2005. *Moral courage.* New York: HarperCollins.

Lee, H. 1960. *To kill a mockingbird.* New York: HarperCollins.

Mahoney, J. 1998. "Editorial adieu": Cultivating moral courage in business. *Business Ethics: A European Review* 7(4), 187–192.

Marino, G. 2004. Before teaching ethics, stop kidding yourself. *Chronicle of Higher Education,* February 20, Observer section, B5.

Meisel, S.I., and Fearon, D.S. 2006. "Choose the future wisely": Supporting better ethics through critical thinking. *Journal of Management Education* 30(1), 149–176.

Miller, W.I. 2000. The mystery of courage. Cambridge, MA: Harvard University Press.

Moberg, D.J. 2006. Best intentions, worst realities: Grounding ethics students in the realities of organizational context. *Academy of Management Learning & Education* 5(3), 307–316.

Morris, D. 2001. Business ethics assessment criteria: Business v. philosophy—survey results. *Business Ethics Quarterly* 11(4), 623–650.

Nordgren, L.F., van Harreveld, F., and van der Pligt, J. 2009. The restraint bias: How the illusion of self-restraint promotes impulsive behavior. *Psychological Science* 20(12), 1523–1528.

Ozick, C. 1992. Prologue. In *Rescuers: Portraits of moral courage in the Holocaust,* by M. Drucker and G. Block, xi–xvi. New York: Holmes & Meier.

Peterson, C., and Seligman, M.E.P. 2004. *Character strengths and virtues: A handbook and classification.* Washington, DC: American Psychological Association.

Rest, J. 1994. Background: Theory and research. In *Moral development in the professions: Psychology and applied ethics,* ed. J.R. Rest, and D. Narvaez, 1–26. Hillsdale, NJ: Lawrence Erlbaum Associates.

Roussouw, G.J. 2002. Three approaches to teaching business ethics. *Teaching Business Ethics* 6(4), 411–433.

Sayette, M.A., Loewenstein, G., Griffin, K.M., and Black, J.J. 2008. Exploring the cold-to-hot empathy gap in smokers. *Psychological Science* 19(9), 926–932.

Schonsheck, J. 2009. Pillars of virtue. *BizEd* 8(3), 46–50.

Sims, R.R. 2002. *Teaching business ethics for effective learning.* Westport, CT: Quorum.

Solomon, R. 1999. *A better way to think about business: How personal integrity leads to corporate success.* New York: Oxford University Press.

Wayne, L. 2009. A promise to be ethical in an era of temptation. *New York Times,* May 30, Business section, B1, B4.

Williams, S.D., and Dewett, T. 2005. Yes, you can teach business ethics: A review and research agenda. *Journal of Leadership and Organizational Studies* 12(2), 109–120.

Moral Courage in Organizations

Part I

The Organizational Pressures That Make Moral Courage Necessary

1

A Short Primer on Moral Courage

AL GINI

It is curious—curious that physical courage should be so common in the world, and moral courage so rare.

—Mark Twain

In a colloquial sense, the concept of courage is usually associated with acts of daring deeds that involve danger, risk, and behavior that overcomes seemingly insurmountable obstacles and odds. The word "courage" conjures up images of individuals' performing difficult actions while risking physical injury or death. A courageous act is one in which the actor disregards concern for personal safety or well-being and exerts himself or herself in the service of another. The courageous act is seen as the heroic act. In popular culture, we use the word "hero" to honor soldiers, firefighters, rescue workers, and, sometimes perhaps inappropriately, even athletes who are severely tested and challenged in the heat of competition. From this perspective, courage is a supra virtue, an extraordinary achievement, and not part of the common repertoire of traits and behaviors associated with the more mundane and pedestrian aspects of our lives.

From a psychoanalytic perspective, Ernest Becker deconstructs our commonsensical definition of courage to mean not an altruistic concern for others but rather a myopic preoccupation with self. Becker argues that the "primary mainspring" of human action is not the pursuit of sex, as Freud proposed, but rather the pursuit of "distractions" that will counterbalance our overwhelming fear of the immensity of eternity and the awareness of our finitude. As a species, says Becker, human beings have a basic existential dilemma: we are both burdened and blessed with a paradoxical nature, half animal and half symbolic. That means that we are simultaneously aware of the possibility of infinity and the absolute certainty that we are finite. We live our whole lifetimes, said Becker, with the "fate of death haunting our dreams" even on the "most sun-filled days."[1]

3

The idea of death, says Becker, the fear of it, haunts us like nothing else. It is the "motivating principle" of human activity. And all human activity is consciously and unconsciously designed to deny and combat our fear and terror of death.[2] "The painful riddle of death" haunts us, says Becker, causing us mental and physical grief and despair. Our fear wears us out, and so, says Becker, out of necessity we seek to repress it, sublimate it, take it off the table of our immediate sense of consciousness. We create mental defenses, illusions, myths, stories, tasks, crusades, causes, work, rituals, and bizarre behaviors to distract us from our discomfort and despair. Becker writes that the most dramatic way to deny the terror of death is to act as if fear means nothing to us, as if we are not helpless and abandoned in the world and fated for oblivion. If we cannot beat death, we can at least temporarily ignore and deny it through culturally sanctioned heroic acts as well as outrageous acts of violence and evil. For Becker, it is only in choosing to act that we assert our "being" and, at least temporarily, overcome "nothingness." Heroism, he writes, "is first and foremost a reflex of terror and death. We admire most the courage to face death; we give such valor our highest and most constant adoration; it moves us deeply in our hearts because we have doubts about how brave we ourselves would be. . . . Man has elevated animal courage to a cult."[3]

Becker argues that the "hero project" is a pose, a learned character trait, a grand illusion, and a "neurotic defense against despair."[4] In the "hero project," we put on the "character armor" (William Reich's term) of the action hero, "lay away" our fears, and pretend to make the world more manageable. Evoking William James's notion of acting oneself into being, the hero, through his or her actions, seeks reinforcement of self, recognition, unabashed self-esteem, ersatz immortality, and, if possible, cosmic significance. For Becker, hero acts are neither selfless nor sincere. They are, rather, sublimated forms of escapist behavior.

Neither Becker's description of courage nor our colloquial understanding of it captures the essence of "courage" or "moral courage" accurately from an ethical point of view. To paraphrase the words of Winston Churchill, moral courage is the first of the human qualities because it is the quality that guarantees all others.[5] Courage is not an extra or a supernumerary virtue, but rather a critical human quality that serves as a necessary precondition for all other forms of moral conduct. Moral courage is the readiness to endure danger for the sake of principle.[6] Moral courage rejects voyeurism and seeks engagement. Moral courage is a stimulus, a catalyst for action. As Nelson Mandela has suggested, moral courage is not the absence of fear; rather, it is the strength to triumph over one's fear and to act.[7] Moral courage is the ability to transcend fear and endure risk to put ethics into actual practice. It means standing up and standing out in defense of a principle. Without it, ethics would simply be a naming noun, and not an action verb. Sadly, however, as Robert F. Kennedy so poignantly phrased it, "moral courage is a more rare commodity than bravery in battle or great intelligence. Yet it is the one essential, vital quality of those who seek to change a world which yields most painfully to change."[8]

The Problem of Ethics

It is not a lack of moral reasoning that causes so much unethical behavior, but rather a lack of moral engagement, or a lack of moral courage.[9] There is insufficient willingness to take on ethical issues and questions, to extend ourselves, to put ourselves in harm's way because we are concerned about the well-being of others.

Publicly, we may live lives that are economically and electronically interconnected and interdependent, but privately, we are emotionally and ethically withdrawn, insensitive to the wants and needs of others. If we care about anyone else at all, it is only after we have first taken care of our own self-centered desires and interests.

People find it hard to do the right thing because they find it hard "to stand outside the shadow of self."[10] Ethical behavior is possible only when we are able to step away from ourselves or, to borrow a phrase, "to forget [about] ourselves on purpose."[11] We must be able to see beyond our self-contained universe of personal concerns. We must be able to become, if only momentarily, more selfless than selfish. Ethics requires recognition that we are not alone or at the center of the universe. Ethics is always about self in the context of others. Ethics must be open to the voice of others; being ethical begins with having the courage to stand outside of the needs of self and to talk and listen to others.

Without moral courage to propel us forward, we become captives of our own needs and desires. We become prisoners enclosed in the fortress of self. Getting free of self, overcoming our natural tendency to put ourselves first in our interactions with others, is the central problem and paradox of communal existence. Although the terms "narcissism" and "narcissistic type" do not often come up in conversations about ethics, these concepts neatly encapsulate why it is so hard to get free of the shadow of self.

Narcissists do not see past their own needs and wants. They have a heightened sense of self-importance and grandiose feelings that they are unique in some way. They consider themselves special people and expect special treatment. They always want their own way and are frequently ambitious, desiring fame and fortune. Their relationships with others are fragile and limited. They are unable to show empathy, and they feign sympathy with others only to achieve their own selfish ends. Interpersonal exploitation is commonplace. The narcissist is totally self-absorbed and either cannot or will not focus on or imagine the needs of others.[12]

Ethical decision making requires us to look beyond the immediate moment and beyond personal needs, desires, and wants to imagine the possible consequences of our choices and behavior on self and others. In its most elemental sense, moral imagination is about picturing various outcomes in our interactions with others. In some sense, moral imagination is a dramatic virtual rehearsal that allows us to examine and appraise different courses of action to determine the morally best thing to do. The capacity for empathy is crucial to moral imagination. As Adam Smith wrote, "As we have no immediate experience of what other men feel, we can form no idea of the manner in which they are affected, but by conceiving what we ourselves should feel in the situation."[13]

According to philosopher Patricia H. Werhane, a failure of this capacity—an inability to imagine and to be sympathetic to the needs, passions, and interests of others—is the main cause of moral ineptitudes. To sympathize is to place myself in another's situation, "not because of how that situation might affect me, but rather if I were that person, in that situation."[14] Using moral imagination allows us to be self-reflective, to step back from our situation so as to see it from another point of view. In taking such a perspective, says Werhane, a person tries to look at the world or herself from a more dispassionate perspective or from the point of view of an impartial, reasonable person who is not wholly absorbed with self. Within this perspective, which Werhane calls "a disengaged view from somewhere," these questions become obligatory:

1. What would a reasonable person judge is the right thing to do?
2. Could one defend this decision publicly?
3. What kind of precedent does this decision set?
4. Is this decision or action necessary?
5. Is this the least worst option?[15]

What Werhane is suggesting is that one must, in making an ethical decision, determine the answers to some crucial questions: What is at stake? What are the issues? Who else is involved? And what are the alternatives? Moral imagination allows us the possibility of addressing these questions from a perspective that is both inside and outside the box, a perspective that focuses on self and others.

Without the ability to see beyond the needs of self, we treat the rest of the world as other, as irrelevant, as inconsequential. This leitmotif completely ignores a whole series of questions. What are our obligations to the great sea of others, our neighbors? Are we obligated to help neighbors when doing so is reasonable and does not entail a serious inconvenience or risk of harm? Are we obligated to help neighbors where the price we pay may include the risk of inconvenience and/or great danger? Are we required to endanger ourselves for our neighbors? Finally, do we at least have a minimal responsibility to help our neighbors?

On March 13, 1964, at 3:15 A.M. on a brisk winter morning along a quiet, picturesque, respectable, tree-lined street in Kew Gardens of Queens, New York City, Catherine "Kitty" Genovese, the twenty-eight-year-old daughter of middle-class Italian-American parents, was brutally stabbed to death. At least three factors make Kitty Genovese's murder especially heinous and unforgettable. To begin with, it was a random act that occurred without rhyme or reason (the killer was simply out roaming the streets looking for "a little action"). The second startling aspect of this crime was its sheer brutality. In the course of three separate stabbing events, which lasted more than thirty-five minutes, Kitty endured at least seventeen wounds. Finally, and most horribly, Kitty Genovese's cries and death agonies were heard or seen by thirty-eight people living in the apartment buildings surrounding the crime scene, but none of them called the police or tried to help her.

These witnesses, these neighbors, these fellow human beings later explained their lack of action to the police by saying: "It was none of my business"; "So many, many [other] times in the night I heard screams"; "I'm not the police"; "I couldn't make out what she said"; "I just saw the guy kneeling over her"; "I thought it was some kids having fun"; "I thought there must have been thirty calls already"; "Frankly, we were afraid." And the saddest one of all: "I was tired."

As a newspaper reporter wrote:

> Four decades after her death, Kitty Genovese is remembered not so much as a human being but as a cultural catch phrase for inexcusable indifference. The term "The Genovese Syndrome" has now become synonymous with one of the worst aspects of urban existence. Too often, we are too frightened, too alienated, too self absorbed to get involved in helping a human being in dire trouble.[16]

The allied notions of narcissism, the inability to forget about ourselves on purpose, and the cool moral detachment of the bystander result in a myopic view of reality that reduces all moral calculations to the overly simplistic—"me, myself, and I."[17] And this syndrome of self-importance is pervasively found where we work, in what we do to earn a living, and in our ethical perspective on the purpose of business.

Work and Self

In this society, we have made a fetish out of being ambitious and achieving financial success. Competition and rugged individualism are part of our collective myth and mantra. Looking out for one's own best interest has become a way of life, even though it regularly means stepping on others in the process. Astonishingly, the notion that such behavior might be destructive to others as well as debasing to ourselves is rarely raised, let alone seriously considered. We live, seemingly, in a society that elevates laissez-faire to a national credo. As a consequence, it has become terribly easy to lose our way. And the only time we have to apologize for our misdeeds or the misfortune we cause others is if we get caught.

Too many of us believe that the stakes and standards involved in business are simply different from, more important than, and, perhaps, even antithetical to the principles and practices of ethics. Ethics is something we may preach and apply at home in our private lives, but not in business. After all, it would cost us position, prestige, profits, and prosperity. Just as it is difficult in our personal lives to keep our narcissism in check, the task becomes much more difficult in our work and our professional lives when cash, comfort, and sinecure are on the line.

Given the centrality of work in our lives—the sheer number of hours we put into the job, the money we make, the stuff it allows us to acquire, the kinds of status and success we can achieve on the job—how can work *not* affect our values and sense of ethics? How is it possible to retain a private sense of objectivity and impartiality and a respectful concern for others? How is it possible not to be co-opted by the needs and demands of the workplace? How is it possible to avoid being at least swayed, if not totally compromised, by the work environment that sustains us?

Work, all work, creates its own self-contained moral universe. Every job, good or bad, creates its own experiences, its own standards, its own pace, and its own self-defined *Weltanschauung* (worldview). Every job, depending on the intensity, depth, and duration of the individual worker's involvement, can have immediate and/or long-term effects on the worker. The habits we acquire on the job, what we are exposed to, what is demanded of us, and the pressure of peers can change, influence, and/or erode our personal conduct and standards. When everybody else in the workplace is doing "it" (whatever "it" is), is it not natural at least to ask yourself, "Why not me, too?"

Two writers who have eloquently explained the phenomenon of the institutional co-option of the individual worker on the job are Howard S. Schwartz and Robert Jackall.[18] Schwartz argues that corporations and businesses are not bastions of benign, community-oriented ethical reasoning, nor can they, because of the demands and requirements of business, be models of moral behavior.[19] The rule of business, says Schwartz, remains the survival of the fittest, and the goal of survival engenders a combative us-against-them mentality that condones getting ahead by any means necessary. Schwartz describes the phenomenon of "organizational totalitarianism": Organizations and the people who manage them create for themselves a self-contained, self-serving worldview, which rationalizes anything done on their behalf and does not require justification on any grounds outside of themselves.[20]

This narcissistic perspective, Schwartz suggests, imposes Draconian requirements on all participants in organizational life: do your work; achieve organizational goals; obey and exhibit loyalty to your superiors; disregard personal values and beliefs; obey the law when necessary, obfuscate it when possible; and deny internal or external information at odds with the stated organizational worldview. Within such a "totalitarian" logic, neither leaders nor followers operate as independent agents. To maintain their place or to get ahead, all must conform.

According to Robert Jackall, organizations are examples of "patrimonial bureaucracies," wherein "fealty relations of personal loyalty" are the rule of organizational life.[21] Jackall argues that all corporations are like fiefdoms of the Middle Ages, wherein the lord of the manor (CEO or president) offers protection, prestige, and status to his vassals (managers) and serfs (workers) in return for homage (commitment) and service (work). In such a system, says Jackall, advancement and promotion are predicated on loyalty, trust, politics, and personality at least as much as on experience, education, ability, and accomplishments. The central concern of the worker minion is to be known as the "can-do" employee, a "team player," being at the right place at the right time and "master of all the social rules." That is why in the corporate world, says Jackall, a thousand "attaboys" are wiped away with one "oh, shit!"[22]

Jackall contends that the logic of every organization and the collective personality of the workplace conspire to override the desires and aspirations of the individual worker. No matter what someone may believe off the job, on the job all of us are required to some extent to suspend, bracket, or conceal our personal convictions. "What is right in the corporation is not what is right in a man's home or his church. What is right in the corporation is what the guy above you wants from you."[23] The workplace tests what we believe in and are willing to act on. Too often we are left with options that are less than appealing: critique, capitulation, or compromise.

In Jackall's analysis, the primary imperative of every organization is to succeed. This goal of performance leads to the creation of a private moral universe that is self-defined, self-centered, and self-sustained. Within such an environment, moral behavior is determined solely by organizational needs. The key virtues for all are the virtues of the organization: goal preoccupation; problem solving; survival or success; and, most important, playing by the "house rules." In time, says Jackall, those initiated and invested in the system come to believe that they live in a self-contained world that is above external critique and evaluation. As sociologist Kathleen McCourt has suggested:

> It is difficult to be a good person in a society that is itself not good. People, after all, live and learn through the institutions of society—family, school, church, community, and the workplace—and these institutions must support the positive development of individuals if society is to produce succeeding generations of positive individuals.[24]

The Need to Overcome Self

We are not herd animals, but we are communal creatures. We are dependent on one another to survive and thrive. Good choices or bad choices, our collective existence requires that we continually make choices about "what we ought to do" in regard to others. Like it or not, we are by definition moral creatures. Ethics is primarily a communal, collective enterprise, not a solitary one. It is the study of our web of relationships with others. As a communal exercise, ethics is the attempt to work out the rights and obligations we have and share with others. Defining ethics is not difficult, but living ethically is. Why? Because ethics requires us to be concerned about the rights and well-being of others. It requires us to stop thinking of ourselves as the sole center of the universe. It requires us to transcend the simplistic equation of "me, myself, and I." It requires us to be just, reasonable, and objective. It requires us to be our rational selves in regard to others, to face personal inconvenience or even harm. It requires us to have the moral courage to live out what we value, what we hold dear, what we believe in.

Notes

Portions of this chapter are reprinted with the permission of Routledge.
1. Becker, 1997, 27, 36.
2. Becker, 1997.
3. Ibid., 11–12.
4. Ibid., 57.
5. Churchill, 1937, 218.
6. Kidder, 2005.
7. Stengel, 2008.
8. Kennedy, 1966.

9. Hendry, 2004.
10. Gini, 2006, 120.
11. Mahan, 2002.
12. Kaplan, Sadock, and Grebb, 1994.
13. Werhane, 1998, 81–82.
14. Ibid.
15. Werhane, 1998.
16. Pearlman, 2004, 14.
17. Gini, 2006, 11.
18. Matt and Shahinpoor, in chapter 12 of this book, discuss the ideas of Schwartz and Jackall with respect to squelching dissent in organizations.
19. Schwartz, 1990.
20. Schwartz, 1991.
21. Jackall, 1989, 11.
22. Ibid., 72.
23. Ibid., 6.
24. McCourt, 1994.

References

Becker, E. 1997. *The denial of death*. New York: Free Press.
Churchill, W.S. 1937. *Great contemporaries*. New York: Putnam.
Gini, A. 2006. *Why it's hard to be good*. New York: Routledge.
Hendry, J. 2004. *Between enterprise and ethics*. New York: Oxford University Press.
Jackall, R. 1989. *Moral mazes*. New York: Oxford University Press.
Kaplan, H., Sadock, B., and Grebb, J. 1994. *Synopsis of psychiatry*, 7th ed. Baltimore: Williams and Wilkins.
Kennedy, R.F.K. 1966. Day of Affirmation Address, University of Capetown, June 6, Capetown, South Africa.
Kidder, R. 2005. *Moral courage*. New York: HarperCollins.
Mahan, B.J. 2002. *Forgetting ourselves on purpose: Vocation and the ethics of ambition*. San Francisco: Jossey-Bass.
Matt, B.F., and Shahinpoor, N. 2011. Speaking truth to power: The courageous organizational dissenter. In *Moral courage in organizations: Doing the right thing at work*, ed. D.R. Comer and G. Vega, 157–170. Armonk, NY: M.E. Sharpe.
McCourt, K. 1994. College students in a changing society: Learning from the past, preparing for the future. Discourse and leadership in service to others in Jesuit higher education. Keynote speech at the Heartland Conference, May, Loyola University, Chicago.
Pearlman, J. 2004. Infamous '64 murder lives in heart of woman's "friend." *Chicago Tribune*, March 12, Section I.
Schwartz, H. 1990. *Narcissistic process and corporate decay: The theory of the organization ideal*. New York: New York University Press.
———. 1991. Narcissism project and corporate decay: The case of General Motors. *Business Ethics Quarterly* 1(3), 249–268.
Stengel, R. 2008. Mandela: His 8 lessons of leadership. *Time*, July 9, 23.
Werhane, P.H. 1998. Moral imagination and the search for ethical decision making in management. *Business Ethics Quarterly*, Ruffin Series (1), 75–98.

Additional Readings

Blackburn, S. 2003. *Ethics: A very short introduction*. New York: Oxford University Press.
———. 1999. *Think: A compelling introduction to philosophy*. New York: Oxford University Press.
Carr, D. 1998. The cardinal virtues and Plato's moral psychology. *Philosophical Quarterly* 38(151), 186–200.
Coles, R. 2000. *Lives of moral leadership*. New York: Random House.
Cox, D., La Caze, M., and Levine, M. 2008. Integrity. In *The Stanford encyclopedia of philosophy* (Fall 2008 Edition), ed. E.N. Zalta. http://plato.stanford.edu/archives/fall2008/entries/integrity/, accessed July 24, 2009.
Craig, E. 1998. *Routledge encyclopedia of philosophy*. London: Routledge.
Cunningham, S.B. 1985. The courageous villain: A needless paradox. *The Modern Schoolman* 62, 97–110.
Grant, C. 2002. Whistleblowers: The saints of secular culture. *Journal of Business Ethics* 39(4), 391–399.
Kidder, R. 2003. *How good people make tough choices: Resolving the dilemmas of ethical living*. New York: HarperCollins.
Lowney, C. 2003. *Heroic leadership*. Chicago: Loyola Press.
McCoy, B.H. 2007. *Living into leadership: A journey in ethics*. Stanford: Stanford University Press.
Miller, W.I. 2000. *The mystery of courage*. Cambridge: Harvard University Press.
———. 2002. *Lincoln's virtues: An ethical biography*. New York: Alfred A. Knopf.
Monroe, K.R. 2001. Morality and a sense of self: The importance of the identity and categorization for moral action. *American Journal of Political Science* 45(3), 491–507.
Roberts, R.C. 1984. Willpower and the virtues. *Philosophical Review* 93(2), 227–247.
Wills, G. 1994. *Certain trumpets: The call of leaders*. New York: Simon & Schuster.

2

"But Everybody's Doing It"

Implications of the Cheating Culture for Moral Courage in Organizations

DAVID CALLAHAN AND DEBRA R. COMER

David Callahan, author of *The Cheating Culture*, has characterized the pervasive cheating across occupations and institutions as a "profound moral crisis that reflects deep economic and social problems in American society" and has asserted that "Americans are not only cheating more in many areas but are also feeling less guilty about it. When 'everybody does it,' or imagines that everybody does it, a cheating culture has emerged."[1] By drawing attention to systemic societal pressures that provide the backdrop to organizational life, he helped to illuminate factors that facilitate unethical behavior by and within our organizations. Debra Comer interviewed David Callahan about the implications of the "cheating culture" for moral courage in organizations.

Comer: You attributed the cheating culture to a confluence of developments over the past quarter-century: a misguided conservative agenda that focused myopically on restoring traditional values threatened by sex, drugs, and rock-and-roll lyrics but ignored dollar-deifying greed and materialism; increased competitiveness and job insecurity that put pressure on companies and employees to do whatever they could (get away with) to succeed, coupled with huge payoffs for the few victors; lower risks of being caught and punished for wrongdoing, resulting from weakened governmental agencies; and individualism taken to the extreme of coldhearted selfishness. In the years since the publication of *The Cheating Culture: Why More Americans Are Doing Wrong to Get Ahead,* how, if at all, have these macro-level conditions changed, either to intensify or to diminish the problems you described in your book?

Callahan: The Cheating Culture was published when the United States was on a very troubling path. The book came out in the wake of a wave of corporate scandals at companies like Enron and WorldCom and during a period of growing economic inequality and rising insecurity for ordinary Americans. Free-market Republicans dominated Washington and were busy rolling back government regulation. Materialism was on the rise in American culture. I argued that such conditions inevitably fostered cheating: inequality had made the carrots bigger, increasing the incentives to cheat one's way to the top, while insecurity meant the sticks of economic life were hitting hard, tempting more people to cut corners to make their lives a little easier. And sleeping watchdogs—or watchdogs that had been put to sleep—reduced the chances of getting caught. I argued that as these forces produced more cheating, the problem took on a self-perpetuating dynamic: when it seems that everyone is cheating, more people feel that cheating is normal and feel more license to cut corners. This is what I meant by a cheating culture.

Are things different today? In many ways, yes. In the wake of the financial crash, there is much wider recognition of the downsides, both economically and morally, of unchecked markets. More Americans understand that greed has gone too far and private power needs to be held more accountable. There is growing support for a stronger government role to enforce the rules of fair play in economic life, and that will make cheating harder in business and the professions. More broadly, the crash and hard times have brought a shift in the culture away from materialism. The go-go days are over, at least for now. In an America that is less focused on money and "stuff"—where people's self-worth is less tied up in their net worth—there is likely to be less cheating. As well, calls for greater service and sacrifice from public leaders like President Obama, who has already expanded the AmeriCorps program, may awaken the nation's dormant idealism—and this, too, could produce less cheating. Cheating thrives in a climate that legitimizes the boundless pursuit of self-interest; it is less widespread when there is a greater focus on the common good, and I like to think we have entered such a moment.

On the other hand, let's not fool ourselves—many of the structural drivers of cheating remain in place. Inequality is still at record levels, insecurity is widespread, watchdogs still remain weak, and materialism and selfishness remain powerful in the culture.

Comer: The Cheating Culture told how companies misrepresent their earnings, accountants sign off on deceptive numbers, analysts inflate stock ratings to curry favor with investment banking clients, and job seekers falsify their resumes by listing degrees they never earned and positions they never held. You argued persuasively that these incidents of cheating within organizations are shaped by the broader societal context. But which *organizational*-level factors do you think contribute most to unethical behavior in businesses? That is, how do organizations bring about their individual members' wrongdoing?

Callahan: The fish rots from the head down. Organizations with unethical leaders are more likely to spawn wrongdoing further down the ranks. If people feel that company policies are subjectively applied or that there are no moral absolutes, they'll find it easier to rationalize their own bad behavior. People are more willing to play by the rules when they feel that those rules are enforced across the board. The second it seems that some people are above the rules and that the rules lack moral legitimacy, it is easy to start making up your own rules—and moral chaos lies ahead. Nobody wants to be the chump who dots every "i" and crosses every "t" when other people are cutting corners and reaping huge rewards. If you're working for crooks, it may be more tempting to become one yourself. So ethical leadership is critical here, and surveys show that there is a real crisis at this level, with large percentages of workers believing that their managers are not ethical. One reason such problems persist is that organizations typically direct the most surveillance and oversight at their lowest-level workers. Even as fraud experts tell us that the biggest, most expensive frauds are committed by middle-aged senior executives, organizations are more likely to focus on the nickel-and-dime stuff at the lowest level. Cronyism on corporate boards and other conflicts of interest often impede efforts to ensure accountability higher up the food chain. These priorities need to be reversed.

On another front, we know that commission- or quota-based compensation systems carry great risks. The mortgage meltdown illustrates this problem well, because front-line brokers and lenders had powerful financial incentives to make bad or predatory loans. Other examples abound, including the infamous case of the Sears auto repair chain. When Sears switched to a compensation system for its mechanics based on the number and expense of repairs, complaints of consumer fraud exploded. In an altogether different arena, we saw the grassroots group ACORN [the Association of Community Organizations for Reform Now] get in trouble in the 2008 election when some of its field canvassers, whose compensation was tied to the number of voters they registered, made up names. What's the moral of these stories? That tying compensation to performance requires vigilant oversight if there is an easy potential for people to boost their pay through unethical practices.

Comer: You asserted in *The Cheating Culture* that people who consider themselves honorable are behind a lot of the cheating. How is it that these decent individuals come to engage in cheating in their workplaces in the first place?

Callahan: Aristotle said that there are some jobs in which it is impossible for a man to be honest. This is especially true in an age of ever-intensifying bottom-line pressures in corporations. I have a number of stories in my book of people who felt the only way to keep their job or stay afloat financially was to take unethical shortcuts. I've collected many more such stories since publishing the book and keep hearing yet more. For instance, I heard an interview with a former mortgage broker explaining how his commission was tied to the interest rate on the loans he closed. The higher the interest rate was on the loan, the bigger his commission. A lot of home owners had no idea what they were getting into. The guy knew this was terrible. He knew people might lose their homes as a result. But he needed the job, so he did it. These days, with so much pressure to perform at work, it is easier than ever to believe that we need an entirely different moral compass in our professional lives than the one that guides our personal lives. It is a bitter truth that when people perceive a choice between financial security on the one hand and personal integrity on the other hand, many people will go for the security. We can and should ask people to take a hit for the sake of a more ethical society—to show moral courage—but that's not an easy sell, and another ineluctable truth is that most of us don't have an appetite for martyrdom. We just want to go about our lives. None of this is to say that there aren't plenty of bad people who cheat in the workplace. There are, and we need stronger systems to root them out. But as long as systemic pressures thrive that can corrupt even the best of us, we are fighting an uphill battle to create a more honest workplace.

Comer: When these workplace pressures influence good people to behave badly, what happens to their values? Do you think that they are rationalizing to themselves what they are doing or, instead, that they are suppressing what they are doing because their immoral behavior is at odds with their self-identity, or that something else is happening? Why?

Callahan: When people are worried about making the next mortgage payment, they can rationalize just about anything. But maybe the bigger problem is that in some workplaces there is the perception that corruption is rife and "everybody else is doing it." For instance, polls of workers routinely find that large percentages say that they have seen unethical things at the office or that their managers lack integrity. The tendency of many people is to adapt their ethics to those that prevail in the environment they inhabit. For example, a large body of evidence shows that overbilling by lawyers is rampant at large corporate firms and at smaller ones, too. Clients are being cheated out of millions or even billions of dollars annually because of these practices. If you talk to lawyers about this, some will readily acknowledge that they have engaged in these practices and quickly blame the culture in their firm—saying that "everyone" in the firm padded their hours. Many firms have annual billing requirements for associates, which creates a strong incentive to pad hours, especially if you perceive that others are doing the same. Nobody wants to look like a laggard. A similar kind of dynamic was visible in major league baseball. Some players who took steroids rationalized it by saying that steroid use was so rife that they couldn't compete without juicing up themselves. If everyone else is cheating, you have to cheat as well just to operate on a level playing field. And that is a pretty easy thing to rationalize.

Comer: How is moral courage—the courage to do the right thing—in organizations related to your advice in *The Cheating Culture* to be a "pain in the ass"?[2]

   Callahan: Being a "pain in the ass" is often the essence of moral courage. For most of us, there is nothing more difficult than personal confrontation or telling people things they don't want to hear. It's hard enough to tell your neighbor to turn down the stereo—much less to tell your boss to act ethically.

Comer: You wrote, "Many of us won't give in to pressures to cheat even when we perceive that everybody else does it. . . . But . . . this means playing by our own rules rather than the prevailing rules, which makes life harder in the process. It means being a hero."[3] Cynthia Ozick, referring to rescuers during the Holocaust, observed that we cannot comprehend why these heroes would take such enormous risks. We revere and honor those few extraordinary individuals who display courage, but do not blame—in fact, we tend to excuse—those who do nothing to thwart the perpetrators of evil.[4] Doing the right thing at one's place of employment does not (generally) imply life-or-death stakes. So why don't we expect people to act with moral courage at the workplace?

   Callahan: The incentives are overwhelmingly arrayed against acting with moral courage in the workplace. First, there is the possibility of losing your job, which can seem like hugely high stakes to many people, especially in a recession and/or if you have a family. Many, if not most, whistleblowers suffer retaliation even when there are laws in place to protect them.[5] Second, while the downsides of moral courage can be clear, the upsides may be murky. Trying to save Jews in the Holocaust is not the same as, say, trying to rectify misleading circulation figures at the newspaper where you work so that advertisers aren't being cheated. In truth, many workers may not care that deeply about the unethical goings-on at their workplace—or at least not enough to put their job on the line. Third, there is the problem of efficacy. It's one thing to take risks and blow the whistle if you're pretty sure you can nix bad behavior for good. But people often doubt that will be the outcome, and for good reason. Consider the case of the young associate at a large corporate law firm: How likely is it that raising a ruckus about overbilling will change anything? Not very likely, since this problem has already been repeatedly exposed in the media and nothing has changed. If the unethical behavior at your workplace seems long entrenched and earlier efforts at reform have failed, it may seem fruitless to crusade for improvement. It's a lot easier just to leave quietly or go along to get along. None of this is meant to exculpate those who sit back and do nothing while terrible things happen at work. It is to say that we need to find ways to deal with the incentive problem if we want more people to push for ethical changes at work.

Comer: Recognizing the difficulties of effecting change at the societal level, you advised readers to make a personal dent in the cheating culture by refraining from dishonesty and encouraging friends and family to follow suit. Can you translate this general advice into specific prescriptions or guidelines as to what someone can do in his or her own workplace to chip away at the cheating culture?

Callahan: One thing to do is to learn the ethics governing your industry or profession, as well as pertinent laws, and to remind your colleagues of these rules at different points. For example, you might ask that a discussion of ethics be included as a topic at a staff meeting or retreat. Or you might suggest that internal ethics policies, like conflict-of-interest rules, be reviewed and updated. If you work at a large organization, you might suggest hiring a chief ethics officer or otherwise creating a stronger ethics and compliance operation. There are numerous ideas and models to choose from and plenty of consultants who specialize in this area. All these suggestions can be couched in terms of protecting the organization's reputation, business, and assets. After all, preventing fraud and scandals should be a key part of risk management.

Another thing to do, at a larger level, is to get involved in a professional association. Many professions have an ethical code of conduct and an association that plays some role in enforcing that code. Yet such codes may be outdated or weak or not adequately enforced. So getting involved in pushing for tougher rules or more enforcement is one thing that professionals concerned about ethics can do. Ultimately, self-regulation is preferable to government regulation, and professions that are proactive in cleaning their own houses are less likely to be subjected to heavy-handed government oversight. Also, strong codes of professional conduct provide a cover for workers who don't want to go along with unethical practices. If you can point to a rule that prohibits your participation and cite possible punitive measures you might face, you're in a stronger position to resist getting dragged into something unethical. These arguments can also be persuasive with colleagues in your same profession.[6]

Comer: How hopeful are you that these individually oriented instructions will have any kind of meaningful impact on the entrenched cultural woes you underscored in your book?

Callahan: Obviously, problems that are systemic cannot be solved purely by personal actions, and it is naïve to imagine that even large numbers of moral individuals could eliminate the cheating culture. On the other hand, a sure way to perpetuate the problem is for all of us to blame "the system" and feel no obligation to lift a finger until that system changes. Mahatma Gandhi's advice—to be the change you want to see in the world—is useful here. Yes, we need broad shifts in the economic incentives, in the culture, and in institutions to dismantle the cheating culture. We need less inequality, more security, stronger watchdogs, and more. But we also need individuals who stand up to wrongdoing on a daily basis, and we need more of us to put the common good above self-interest. Is it futile to imagine such behavior? Of course not. Self-interest is not the only motivation behind human actions. In fact, people often act in ways that are irrational in order to advance the common good. And they are more likely to make these choices if they find support among their peers and the culture at large. If it's true that American culture is shifting away from some of the extremes of selfishness and materialism we've seen in recent years, then more people will find a supportive climate in which to act for the common good. In turn, that could create a virtuous cycle in which self-interested behavior becomes less common and attracts more social opprobrium. Just as there can be a tipping point where "everybody is doing it," and cheating becomes normalized and thus morally acceptable, the dynamic can work in the reverse. Individual actions can help set this cycle in motion.

Comer: In addition to individual actions, how can collective actions help to combat the cheating culture?

Callahan: In my book I advised readers to join a resurgent progressive movement that challenges the structural drivers of the cheating culture: inequality, insecurity, and deregulation. That movement was gathering steam in 2004 and has since helped to remake American politics with Democrats now controlling both the executive branch and the Senate. In any case, I think people need to be pushing for change at every level: creating an economy and a regulatory structure that support ethical behavior; strengthening self-regulation at the professional or industry level; pushing for a more ethical workplace; working to influence our peers and family members; and—finally—changing our own individual behavior. My tendency is to believe that structural changes are most important, but it's not either/or. Few problems in our society can be solved without both structural and individual-level changes.

Comer: You proposed "reforming business and professions" in order to dismantle the cheating culture.[7] What specific action(s) do you recommend?

How can each individual participate in such reform? What steps should organizational leaders take?

Callahan: I argue for a range of institutional and regulatory reforms that aren't easy to summarize in this space, but let me highlight a few illustrative points. First, we have overwhelming evidence of eroded ethics in some of our leading professions, such as law, medicine, and accounting (we can now add real estate professionals to this list), and equally powerful evidence that these professions have failed to police their own ranks. I advocate reforms to strengthen such entities as state bar associations and state medical societies, as these entities are charged with policing their respective professions. If our key professions can't regulate themselves, then the government should take stronger action. Second, in terms of keeping business honest, we need better self-regulation here, as well, through strengthening independent corporate boards and the like. Also, we must strengthen a variety of government watchdogs that oversee business but have been weakened by thirty years of deregulation, including the Securities and Exchange Commission, the Department of Labor, and the Food and Drug Administration. We need a better balance of power between the public and private sectors. Fortunately, there is now wide recognition that deregulation has gone too far and new efforts are afoot to strengthen a variety of watchdogs.

The easiest way for individuals to participate in the reformist push that I advocate is to get involved in self-regulatory efforts in their own industry or profession. This is to everyone's benefit. Nobody wants to be undercut by the cheaters in their field, and all of us aspire to compete on a level playing field. Also, self-regulation—when it works—is both more effective and less cumbersome than government regulation. If individuals can be proactive in self-regulating their profession or industry, then government won't have to act and everyone's lives will be easier.

Comer: In the next chapter, Gina Vega and I present our concept of the "Personal Ethical Threshold," which has to do with how much (or, in some cases, how little) it takes in the way of organizational pressures to induce a person to abandon, rather than to adhere to, his or her moral values and principles.[8] We argue—and, in fact, it is our rationale for putting together this book—that *the issue when it comes to (un)ethical behavior in organizations is that there are individuals who know what the right thing to do is and, further, would *like* to do it, but are diverted from doing it by organizational pressures.* You wrote in *The Cheating Culture* that "when you put people under pressure and give them a choice of preserving either their integrity or their financial security, many will go for the money."[9] How many of these people who forsake their integrity struggle with their decision? In other words, what proportion of those people who "go for the money" feel regret about going against their principles—and what proportion just weigh the personal consequences and choose the more rewarding path, without regard for what is morally appropriate?

Callahan: It is hard to know how many people who compromise their integrity experience regret, or the ways that people calculate the trade-offs between integrity and financial security. Many people do not reflect on their own moral evolution. One thing about slippery slopes is that people often get onto them gradually as they are drawn into unethical situations over time or inculcated with the corrupt values that dominate their institutional setting. They may experience few crystal-clear forks in the road—with moral purity leading in one direction and moral corruption in another. Instead, the road they are traveling may lead slowly into corrupting territory, and, after a while, the scenery may look perfectly normal. This journey can unfold over years. People can take the first step toward selling out their values when they choose a career that prioritizes financial security over social contribution. Then, over time, they may come to embrace a new value system that exalts the market and the bottom line. Then they may end up working in a sector where corruption is common and come to see that corruption as normal. By the time they themselves participate in unethical behavior, they may barely notice. In those cases where they do perceive clear moral forks in the road, they may be well equipped with a set of rationalizations that allows them to choose the easier and more lucrative path with few second thoughts.

Of course, the problem is not just good people who slowly sell out their integrity. Organizations can also have *bad* people who lack a moral compass and consistently put self-interest above all other concerns. These people—especially if they are in positions of power—can foster a climate that drags down everyone else's integrity.

Comer: As you observed in *The Cheating Culture*, each of us has responsibility for how we behave. How can we remind ourselves that, regardless of the pressures in the workplace—including bad people in positions of power over us—that may threaten our livelihoods, *we* are ultimately responsible for our actions?

Callahan: Go back for a moment to Gandhi's advice, that we should be the change we want to see in the world. Nearly all of us would like to see a world with more integrity. Polls show that integrity is a highly prized value in our society; vast majorities of people say that integrity matters to them—both in themselves and others. So, although there is rampant dishonesty in America, most of us aspire to live differently, and there is strong societal consensus that integrity is a value we should encourage. Nobody likes to be a hypocrite, and most of us feel a responsibility to align our behavior with our beliefs. If most of us want a more honest world, it's hypocrisy when our behavior helps to foster an unethical world. We need to remind ourselves what alignment looks like, be reminded constantly by others, and also receive support from institutions and the culture.

This is one reason that America needs an expanded values debate. Most discussion of values since the 1960s has focused on a narrow swath of moral issues around the topics of sexuality, marriage, and drugs. The societal focus on these issues has led to more self-examination and changes in personal behavior: the teenage pregnancy rate is way down, as are the divorce rate, drunken-driving deaths, and the use of drugs, alcohol, and tobacco. But a host of moral issues that relate to greed, materialism, self-interest, and—broadly—the moral downsides of capitalism has been left off the table. If we as a society can focus more attention on these issues, individuals will lead more self-examined lives when it comes to ethics in the workplace and other settings.

Comer: You wrote, "In today's competitive economy, where success and job security can't be taken for granted, it's increasingly tempting to leave your ethics at home every morning."[10] Do you think that the repercussions of the hibernating bear market at the end of the 2000s decade will exacerbate cheating within organizations—or, instead, that collectively hitting rock bottom will somehow spur a change for the better?

Callahan: I hope that we have come to the end of an era, that an economy built on unchecked self-interest and a culture saturated with materialism have finally crashed and burned. There is a new opening for a variety of reformist measures to change how this country operates. My concern is that our political leaders have framed the post-crash challenges strictly in economic terms, arguing for reform because the financial and housing markets grew too unstable and hurt people financially. These arguments won't have much traction once the economy rebounds and good times return. We need a stronger values-based critique of what went wrong with American capitalism and how its excesses served to corrupt us morally by weakening ethics in business, the professions, and elsewhere. This deeper critique will have a better chance of resonating into the future when nobody can remember why credit default swaps were so bad or what AIG did wrong.

Comer: In the immediate aftermath of the Madoff scandal,[11] Rabbi Benjamin Blech, a professor at Yeshiva University, remarked, "In elevating people with "big bucks" to a level of demiworship, we have been destroying the values of our future generation. We need a total rethinking of who the heroes are, who the role models are, who we should be honoring."[12] How would you respond to Rabbi Blech?

Callahan: Worship of the rich and famous is a major source of our moral problems and not easily dealt with. After all, it is the mass media that largely decide who gets attention and why, and members of the media are market actors who, for the most part, are unaccountable to democratic control. But there are a few ways we can confront this challenge. First, our democracy needs to reassert control over mass media by dramatically expanding every kind of public broadcasting and demanding more public-interest content from broadcasters in exchange for their use of the airwaves, which was the original goal of the Federal Communications Act. This can make a difference to the extent that there is available more cultural content that is not market-provided, ratings-driven, and—too often—designed to cater to our basest instincts. Second, we need to take steps to reduce the excessive concentration of wealth at the top of our society. Although there will always be rich people—and should be—we can use public policy to channel more wealth to public investment instead of private consumption. Public policy can bring the rich down a few notches and help usher in a more egalitarian era, similar to the post–World War II period when so-called "equity norms" prevailed in the corporate world and upper class more broadly, militating against conspicuous consumption and imperial behavior. Third, it's crucial that our schools and universities introduce young people to the real heroes of our time by bringing these heroes in as speakers and visitors.

Comer: Speaking of young people, let's talk about individuals in their first full-time jobs, who might unthinkingly fall into step with socialization pressures in their organizations, where cheating becomes accepted, if not expected. Consider reports about the twenty-somethings of today and tomorrow. These Millennials, or Gen Yers, have been characterized as conventional, achievement-oriented, and highly attuned to their peers' opinions. But it has also been said that they seek greater balance between their work and personal lives than Gen Xers or baby boomers and are less willing to make sacrifices for their career. Do you think that Millennials, the next generational cohort poised to swell the ranks of the workforce, will be more likely to cheat because everyone else is doing it—or more likely to act with moral courage? Why?

Callahan: There is strong evidence that the Millennials are shaping up to be the most progressive generation in American history. They have a much stronger belief in government and service, as well as greater concerns about the environment. Their focus on life balance makes them less likely to elevate materialist ends over means. All that bodes well in terms of the possibility that American culture could pivot into a new kind of moment when wealth is less exalted and self-interest is less triumphant.

Comer: Thank you for your thoughtful and encouraging comments.

Notes

1. Callahan, 2004, 13.
2. Ibid., 293.
3. Ibid., 26.
4. Ozick, 1992.
5. In chapter 5 of this book, Kohn looks at the personal price whistleblowers often pay.
6. Comer and Baker, in chapter 13 of this book, also advise employees to refer to professional codes and standards to convince colleagues to join their morally courageous coalition.
7. Callahan, 2004, 293.
8. Comer and Vega, chapter 3 of this book.
9. Callahan, 2004, 62.
10. Ibid., 20.
11. Vega considers Madoff's Ponzi scheme in chapter 4 of this book.
12. Hernandez, 2008, A26.

References

Callahan, D. 2004. *The cheating culture: Why more Americans are doing wrong to get ahead.* New York: Harcourt.

Comer, D.R., and Baker, S.D. 2011. I defy with a little help from my friends: Raising an organization's ethical bar through a morally courageous coalition. In *Moral courage in organizations: Doing the right thing at work,* ed. D.R. Comer and G. Vega, 171–187. Armonk, NY: M.E. Sharpe.

Comer, D.R., and Vega, G. 2011. The personal ethical threshold. In *Moral courage in organizations: Doing the right thing at work,* ed. D.R. Comer and G. Vega, 25–44. Armonk, NY: M.E. Sharpe.

Hernandez, J.C. 2008. Betrayed by Madoff, Yeshiva U. learns a lesson. *New York Times,* December 23, A26.

Kohn, S.M. 2011. For the greater good: The moral courage of whistleblowers. In *Moral courage in organizations: Doing the right thing at work,* ed. D.R. Comer and G. Vega, 60–74. Armonk, NY: M.E. Sharpe.

Ozick, C. 1992. Prologue. In *Rescuers: Portraits of moral courage in the Holocaust,* by G. Block and M. Drucker, xi–xvi. New York: Holmes & Meier.

Vega, G. 2011. How the mighty have fallen. In *Moral courage in organizations: Doing the right thing at work,* ed. D.R. Comer and G. Vega, 47–59. Armonk, NY: M.E. Sharpe.

3

The Personal Ethical Threshold

Debra R. Comer and Gina Vega

Organizational Factors That Impede Moral Behavior

This chapter introduces the concept of the *Personal Ethical Threshold*.[1] Learning about your own Personal Ethical Threshold, or PET, will help you to understand how organizations can at times make it more difficult to act with moral courage. In the appendix at the end of this chapter is a ten-item questionnaire that assesses your PET.[2] Read the instructions and each of the ten scenarios carefully, and respond to the questions as accurately as you can. The material that follows will be much more meaningful and useful to you if you take a few moments now to complete the questionnaire *before* you continue reading.

Think about what you would do if you saw a coworker stealing money or goods from your employer or if you observed a classmate (or colleague) cheating on an important (qualifying) exam. Would you say anything to this coworker or classmate? Would you report him or her? Would you act differently if your coworker's theft involved less than twenty-five dollars versus hundreds of dollars or if the coworker were your boss's nephew? Would your response change if the exam were being graded on a curve or if you would have to face the scorn of people who might consider you a tattletale? Now try to imagine what you would do if your employer asked you to sell a dangerous product, or to sell a product that posed no health or safety risks but did not deliver on its promised results. Would it matter to you if the average customer paid only a few dollars as opposed to thousands of dollars for the product? Would you act differently if you were likely to lose your job for refusing to sell the product?

All of the above scenarios involve unethical acts. How we behave in scenarios such as these is likely to depend on the consequences for us personally and for others. Indeed, these two types of consequences affect our Personal Ethical Threshold—what it takes for us to cross our proverbial moral line to act in a way that violates our standards and values. Even when we know the right thing to do and want to do it, we all fail from time to time to have the moral courage to follow our beliefs. We are more likely to abandon our moral principles when:

- there are relatively high *situational pressures* to act against our moral standards, that is, when we will experience greater personal loss by adhering to our standards or when we will experience greater personal gain by abandoning them; and/or
- the *moral intensity* of the circumstances is relatively low, that is, when violating our moral standards will have minimal negative impact on others.

Throughout this chapter, we will use examples from films and from real life to illustrate that people tend to dishonor their principles when the situational pressures are high and/or the moral intensity is low.[3]

Situational Pressures: The Costs to Ourselves of Our Moral Behavior

Situational factors can cause individuals to act in ways that go against their moral principles.[4] The PET represents how little or how much in the way of situational pressures it takes for a member of an organization to act in a way he or she considers unethical. A person with a lower PET is more susceptible to situational forces that may exact costs on his or her job or career than is someone with a higher PET. But even someone with a relatively high PET has a limit: "Good people will do bad things if they are placed in an environment where doing anything else threatens their livelihood and ability to support their dependents."[5] For example, Peter Parker (Tobey Maguire) has an admirably elevated PET in *Spider-Man 2*.[6] Yet, after two years of saving the people of New York City as Spiderman, he is spent. The 24/7 demands of his superhero alter ego have cost him his beloved and are increasingly interfering with his performance at work and school. Once doing the right thing becomes too personally onerous for Peter, he sheds his Spiderman costume.[7]

Situational pressures that cause someone to act at odds with his or her principles do not necessarily entail dodging personally negative outcomes. Instead, they may involve opportunity costs. That is, the possibility of acquiring extra benefits may tempt an individual to violate his or her moral preference. *Eight Men Out* is a dramatization of the 1919 scandal in which tremendously talented but abysmally underpaid Chicago White Sox ballplayers conspired with gamblers to lose the World Series.[8] Pitcher Eddie Cicotte (David Straitharn) is asked to throw the World Series so that the players can make more money than they are paid by miserly team owner Charles Comiskey. Eddie declines, but changes his mind after a meeting with Comiskey (Clifton James). Comiskey had promised Eddie a $10,000 bonus for winning thirty games that season but refuses to pay up, on the grounds that Eddie won only twenty-nine games. Eddie objects that he would have won at least one more game during the last two weeks of the season but was required to rest his pitching arm to prepare for the World Series. When Comiskey does not budge, Eddie learns that playing by the rules does not pan out—and changes his mind about losing the Series.

Thus, whereas Peter Parker leaves the unrailed, tortuous slopes of the high road, Eddie Cicotte takes the payoff-paved low road. Likewise, organizational situations can present disincentives for moral behavior, by either punishing individuals or depriving them of rewards for following the path they know and value as morally correct. Take the example of Melinda Swann, a human resources professional at a regional department store. For each of the past few summers, Melinda has collaborated with the career center at a neighboring university to identify high-potential students for two coveted management training internships. This year Melinda's manager decides to give both internships to the children of his friends. Melinda, disgusted by such unfairness, begins to conduct an unbiased and more comprehensive search through the university. But her coworker warns her that their manager fired the last person who defied him. Melinda is angry and frustrated, but she cannot afford to lose her job. She decides, reluctantly, to follow her coworker's advice instead of her moral compass.

Diann Cattani, a well-educated woman raised in a loving, religious family, was the proverbial girl next door. Yet, over a period of time, she took a half-million dollars from her trusting employer until, guilt-stricken, she turned herself in and served more than a year for fraud and embezzlement in a federal prison. How did this happen? When Diann's travel agency mistakenly charged her vacation trip to the corporate account, she never corrected the error. Meanwhile, although she and her husband made a comfortable combined income, their expenses increased dramatically after the birth of their first child, as they paid for childcare while trying to keep up with professional and social commitments. As their family grew, Cattani's perceived financial pressure led her to continue to steal from her employer.[9]

To make their own lives easier, Melinda Swann (a fictitious character based loosely on a real person) stopped doing the right thing and Diann Cattani (a real person) started doing the wrong thing. Whereas Melinda, like Peter Parker (Spiderman), took the exit off the high road, Diann Cattani, like Eddie Cicotte, took the entrance ramp onto the low road. Perhaps, as Noah Cross (John Huston) advises Jake Gittes (Jack Nicholson) in *Chinatown*, everyone has a price: "[M]ost people never have to face the fact that, at the right time and the right place, they're capable of . . . *any*thing."[10] Although some people may be more inclined to fold in the face of slight external forces whereas others may have the fortitude to withstand greater pressures, we *all* have a breaking point at which we jettison our morals.

Moral Intensity: The Costs to Others of Our Immoral Behavior

Even for the same person, the PET may fluctuate according to the issue in question. Specifically, for a given amount of situational pressure, a person will more likely abide by his or her moral standards—that is, act with moral courage—to the extent that the issue has greater moral intensity (i.e., the consequences for others are of a greater magnitude).[11] *On the Waterfront* depicts how moral intensity affects the PET.[12] Marlon Brando's Terry Molloy "coulda been a contender," had he not sacrificed his boxing career by throwing a key fight for some quick cash. As a longshoreman under corrupt union boss Johnny Friendly (Lee J. Cobb), who bumps off anyone who gets in his way, Terry avoids thinking about issues of right and wrong—until his own brother (Rod Steiger) becomes Johnny's latest victim and an activist priest (Karl Malden) underscores the bleak repercussions of allowing Johnny's crookedness to persist. Terry, with his conscience restored, reports Friendly's racketeering to the waterfront commission.

Simply put, people are more likely to do the right thing when moral intensity is higher. Linda, an IT specialist at a hospital, habitually ingratiates herself with her boss by laughing at his unoriginal jokes. Yet, she refuses to comply with his request to change a patient's computerized records so that the patient, her boss's cousin, can receive insurance reimbursement for pricey, medically unnecessary cosmetic surgery. Although both acts involve lying, the latter has greater moral intensity. Likewise, Sam, who works at a convenience store, feels uneasy when the assistant manager instructs him to shortchange by up to seventy-five cents any customer who seems too distracted to count (such as a parent with a young child or anyone making a purchase during the pre-dinner rush). Nonetheless, he carries out the request. When the assistant manager tells him to replace expired last-sale-date stickers on prepared food items, Sam objects and quits. Sam did not take a stand against stealing customers' pocket change, but he will not jeopardize their health.

Whereas the moral intensity of an issue involves an individual's perception of its collective importance, the situational pressure involves the individual's own interests. As Figure 3.1 shows, the line depicting how we respond to increasing situational pressure for an issue of higher moral intensity is not as steep as the line depicting how we respond to corresponding situational

Figure 3.1   **Likelihood of Violating Our Moral Principles as a Function of Situational Pressure and Moral Intensity**

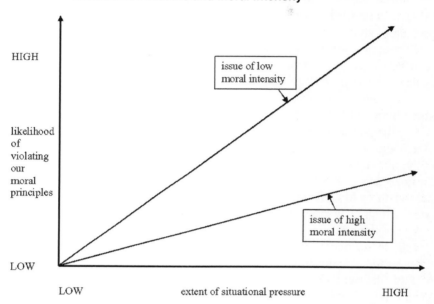

Source: Comer and Vega, 2008. Reprinted with kind permission from Springer Science+Business Media.

Note: The moral intensity of an issue represents its collective importance, whereas the situational pressure represents the interests of the individual.

pressure for an issue of lower moral intensity. Our PET tends to be higher for an issue of greater moral intensity because we consider the consequences of our actions on other people. We are more likely to do the right thing, even at personal expense, to the extent that our behavior affects others.[13]

A murder trial, a situation of indisputably high moral intensity, is at the center of *Twelve Angry Men*.[14] Immediately following closing arguments, a straw vote reveals that eleven jurors have already concluded that the young man whose fate they will be deciding did commit murder. Juror 8 (Henry Fonda), however, tells his fellow jurors that he would feel uneasy sending the defendant to his death without any deliberations. His insistence on scrutinizing and discussing the evidence angers several of the other jurors (who were selfishly hoping for the convenience of a quick verdict, which would have allowed them to leave the stifling room in a New York City courthouse and attend to their own business). Nonetheless, Juror 8 chooses to contend with their wrath. When deciding whether or not to follow what we perceive and value as the moral course of action, we tend to weigh the costs and benefits to ourselves (situational pressures) and to others (moral intensity) that our (un)ethical behavior would likely elicit—and how strongly we feel about these outcomes.[15] Even in cases of high moral intensity, imposing situational pressures can dissuade us from doing what we know is right.

Contrast Juror 8's moral courage with the decision of Harry Markopoulos or of Valerie Young. Whereas Juror 8 would, at the end of the trial, likely never again see any of his fellow jurors, higher stakes were at play for both Markopoulos and Young. For nearly a decade, Harry Markopoulos tried to warn regulators about Bernard Madoff. Markopoulos recognized as early as 2000 that Madoff was dealing dishonestly, because the trading strategy Madoff claimed his fund used could not have yielded the consistently high returns he reported. Because of the scale of Madoff's Ponzi scheme and the extent of Madoff's influence in the financial world, Markopoulos worried that he was risking his life by blowing the whistle on Madoff and did so only anonymously.[16] Perhaps if Markopoulos had acted more overtly, he could have reduced the devastation to thousands of investors victimized by Madoff's duplicity.

Like Harry Markopoulos, Valerie Young, the pseudonym of a marketing manager for an international fragrance firm,[17] weighed the high costs to herself of doing the right thing against the high costs to others of not doing it. When Valerie joined the firm, her department did business with perfumers from a variety of fragrance companies. Shortly thereafter, however, the number had dwindled to just two. Valerie did not know why, until the day she fixed a paper jam in the office copy machine. Documents she found in the output tray indicated that her boss was receiving thousands of dollars per month in kickbacks from the two fragrance companies with which her department still worked. She surmised that all of the other companies had refused to play her boss's slippery game and that he had reciprocated by severing ties with them. Valerie was outraged by her boss's unethical behavior, but considered the price she would pay for reporting it. Because she had only a working visa, she knew that she could lose the right to work and remain in the United States if her employer were found to be involved in unfair dealings. She decided against blowing the whistle.

When We Look at Ourselves in the Mirror After Violating Our Personal Principles, Why Do Our Reflections Show No Shame?

All other factors being equal, the more situational pressure we encounter, the more likely we are to discard our standards, particularly for issues of low moral intensity. So how do we let ourselves make moral compromises without feeling regret? We use two processes: (1) dissonance reduction and (2) desensitization.

Dissonance Reduction

Ordinarily, we strive to live up to our moral standards to avoid self-censure,[18] and we experience distress when we do not.[19] When our actions violate these standards, we experience cognitive dissonance, an uncomfortable feeling of inconsistency between our behavior and attitudes.[20] After doing something that does not fit with our sense of ourselves as morally decent, we try to reduce dissonance by creating an explanation for the discrepancy between our positive self-concept and the knowledge that we have behaved wrongly.[21] It is important to note that we experience no dissonance for abandoning our moral standards in the face of hefty situational pressure (e.g., the threat of losing one's job or the promise of landing a big account that will pay handsome commissions for a long time to come), because we can attribute our nonexemplary behavior to the commanding condition.[22] If, however, we have disregarded our principles after experiencing relatively minimal situational pressure (e.g., the possibility of forfeiting a day off or the opportunity to accrue a few extra paid vacation days), cognitive dissonance results from the lack of external justification for our bad behavior.[23] When we succumb to slighter pressures, we feel a greater need to justify our unethical behavior to ourselves than we do when we bow in the face of more extreme ones.[24]

When we do experience dissonance, we need to reduce inconsistency, either by lowering our standards, that is, adjusting our attitude as to what constitutes (un)ethical behavior; or reinterpreting the issue as less morally intense, which permits us to view our own behavior as inoffensive. In the latter case, we convince ourselves that behaving at odds with our values does not matter much because what we do has only a trivial impact on others.[25] So, for instance, we can maintain the attitude that stealing is wrong, even as we fail to report that a few of our coworkers occasionally take home company merchandise, if we rationalize that our employer will be no worse for wear for their petty thefts.

Desensitization

We have described how the PET is higher for issues of greater moral intensity. Over time, however, if people violate their moral standards in response to situational pressures, they may gradually become inured to substandard behavior and desensitized to the intensity of moral encounters. Just as virtuous character develops through habitual good acts,[26] dishonorable character may develop as individuals habituate to performing immoral deeds of incrementally greater intensity. Through a process of desensitization, we grow accustomed to acting in ways we once thought we never would or could.[27] As Sherron

Watkins described her former Enron colleagues, "These people did not start their careers intending to become felons, but that's where they ended up."[28] Crossing one's line for an issue of relatively low moral intensity may make it more likely, at some point in the future, that one will cross the line for an issue of somewhat greater intensity, until, ultimately, an act formerly deemed egregious seems acceptable. We may proceed to behaving badly even when issues are of relatively high moral intensity and/or when situational pressures are relatively low.

Your Personal Ethical Threshold

At what point do *you* forsake your moral values and principles? The questionnaire you completed presents ten scenarios you might very well encounter. In fact, the scenarios are based on actual incidents, and you have probably already experienced situations that resemble these everyday tests of your moral courage. Use Table 3.1 to record the scores from your questionnaire. To find your overall PET score, add up the numbers in the ten cells and then divide the total by ten. The questionnaire is designed so that higher scores represent a higher PET, that is, greater adherence to the morally stainless path, regardless of the heaviness of the situational pressure or the low moral intensity of the issue. The ten scenarios describe incidents of varying levels of situational pressure *or* varying levels of moral intensity. In the first five scenarios (Questions 1–5), the moral intensity varies among response choices, while the situational pressure remains constant. Each successively higher response choice for a given question involves an issue of incrementally lesser moral intensity, with the fourth response choice entailing the least impact on others. Your responses to these first five scenarios suggest the types of issues, in terms of their effect on others, for which you would succumb to pressure to perform in a morally distasteful way. In the remaining five scenarios (Questions 6–10), the situational pressure varies among response choices, while the moral intensity stays the same. Each successively higher response choice for a given question involves an incrementally greater situational pressure, with the fourth response choice entailing the greatest personal price. Your responses to these last five scenarios suggest what it would take, in terms of personal gains or losses, for you to perform in a morally distasteful way.

A higher PET score *suggests* that you are more likely to follow your moral compass, even when situational pressures are substantial (you will incur personal difficulties and/or forfeit personal gains for doing the right thing) and/or when moral intensity is low (your behavior has a negligible impact on others). It is highly unlikely that anyone would answer all the questions

Table 3.1

Scoring the PET Questionnaire

Moral Intensity Varies		Situational Pressure Varies	
Question #	Score	Question #	Score
1	_____	6	_____
2	_____	7	_____
3	_____	8	_____
4	_____	9	_____
5	_____	10	_____
Sum of questions 1–10		_____	
Overall score (mean of questions 1–10)		_____	

For questions 1–5, no matter how many lines you have checked, the *highest* one gets the score. For example, if you checked lines 2 and 3 for question 1, score it as 3.

For questions 6–10, you were instructed to choose only *one* response. For these questions, choosing multiple responses would produce contradictions. If you chose more than one response for any of these questions, it may be worthwhile for you to redo them.

with a "4" because nobody is perfect. Do not despair if your PET score is lower than you would like. Instead, focus on your future behavior. With enough practice, people eventually stop feeling guilt and regret about their misdeeds and simply accept unethical behavior as normal. Therefore, it is important not to establish bad habits. Understanding your PET can help you to be vigilant not to excuse your misbehavior by attributing it to situational pressures or rationalizing that nobody is really being hurt. If you have been entrenched in an organizational culture where you have copied the unethical actions of your coworkers, mindlessly mimicking their unsavory responses and incorporating them into your own repertoire,[29] we hope that the PET concept has been a wake-up call.

Conclusion

As a boy, Frank Serpico dreamed of becoming a policeman to protect and help the public. As a cop, he refused to participate in or even to condone the pervasive corruption in the New York City Police Department in the mid-1960s. For five years he persisted in reporting wrongdoing in the department, even though his superiors ignored him and his fellow officers ostracized and threatened him. Serpico almost lost his life for breaking the code of silence when he was shot in the face during a drug bust in 1971. His partners had not answered his calls for backup prior to the shooting—nor did they report the shooting. Four decades later, he still has bullet fragments in his head, deafness in his left ear, and nerve damage in his left leg.[30]

The concept of the Personal Ethical Threshold does not address why some individuals have lower moral awareness, use flawed ethical reasoning processes, and/or care little about ethical values and principles. Instead, it aims to help make sense of when and why people of solid character, that is, those who *are* morally sensitive, *have* intact moral judgment, and *want* to behave morally, still do not always do what they believe is right in their workplace.[31] We would not suggest condoning those who forsake their principles. On the contrary, we offer the concept of the PET to *explain*—not to excuse—immoral behavior that occurs when "situational pressures make us lose our moral compass."[32] You took a questionnaire to focus your attention on the effect on *your* moral behavior of (1) situational pressures in organizations that can divert you from following your moral standards and (2) the rationalizations you may use to convince yourself that matters of lesser moral intensity do not require moral responses. Recognizing the twin threats of external pressures and internal rationalizations can help you follow your principles to behave with moral courage.

The Nazi Party had only 108,000 members in 1929. But by 1933, more than 1.6 million Germans, worn down by the Depression, had joined the party, seeking preferential treatment in snapping up jobs left vacant by the incarceration of Jews, communists, and socialists.[33] As members of a society that often accepts the abdication of personal responsibility,[34] we tend to attribute our misbehavior too readily to forces beyond ourselves. Yet, we continue to praise the rare individuals like Frank Serpico who make personal sacrifices in order to uphold their high moral standards.[35] We hope that understanding the obstacles to doing the right thing will encourage you to take ownership of your ethical choices, to prepare yourself to become less vulnerable to organizational factors, and to act in concert with your moral values.

Appendix: PET Questions

For the first five questions, check at least one response and any other/others that also applies/apply.

1. You are an associate management consultant who has just completed an expensive and comprehensive project for a client company. You know you can offer no more service of value to this client and that any further research would waste the client's time and money. However, your superiors, the partners of the consulting firm, insist that this thriving company can afford more research. You believe it would be wrong to undertake any additional research for this client, but the partners, who are very strong-willed, are pressuring you.

Under what conditions, if any, would you voice your objections to the partners? Check at least one response and any other/others that also applies/apply.

_____ 1. I would not voice my objections to the partners under any conditions.
_____ 2. I would voice my objections to the partners if they asked me to conduct as many studies as this deep-pocket company could afford.
_____ 3. I would voice my objections to the partners if they asked me to conduct just one more large project.
_____ 4. I would voice my objections to the partners if they asked me to conduct any additional project, no matter how small.

2. You believe that lying is wrong, but understand that telling the truth sometimes has unpleasant personal consequences. Nonetheless, there are some lies you would find so objectionable that you'd avoid telling them regardless of the consequences you'd have to face.

What would you avoid? Check at least one response and any other/others that also applies/apply.

I would avoid:
_____ 1. complying with my boss's instructions to conceal a product flaw that could, under certain circumstances, cause injuries
_____ 2. going along with my boss's instructions to falsify a financial document
_____ 3. glossing over a product's drawbacks to make the sales needed to meet a tough quota
_____ 4. calling in sick (when I was feeling fine) because I had already used up all of my personal days for the year

3. You are a junior partner at Fields and Wellington. Chris, who recently joined your firm as a junior partner, has an office next to yours. Late one evening, Chris and you are the last to leave the building. As you ride the elevator to the lobby, Chris (who is in the same ethnic and racial groups as you) makes a racist remark. You are surprised and offended, but recognize that saying something—no matter how tactfully—may not change Chris's attitudes and may serve only to make your working relationship strained and awkward. Besides, the senior partners at the firm think especially highly of Chris, whom they hired away from a rival firm.

Under what conditions, if any, would you say something to Chris? Check at least one response and any other/others that also applies/apply.

_____ 1. I would not say anything to Chris under any conditions.
_____ 2. I would say something if Chris told me, after we'd just interviewed a promising candidate for an associate's position, "It would be a big mistake to hire one of those people."
_____ 3. I would say something if Chris commented, "Playing the race card can really help people advance professionally: look where it got C.J."
_____ 4. I would say something if Chris shared a racist joke that had made the rounds at the rival firm.

4. You are a local chef, teaching a cooking class in the adult education program at the high school in your community. The pay is respectable, but you are teaching the class primarily because you enjoy sharing your love of cooking with others. Your class meets every Wednesday for fifteen weeks, from 7:00 to 10:00 P.M. While sipping a cup of coffee before class one evening, you are approached by the entire group of students enrolled in the English-as-a-Second-Language (ESL) class that meets across the hall. They tell you, in broken English, that they are frustrated because their instructor cuts class short each week, even though they have told him how much they want and need to improve their English. They beg you to help them by speaking to him on their behalf, which they are reluctant to do because of their difficulty expressing themselves and, especially, their fear of retaliation from their instructor. You have noticed yourself that the instructor has been leaving early each week. You think it is unfair for this instructor to shortchange these students and the school district, but you recognize it would be much easier for you not to get involved. Besides, you've heard that this instructor got the job because he is the program director's childhood friend. This instructor is scheduled to teach the same course the following season.

Under what conditions, if any, would you speak to the instructor? Check at least one response and any other/others that also applies/apply.

_____ 1. I would not speak with the instructor. Even though he is shortchanging the students and the school district, I wouldn't want to deal with the hassle of getting involved.

_____ 2. I would speak with the instructor if he dismissed the students two hours before the end of each three-hour class every week.

_____ 3. I would speak with the instructor if he dismissed the students one and one-half hours before the end of each three-hour class every week.

_____ 4. I would speak with the instructor if he dismissed the students one hour before the end of each three-hour class.

5. You are a salesperson at a small fitness club. You found out just last week that the gym's owners have been losing money for quite some time and have decided to close within the next few days. The members have no clue; in fact, the locker room has just been renovated. You've been instructed to continue signing up any new members and renewing current memberships, to conceal the imminent closing and to generate cash. You know it is not right to deceive people and sell them worthless memberships. On the other hand, you do not want to alienate the owners, who are well connected and have already arranged for you to get a job at a larger club.

Under what conditions, if any, would you tell the truth to someone asking to purchase a new or renewed membership? Check at least one response and any other/others that also applies/apply.

_____ 1. I would not tell the truth to any customer. Let the buyer beware.

_____ 2. I would tell the truth to someone asking to purchase an annual membership.

_____ 3. I would tell the truth to someone asking to purchase a six-month membership.

_____ 4. I would tell the truth to someone asking to purchase a one-month trial membership.

For the last five questions, check only one response.

6. You are completing your degree while working full time. During the past few weeks, you have been consumed at work by a complex and critical group project, which is in its final stages. You are exhausted from the sixty-plus hours per week you have been working. On your way home from work, you suddenly remember that a twenty-page paper is due tomorrow evening for one of your classes. Unless you earn at least a B in this course, you will

not qualify for your company's tuition remission program—and will have to pay a few thousand dollars for the course out of your own pocket. The professor has an unyielding policy against granting extensions, and you know that even if you stayed up all night to do the paper, you would be submitting something that would fall short of your best work. You won't have the time you'd like to devote to this paper unless you call in sick and take tomorrow off from work, but you know that bailing out on your project group, which would require all the other members to work even harder to pick up the slack, would be wrong.

Would you call in sick, even though everyone else would have to work much harder in your absence, so that you could have the whole day to prepare a decent paper? Check only one response.

_____ 1. Yes. I'd call in sick, even if the paper were worth only twenty percent of my course grade.
_____ 2. Yes. I'd call in sick, but only if the paper were worth forty percent of my course grade.
_____ 3. Yes. I'd call in sick, but only if the paper were worth sixty percent of my course grade.
_____ 4. No. I would go to work, no matter how much the paper was worth.

7. You are anxious about an upcoming interview this afternoon for a managerial position within your company. The new position would be a real break, with exciting challenges and a substantial salary increase. Your qualifications are very strong, but you face tough competition from Pat, your colleague and chief rival for the position. Pat, whom you find unbearably arrogant, is less technically competent than you, but more skilled at flattering people in high places. Midmorning on the day of the interviews, you and Pat are attending a staff meeting. You step out of the meeting to use the restroom, and on your way back to the meeting, you pass by your cubicle, where you find a Post-it note stuck to your computer screen (company policy prohibits the use of sending and receiving text messages during meetings). The note indicates that the interview schedule has been moved up by one hour. You notice an identical note on Pat's nearby computer. You believe it would be wrong to destroy Pat's note. But you know that the interviewer, who takes pride in being a real stickler for punctuality and has no patience for excuses, would hold it against Pat in a big way if the interview had to be rescheduled. This would help clinch the job for you. With everyone else in the meeting, the office is empty; nobody would ever know if you took Pat's note.

What would you do? Check only one response.

_____ 1. I'd destroy the note to increase my chances of getting this great job.

_____ 2. I'd destroy the note, but only if I needed the salary increase to re-decorate my living room.

_____ 3. I'd destroy the note, but only if I needed the salary increase because one of my family members had been laid off unexpectedly and we needed to pay off mounting household bills.

_____ 4. I'd leave the note where I found it, no matter how much I needed and wanted this job.

8. You are the newest analyst at Kesnero Securities, covering the fashion industry. With degrees in marketing and design, you couldn't be happier with your job. After conducting a thorough analysis of a major clothing retailer, you report that customer purchases have been softening and recommend a "hold" rating on the company's stock. An executive from the retailer phones you to complain about your neutral rating. He tells you that if you don't up-grade it to something more favorable, he will thwart your future attempts to do research at his company. Lying would go against your value system, but, on the other hand, you don't want to anger your boss, who prefers analysts who don't make waves.

Would you upgrade your rating? Check only one response.

_____ 1. Yes. I'd upgrade my rating.

_____ 2. No. I wouldn't upgrade my rating, even if it meant annoying my boss for losing access to this company.

_____ 3. No. I wouldn't upgrade my rating, even if it meant my performance ratings would suffer enough to jeopardize my year-end bonus.

_____ 4. No. I wouldn't upgrade my rating, even if it meant I'd end up being fired.

9. You have applied to graduate school to work toward your master's degree in engineering. The faculty member heading the admissions committee calls to congratulate you upon your acceptance. She invites you to consider pursuing your PhD. Your plan is to acquire your master's in engineering and then to go to law school. Your goal is to become a patent attorney, and you have absolutely no interest in or use for a doctorate in engineering. However, as a doctoral stu-dent, your tuition would be waived and you would even receive a small stipend, whereas you would have to pay full tuition as a student in the terminal one-year master's program to which you applied. You could enter the doctoral program and leave after completing your master's, but you know this would be deceitful and wrong. Still, this would save you several thousand dollars.

Would you accept the offer to enter the doctoral program, and then leave after completing your master's? Check only one response.

_____ 1. Yes. In order to save the cost of tuition I'd accept the offer to enter the doctoral program and leave after finishing my master's degree. Taking an opportunity to save money is good common sense.

_____ 2. Yes. I would accept the offer if I had to repay thousands of dollars of outstanding student loans I'd accumulated to go to college.

_____ 3. Yes. I would accept the offer if I had to repay thousands of dollars of outstanding student loans I'd accumulated to go to college and I would need to borrow more money to go to law school after completing my master's.

_____ 4. No. Even if I had to repay thousands of dollars of outstanding student loans I'd accumulated to go to college and would need to borrow more money for law school after completing my master's, I would sincerely thank the admissions committee for the offer, but I'd tell them that a PhD doesn't fit my career goals.

10. You are a scientist at a major pharmaceutical concern. The clinical trials research you have just completed provides compelling evidence that a new diet medication may cause severe liver problems in a significant percentage of patients. Because sale of the medication promises to generate handsome revenues for your company, the head of your division has asked you to massage your data. You know that it is wrong to put a dangerous product on the market, especially when many of the individuals taking the diet medication are only moderately overweight; they do not have life-threatening obesity and would most likely be better off changing their diets and exercising.

What would you do? Check only one response.

_____ 1. I'd falsify the data. At times it's necessary to go along to get along at work.

_____ 2. I would not falsify the data even if it meant getting on my boss's bad side.

_____ 3. I would not falsify the data even if it meant being passed over for a deserved promotion.

_____ 4. I would not falsify the data even if it meant losing my job.

Notes

1. Comer and Vega, 2005, 2008.

2. Detailed information about this assessment instrument appears in Comer and Vega, 2008.

3. We hasten to call attention to our ideological and cultural biases about what constitutes moral behavior. Haidt and his colleagues (Graham, Haidt, and Rimm-Kaufman, 2008; Haidt and Graham, 2009) discuss five moral foundations, or key issues by which people around the globe perceive acts as morally right or wrong: (1) harm/care, (2) fairness/reciprocity, (3) in-group/loyalty, (4) authority/respect, and (5) purity/sanctity; see Moberg, chapter 14 of this book, for further explanation. They explain that, whereas members of some cultures are concerned about all five moral issues, Western academics tend to emphasize the first two of these moral foundations. Indeed, not only do our scenarios present situations in which the morally "appropriate" decision involves safe and compassionate, as well as just and honest, treatment of others, but the actors in these scenarios are challenged to contend with pressures to do just the opposite—from either their peers (in-group members) or their boss (authority figure).

4. Blass, 2009; Card, 2005; Moberg, 2006; Pinto, Leana, and Pil, 2008; Zimbardo, 2007.

5. Wines, 2007, 489.

6. *Spider-Man 2*, 2004.

7. Peter eventually resumes his Spiderman persona after his Aunt May (Rosemary Harris) resurrects his PET by reminding him that doing the right thing, even if it necessitates personal sacrifice, is important.

8. *Eight Men Out*, 1988.

9. Cattani, 2006.

10. *Chinatown*, 1974, italics in original. See also Zimbardo (2007), describing the ease with which situations can transform ordinary individuals into perpetrators of heinous acts.

11. Jones, 1991; Roberts, 1984.

12. *On the Waterfront*, 1954.

13. Baumeister and Exline (1999), viewing morality as a set of cultural adaptations designed to allow people to live together, point out that individual members must at times subordinate their own needs and interests to those of their larger societal unit.

14. *Twelve Angry Men*, 1957.

15. Vroom (1964) explains motivation in terms of the desirability of expected outcomes.

16. Henriques, 2009. See Vega's discussion of Madoff in chapter 4 of this book.

17. Dench, 2006.

18. Bandura, 2002.

19. Austin et al., 2005.

20. Festinger, 1957; for a comprehensive review of research stemming from Festinger's original formulation of dissonance theory, see Olson and Stone, 2005.

21. Eagly and Chaiken, 1993.

22. Perloff, 2003; Zimbardo and Leippe, 1991.

23. Aronson, 1999; Cooper and Fazio, 1984.

24. Even some business ethicists, such as Jones and Ryan (1997), have argued that an individual's moral responsibility is reduced in the face of sizable organizational pressures to behave unethically.

25. Simon, Greenberg, and Brehm, 1995.

26. Aristotle, 1962.

27. Bandura, 2002; Bok, 1978; Luban, 2003.

28. Told to Beneen and Pinto, 2009, 280.

29. Ashforth and Anand (2003) describe how corruption becomes so pervasive within an organization that members come to behave unethically without misgivings.

30. Kilgannon, 2010; see also Dillon, 2002; Maas, 1973.

31. Batson and Thompson, 2001, distinguish between "moral hypocrites," who aspire merely to appear to be moral, and individuals of "moral integrity," who truly are motivated to be moral. The PET addresses how the latter may fail to behave morally when conditions that threaten their self-interest overcome them.

32. Alzola, 2008, 354.

33. Nelson, 2009.

34. Greenfield, 2004. In his inaugural address Barack Obama called explicitly for "a new era of responsibility" (January 20, 2009).

35. Weaver, Treviño, and Agle, 2005.

References

Alzola, M. 2008. Character and environment: The status of virtues in organizations. *Journal of Business Ethics* 78(3), 343–357.

Aristotle. 1962. *Nichomachean Ethics*, trans. M. Ostwald. Indianapolis, IN: Bobbs-Merrill.

Aronson, E. 1999. Dissonance, hypocrisy, and the self-concept. In *Cognitive dissonance: Progress on a pivotal theory in social psychology*, ed. E. Harmon-Jones and J. Mills, 103–126. Washington, DC: American Psychological Association.

Ashforth, B.E., and Anand, V. 2003. The normalization of corruption in organizations. *Research in Organizational Behavior* 25, 1–52.

Austin, W., Rankel, M., Kagan, L., Bergum, V., and Lemermeyer, G. 2005. To stay or go, to speak or stay silent, to act or not to act: Moral distress as experienced by psychologists. *Ethics & Behavior* 15(3), 197–212.

Bandura, A. 2002. Selective moral disengagement in the exercise of moral agency. *Journal of Moral Education* 31(2), 101–119.

Batson, C.D., and Thompson, E.R. 2001. Why don't moral people act morally? Motivational considerations. *Current Directions in Psychological Science* 10(2), 54–57.

Baumeister, R.F., and Exline, J.J. 1999. Virtue, personality, and social relations. *Journal of Personality* 67(6), 1165–1194.

Beneen, G., and Pinto, J. 2009. Resisting organizational-level corruption: An interview with Sherron Watkins. *Academy of Management Learning & Education* 8(2), 275–289.

Blass, T. 2009. From New Haven to Santa Clara: A historical perspective on the Milgram obedience experiments. *American Psychologist* 64(1), 37–45.

Bok, S. 1978. *Lying: Moral choice in public and private life*. New York: Pantheon Books.

Card, R.F. 2005. Individual responsibility within organizational contexts. *Journal of Business Ethics* 62(4), 397–405.

Cattani, D. 2006. The courage to live. In *Taking the harder right*, ed. O.G. Halle, 71–89. Smyrna, GA: Concord Bridge Press.

Chinatown. 1974. Directed by Roman Polanski. Paramount Pictures.

Comer, D.R., and Vega, G. 2005. Using the concept of the personal ethical threshold to develop students' moral courage. *Journal of Business Ethics Education* 2(2), 171–198.

———. 2008. Using the PET assessment instrument to help students identify factors that could impede their moral behavior. *Journal of Business Ethics* 77(2), 129–145.

Cooper, J., and Fazio, R.H. 1984. A new look at dissonance theory. In *Advances in experimental social psychology,* vol. 17, ed. L. Berkowitz, 229–266. New York: Academic Press.

Dench, S. 2006. How personal can ethics get? *Journal of Management Development* 25(1), 1013–1017.

Dillon, M. 2002. Frank Serpico: The roots of character. *F&L Primo* 2(7), 21–26.

Eagly, A.H., and Chaiken, S. 1993. *The psychology of attitudes.* Fort Worth, TX: Harcourt Brace Jovanovich.

Eight Men Out. 1988. Directed by John Sayles. Orion Pictures.

Festinger, L. 1957. *A theory of cognitive dissonance.* Palo Alto: Stanford University Press.

Graham, J., Haidt, J., and Rimm-Kaufman, S.E. 2008. Ideology and intuition in moral education. *European Journal of Developmental Science* 2(3), 269–286.

Greenfield, W.M. 2004. In the name of corporate social responsibility. *Business Horizons* 47(1), 19–28.

Haidt, J., and Graham, J. 2009. Planet of the Durkheimians, where community, authority, and sacredness are foundations of morality. In *Social and psychological bases of ideology and system justification,* ed. J. Jost, A.C. Kay, and H. Thorisdottir, 371–401. New York: Oxford University Press.

Henriques, D.B. 2009. At Madoff hearing, lawmakers lay into S.E.C. *New York Times,* February 4, Business section, B4.

Jones, T.M. 1991. Ethical decision making by individuals in organizations: An issue-contingent model. *Academy of Management Review* 16(2), 366–395.

Jones, T.M., and Ryan, L.V. 1997. The link between ethical judgment and action in organizations: A moral approbation approach. *Organization Science* 8(6), 663–680.

Kilgannon, C. 2010. Serpico on Serpico. *New York Times,* January 24, Metropolitan section, B1, B6.

Luban, D. 2003. Integrity in the practice of law: Its causes and cures. *Fordham Law Review* 72, 279–310.

Maas, P. 1973. *Serpico.* New York: Viking Press.

Moberg, D.J. 2011. The organizational context of moral courage: Creating environments that account for dual-processing models of courageous behavior. In *Moral courage in organizations: Doing the right thing at work,* ed. D.R. Comer and G. Vega, 188–208. Armonk, NY: M.E. Sharpe.

———. 2006. Best intentions, worst results: Grounding ethics students in the realities of organizational context. *Academy of Management Learning and Education* 5(3), 307–316.

Nelson, A. 2009. *Red orchestra: The story of the Berlin underground and the circle of friends who resisted Hitler.* New York: Random House.

Obama, B. 2009. Inaugural address. *New York Times,* January 20. At www.nytimes.com/2009/01/20/us/politics/20text-obama.html, (accessed January 21, 2009).

Olson, J.M., and Stone, J.S. 2005. The influence of behavior on attitudes. In *The handbook of attitudes,* ed. D. Albarracín, B.T. Johnson, and M.P. Zanna, 223–271. Mahwah, NJ: Lawrence Erlbaum.

On the Waterfront. 1954. Directed by Elia Kazan. Columbia Pictures.

Perloff, R.M. 2003. *The dynamics of persuasion: Communication and attitudes in the 21st century* (2d ed.). Mahwah, NJ: Lawrence Erlbaum Associates.

Pinto, J., Leana, C.R., and Pil, F.K. 2008. Corrupt organizations or organizations of corrupt individuals? Two types of organizational corruption. *Academy of Management Review* 33(3), 685–709.

Roberts, R.C. 1984. Willpower and the virtues. *Philosophical Review* 93(2), 227–247.

Simon, L., Greenberg, J., and Brehm, J. 1995. Trivialization: The forgotten mode of dissonance reduction. *Journal of Personality and Social Psychology* 68(2): 247–260.

Spider-Man 2. 2004. Directed by Sam Raimi. Columbia Pictures.

Twelve Angry Men. 1957. Directed by Sidney Lumet. MGM/United Artists.

Vega, G. 2011. How the mighty have fallen. In *Moral courage in organizations: Doing the right thing at work,* ed. D.R. Comer and G. Vega, 47–59. Armonk, NY: M.E. Sharpe.

Vroom, V.H. 1964. *Work and motivation.* New York: Wiley.

Weaver, G.R., Treviño, L.K., and Agle, B. 2005. "Somebody I look up to": Ethical role models in organizations. *Organizational Dynamics* 34(4), 313–330.

Wines, W.A. 2007. Seven pillars of business ethics: Toward a comprehensive framework. *Journal of Business Ethics* 79(4), 483–499.

Zimbardo, P.G. 2007. *The Lucifer effect: Understanding how good people turn evil.* New York: Random House.

Zimbardo, P.G., and Leippe, M.R. 1991. *The psychology of attitude change and social influence.* Philadelphia: Temple University.

Part II

The Faces of Moral Courage

4

How the Mighty Have Fallen

GINA VEGA

In 2 Samuel 1: 17–27, David laments the death of his friend Jonathan and Jonathan's father Saul on the battlefield: "How the mighty are fallen," David cries. "In life they were loved and gracious . . . swifter than eagles, stronger than lions. . . . I grieve for you." Jonathan and Saul died at the Battle of Mount Gilboa, Jonathan in battle, and Saul in defeat.

Saul, the first king of Israel, was a modest man. He was humble, honest, and heroic, pious, dedicated, and generous—all reasons that he was anointed the first prince of Israel. Saul lived unassumingly and exhibited none of the excesses that future kings would enjoy—no palaces, rich foods, dancing girls. He studied, he was ritually pure. Saul was a soldier, a military leader who was anointed king, but he was unprepared to handle the role. When it became obvious that David would succeed him, Saul's frustration began to influence his actions and minimize his effectiveness. Events such as losses in battle conspired to hasten his fall and his subsequent erratic and unexpected behavior.

Saul is often seen as a tragically conflicted figure.[1] Despite his reputation as a warrior and leader, Saul committed suicide rather than face the collateral damage his behavior instigated: the death of the entire population of Nob, including eighty-five priests; the defeat of the Hebrews by the Philistines. He ended his career as an "embittered schemer and plotter,"[2] after his jealousy over David's future succession to the throne led him to perform unthinkable acts such as throwing a spear at David twice while he was playing his harp, sending David into battle with the Philistines assuming he would be killed, and plotting (and failing) at multiple attempts on David's life. According to Elie Wiesel, "Despite or because of his complexity, Saul seems profoundly pathetic: one cannot but empathize with his fate."[3] How and why did his personality undergo such a dramatic shift after he became king? This is the same question we ask about today's leaders who have mimicked the various obsessions exhibited by Saul 3,000 years ago.

Values and Leadership

Nearly twenty years ago, Linda Klebe Treviño and Stuart Youngblood suggested that there are multiple inputs to ethical decisions.[4] To reprise their central argument briefly, rather than labeling people "bad apples" or labeling environments "bad barrels," it is a combination of weakness in moral character and poisonous organizational environments that creates unethical decisions. Treviño and Youngblood concluded that ethical decision making is a complex phenomenon that involves the interactions of individuals with organizational rewards and punishment. Organizational development (OD) specialists who examine organizational structure and psychologists and philosophers who consider individual behavior have not reversed their thinking on ethical decision making. The main evolution in ethical decision-making thought concentrates on character and values as epitomized by Rushworth Kidder's focus on moral courage.[5]

In an age where lax standards have led to casual malfeasance and arrogance on the part of organizational leaders, a focus on Aristotelian virtues, the first of which is courage, has enjoyed resurgence. Aristotle argues that courage is the disposition to confront dangerous situations without being too bold or too fearful.[6] We understand innately what this means in relation to physical danger (war, mugging, fire, and the like), but applying the principle of courage to business decision making requires profound consideration.

Courage manifests itself in the area between recklessness/carelessness and cowardice; because of this, the person who is courageous must have previously faced a threatening situation with the likelihood of repercussions from action and acted anyway. It is important to note that courageous actions are not foolhardy actions; they do not involve unnecessary risk or excessive personal jeopardy. Courageous actions are thoughtful and deliberate, relying both on instinct and on reason, as well as careful analysis of the consequences—heart and head. So, why have so many business leaders failed so massively to exhibit courage in their actions? In this chapter, we consider how risk, reward, and moral hazard were involved in three examples of public failure of moral courage and the myths that allowed them to occur.

Failure Writ Large: Risk, Reward, and Moral Hazard

Let's begin with three definitions.

- *Risk:* venturing into the unknown; taking the first step off the flat world; that is, if you don't know what's behind the door, you may be cautious when opening it.

- *Reward:* payback or consequences for actions initiated or completed; that is, the results of your actions may be positive or negative.
- *Moral Hazard:* the lack of incentive to guard against risk when you are protected against the risk, such as with insurance; that is, if your car is insured, you may be less mindful of locking the doors at night. According to InvestorWords.com, moral hazard can be defined as "The risk that the presence of a contract will affect the behavior of one or more parties. The classic example is in the insurance industry, where coverage against a loss might increase the risk-taking behavior of the insured."

These three concepts activate contradictory motivations and together create potentially explosive ethical dilemmas in the business world. Risk may be frightening or it may be thrilling. Rewards may be desirable, but consequences may be unwelcome. Moral hazard can encourage carelessness or conflict of interest. The interaction of these concepts without the mitigation of moral courage has resulted in notable implosions within the past decade. Would any such list be complete without Bernard Madoff and his Ponzi scheme in the number-one position?

2009: The Year of the Disgraced Financier—Bernard Madoff

In 1962, only two years out of college, Bernard Madoff began managing investment accounts under the aegis of his father-in-law's accounting firm.[7] He made money at a time when the stock market was not highly regulated. By the mid-1980s, Madoff had made a name for himself in the stock market and in the new electronic trading processes, and his successes escalated, even as he began the largest stock fraud in history. At his trial, Bernard Madoff claimed to have run his Ponzi scheme successfully since 1991 through his friends, connections, and the elite of philanthropic communities across the country and, later, around the world. Until December 10, 2008, he defrauded billions from investors. Then, on December 11, it was over.

With no affect and no apparent remorse, Madoff turned himself in, confessed his crimes, and acknowledged enormous losses of his clients' funds. Shocked into silence, normally eloquent investors were photographed looking stunned. Newspapers printed articles and letters decrying Madoff's actions. The Web was alive with blogs condemning the events. Formerly wealthy people feared they would become homeless. Philanthropic foundations closed down, creating a domino effect among small nonprofits that depended upon the foundations' donations for existence. Life savings were wiped out. Each time Madoff was photographed with his baseball cap and serene demi-smile, people became more inflamed and more puzzled.

Gradually, the story emerged that the SEC had been warned about the Ponzi scheme more than fifteen years prior, but they failed to act to shut it down. At the time of that investigation, Bernard Madoff was president of NASDAQ, and his business was responsible for an unheard-of 9 percent of all trading on the stock exchange. Although Madoff was unregistered and unlicensed as an advisor, his company traded for 3,200 clients, promising and delivering returns of 15–19 percent regardless of whether the market went up or down. It became clear that no one had done due diligence on the actions of Madoff's firm or of Madoff himself. Claims that he would not describe his trading scheme because it was a proprietary trading model were accepted by the grateful recipients of extraordinary returns on their investments. No one wanted to look too closely, until the economy forced Madoff's hand and the necessity of paying out large sums made him see that he was out of business.

Madoff had managed the significant *risk* and enjoyed very favorable *rewards*. His fraud was protected from discovery by the continuing desire of his clients to participate in the pleasures of receiving something for nothing. His associates, clients, and friends did not simply ask, "How could he do this?" Instead they were outraged: "How could he do this to us?" The moral courage to avoid the easy but illegal dollar was nowhere to be found, on the part of anyone.

2008: The Year of the Mortgage Meltdown— The American Public

Even before Madoff became the poster boy for financial disaster, the economic scene was well set for collapse. The mighty monolith known as the American public, with strength in numbers and faith in capitalism, participated eagerly in the destruction of their own economy. The trusted maxim that real estate is always a good investment and, contrary to the laws of gravity, that housing prices always go up and "never" come down led many into the double trap of the adjustable rate mortgage (ARM) and subprime mortgage loans. The ARM is a mortgage product whose interest rate varies according to one of several government indices. It is possible for the rate to go down (as it did during 2009), but it is more common for it go up, as it did during 2006 to 2007 (as the housing bubble burst). A subprime mortgage is a risky loan (risky for all parties involved) due to the potential inability of the mortgage holder to pay the fees because of the size of the loan, "traditional" or "nontraditional" structure of the loan, borrower credit rating (a FICO score below 640 is considered high risk), ratio of borrower debt to income or assets, ratio of loan to value or collateral, or documentation that does not meet Fannie Mae or Freddy Mac (federal guarantors) guidelines. The granting of one subprime ARM sets the stage for an individual tragedy; the granting of hundreds of thousands of them is a debacle waiting to happen.

Senator Christopher Dodd, chairman of the Banking, Housing, and Urban Affairs Committee, announced in February 2007 that about 80 percent of the subprime mortgages issued in the mid-2000s were adjustable rate mortgages.[8] As money became tighter, interest rates went up, sometimes doubling the monthly load on the mortgage holder.[9] Tantalized by easy access to mortgages and in the name of the American Dream, the vast majority of new home owners put themselves in properties they could not afford. They had overextended themselves from the very start, often buying property with no down payment and no proof of income (so-called "liar loans"). The warnings were clear to anyone who was looking; the loans were a house of cards trembling in the economic breeze. Sadly, no one was noticing. Home ownership had long been an American ideal, and we were all "entitled" to own our homes. The result was first a flood of foreclosures, then the federal takeover of Fannie Mae and Freddie Mac in September 2008 in a desperate attempt to keep the two agencies from defaulting on $5 trillion in mortgage-backed securities.

Where was the moral courage of the American public to take a stand against overextending itself? Against taking on too much debt? Against pretending that nothing could happen to affect income negatively? Backed by mortgage companies and investment banks that had the vision of dollars dancing in their dreams, the American public was complicit in ignoring the *risk* of shouldering more debt than it could possibly cover. The hoped-for *reward* of being a home owner blinded people to the downside of the risk: losing their longed-for home, all their assets, and their possibility of starting anew. They were fearless (but not courageous), deluded by the *moral hazard* offered by their optimistic belief in a perfect future.

2001: The Year of the Profiteer—Enron

The turn of the millennium brought with it a series of semi-apocalyptic events that foreshadowed the economic disasters that followed. Trivialized by the term "scandal," the examples of arrogance and wrongdoing were equated to embarrassing but scarcely horrific stories of sexual capers and political antics, and the longer-ranging implications of the behavior were overlooked. Perhaps because the country was overwhelmed by the tragedy of 9/11, the financial community did not sufficiently take to heart the lessons provided by Enron, Tyco, Adelphia, Worldcom/MCI, and Global Crossing. The response to these "scandals" was limited to a flurry of legislation and the rapid passage of the Sarbanes-Oxley Act (SOX) in 2002. SOX imposed regulation on the management and behavior of public companies and strengthened corporate accounting controls through auditing and the requirement for senior executives to take individual responsibility for the actions of their organizations. It is unclear whether SOX has had an overall positive or negative effect on the workings of the U.S. stock market; some claim that smaller corporations are listing in London rather than in New York because of the restrictions and expense imposed by the act,[10] but others insist that the newly reliable financial statements provide evidence of the efficacy of SOX.[11]

From the time Kenneth Lay became CEO of Enron in 1985, its principals were tainted with accusations of corruption and fraud. The company appeared to be a haven for failed executives and fast operators who functioned just under the legal radar in an effort to push limits and achieve more, ethics be damned. Fraud was a way of life for Kenneth Lay, Jeffrey Skilling, and Andrew Fastow, although Lay, CEO and chairman of Enron from 1985 to 2003, argued until his death in 2006 that he was fooled and misled by his executive subordinates. Skilling, promoted to COO in 1997, introduced "mark-to-market" accounting that allowed Enron to post anticipated future profits as if they were real, creating a fantasy surrounding the value of Enron stock. Andrew Fastow, CFO from 1997 to 2001, provided the number-crunching skills to implement Skilling's creative accounting vision. Caught up as they were in their own personal sense of superiority, this team of rogues destroyed one of the "country's coolest companies."[12]

Fifteen years of shady deals culminated in the events of 2001, including rolling blackouts for California at times of peak demand, securities fraud, conflicts of interest, and a series of complex illegal accounting actions. Bankruptcy and acknowledgment of years of overstated profits closed out 2001. The year 2002 brought admissions from Arthur Andersen that they had destroyed Enron documents in the last quarter of 2001, and a former executive admitted that Enron itself had destroyed documents in the beginning of 2002.

The arrogance exhibited by the Enron principals over the course of fifteen years was stunning, and the financial impact of its corporate improprieties was far-reaching. Overall, over $1 billion was lost in illegal Enron activities;[13] 4,000 people lost jobs at Enron,[14] while another 28,000 lost jobs as a result of the shutdown of Arthur Andersen;[15] and an estimated $800 million in retirement savings for Enron employees disappeared. Lay, Skilling, and Fastow had seriously underestimated the *risk* inherent in their behaviors; they enjoyed the *rewards* until they could do so no longer; and they functioned for more than a decade under the *moral hazard* of being able to control the energy allocations in large geographic areas of the United States. Where was the moral courage that could have sustained the continuing existence of Enron? According to Sims and Brinkmann, "Enron's top executives set the tone for this culture. Personal ambition and greed seemed to overshadow much of their corporate and individual lives. They strove to maximize their individual wealth by initiating and participating in scandalous behaviors. Enron's culture created an atmosphere ripe for the unethical and illegal behavior that occurred."[16]

Debunking the Myths We Fall For

Why do we fall, over and over again, for the same scams and temptations? Some smugly say that it's our greed—we always want to believe that we can get something for nothing. After all, we are not like Saul, modest, unassuming, and pure. In fact, purity does not even appear on the radar of many individuals, according to psychologist Jonathan Haidt.[17] We want more, and our national culture endorses and reinforces that desire. Some condescendingly suggest that most of us are simply not smart enough to recognize a scam when we see one. But the scams we fall for most often are sophisticated and well designed; succumbing is not necessarily a signal of lesser intelligence, but rather a signal of less financial education. Others sneer about naïve adults who believe in fairy tales. Are Americans less cynical and worldly-wise than other nationalities? Perhaps, but people all over the world have fallen for the same scams, frauds, and misdirection. Still others adhere to the "survival of the fittest" maxim, playing on Darwin's theory of natural selection. The theory adaptation would be better named, "All's fair in love and war (and economics)."

I propose that none of these explanations works. I suggest instead that we have unwittingly endorsed a series of communal myths; that our collective unconscious has subscribed to several beliefs that allow our mighty to continue to wreak their economic havoc on our wallets, bank accounts, institutions, and government.[18] These myths are insidious because they are all based on our operationalized values: the one with the most toys wins; if you're not a winner, you're a loser; get something for nothing when you can; and do whatever you like as long as you don't get caught.

Myth 1: The Rational Man
Myth 2: The Allure of Everest
Myth 3: The African King
Myth 4: Rules Work

The Myth of the Rational Man

The rational man, or person, is a construct of the science of economics, which postulates that decisions are made to optimize utility; that is, to get the best possible economic outcome. This ideal-world description has been modified to state that people will make decisions based on their own self-interest, bounded by the information they have and the anticipated utility of the outcome of their decision.[19] This system of decision making is known as "bounded rationality" because the decision maker is bounded by limited information, time, energy, and understanding of potential utility. Utility—the measure of satisfaction received—always underlies this decision-making process. It is here that utility as described in economics and philosophy collides with utility as used in politics and rhetoric, because in the latter pair, "reason" has nothing to do with utility; the effort involved in making political choices requires intensive research disproportionate to the anticipated result.[20]

Decisions made using bounded rationality are emotional decisions based on desired outcomes. Once desire enters the equation, reason dissipates. What is it that we desire? Aristotle would say we all desire happiness. Utilitarians extend this to include the greatest amount of happiness for the largest number of people. Some psychologists would suggest that money is the most powerful extrinsic motivator, while personal satisfaction from self-expression is the most powerful intrinsic motivator. These responses appear to distill to a basic agreement that people want to be happy . . . whatever that may mean to the individual. Unfortunately, rational man is an amoral person, seeking only to maximize the utility of his own decisions, heedless of the impact of his decisions on others. The rational person does not weigh the risk vis-à-vis the reward; his focus is purely on the reward.

Returning briefly to Saul, his original happiness seems to have derived from his personal value system that elevated humility, generosity, purity, and study to the highest rank. When threatened with the loss of his power as king, he experienced an irrational shift in values, and his happiness disappeared concurrently with his moral courage. When the "mighty" described in this chapter lost their ability to exert moral courage and find happiness or fulfillment through legitimate means, their need to make decisions based on pure utility overrode society's generally endorsed values; morality and ethics became irrelevant, perhaps even naïve or foolish.

The Myth of the Allure of Everest

When George Mallory was asked in 1924 why he wanted to climb Mt. Everest, he replied famously, "Because it's there." We can expand his intent to include, "And because I can." Sometimes, the challenge alone is sufficient to encourage people to seek the risk and imagine only the positive reward. Mallory did not expect that he would die in his attempt on Everest, but he was not even concerned about the possibility. His longer quote makes that clear:

So, if you cannot understand that there is something in man which responds to the challenge of this mountain and goes out to meet it, that the struggle is the struggle of life itself upward and forever upward, then you won't see why we go. What we get from this adventure is just sheer joy. And joy is, after all, the end of life. We do not live to eat and make money. We eat and make money to be able to enjoy life. That is what life means and what life is for.[21]

Individuals who are moved by the Allure of Everest are different from the Rational Man and seek happiness through thrills, with risk as its own reward. For people like this, just being able to succeed in a scam is sufficient motivation to conduct one. The appeal of Mt. Everest is universal—bigger than life, the danger is extreme, very few people can conquer it, and conquering it means standing on top of the world. What could be better than to be first among peers? The way that capitalism has evolved, competition is the key to success. Originally, in Adam Smith's formulation, competition was meant to be cooperative and collaborative. Today, competition is a zero-sum game with winners and losers. If you want to win badly enough, if you burn to succeed, you may be willing to set aside any number of moral values. Moral courage hasn't a prayer in a competition with standing on top of the world, but the competitors don't set out with that idea in mind. Saul's goal was not so much to discredit David as to retain power in his own bloodline. When moral courage drops away, it does so incrementally, and, like the frog in cold water that slowly comes to a boil, we don't notice that we are cooked until it's too late.

The Myth of the African King

Somewhere in Africa there is a legitimate ruler who needs your help, but he's probably not in Nigeria and he probably has not asked henchmen to solicit financial aid or bank account information and PINS from innocent e-mail readers. Why do people fall for scams, especially scams that seem so transparent?

One reason is basic human kindness. We do want to help someone in need if we can. After all, we are generous people, right? Babies as young as eighteen months will try to help even unrelated adults who have their hands full and have dropped a clothespin, for example.[22] We've been helped by others before. Now is the time to "pay it forward." Plus, there's a little something in it for us, as well. And it's only right, isn't it, to get reimbursed for your effort? We can easily talk ourselves into believing even the most outlandish of scams if it means that we will benefit and be able to help someone else at the same time. It fits in with all our homespun folk wisdom—killing two birds with one stone, one hand washing the other, your scratching my back and my scratching yours, etc. We *want* to believe that we are helping and that we will get rewarded. We *want* to believe that there is little or no risk to our behavior. We *want* to believe that, because we are good people, we will be looked after and protected (the individual's version of moral hazard). We do not want to hear, as did Saul, that we are about to lose the major battle of our lives. We resist this knowledge. As we saw earlier in this chapter, once emotion makes the decisions for us, our values take a second seat and, almost before we know it, we have been scammed and we are afraid to admit it, because our own role in the process demanded that we be willing to take advantage of someone else (or to believe that we had done so). We are embarrassed.

The Myth That Rules Work

When we make rules, people abide by them. Stop laughing. I mean it. Are you still laughing? What could be sillier than to believe this myth? Yet, we all do. We establish our watchdog organizations, our regulatory agencies, our multivolume rule books. And we are still surprised when people behave badly, don't follow the rules, and don't care that we stamp our proverbial foot to get them to pay attention. Even the simplest of rule-based systems, the Ten Commandments in its various representations, is violated regularly and observed more in the breach than in the adherence. Ten little rules, and we can't follow them. The short version, one rule—the Golden Rule—also fails to move us. One rule. So why do we imagine that building regulations, rule books, and watchdogs will control human behavior, especially when the watchdogs have no teeth?

It is much easier to get people to listen to you when you are right there with them. When a state trooper sees you speeding, catches you on radar, pulls you over to the side of the road, checks your license, and "rewards" you with a speeding ticket, you will have learned that the next time you want to speed, you should check carefully for state troopers and radar. Will you have learned not to speed? Probably not, but you have learned to manage your *risk* in order to avoid the negative and costly consequence.

If a direct personal interaction with a member of the police force does not stop risky behavior, it is unlikely that a long-distance relationship with a rule book or a regulatory agency will have an impact on risk, particularly if the consequence is a slap on the wrist, a small fine, or a warning such as issued by most government agencies. In early 2009, the Peanut Corporation of America and its president, Stewart Parnell, were accused of knowingly shipping contaminated peanut products. These peanuts resulted in multiple deaths from salmonella and illness in forty-four states. The peanuts had been tested according to FDA regulations at a lab that found ten positive samples out of one thousand. Mr. Parnell's response was to switch labs because of the frequency with which this lab found contaminants.[23] Shortly thereafter, the Peanut Corporation filed for bankruptcy protection, and the Texas Department of Agriculture discovered that the plant did not have a state health certificate and that an inspector had "accepted incomplete information."[24] Penalties for this? Peanuts.

Or consider this case: an anesthesiologist published twenty-one studies in medical journals over thirteen years about pain management postsurgery. This would have been a noble endeavor had he not invented most of the data. In many cases, there were no clinical trials at all because there were no patients. Dr. Scott Reuben had accepted funding from Pfizer, the manufacturer of Celebrex and Lyrica, to determine the efficacy of the drugs in relation to orthopedic surgery pain. Not surprisingly, Dr. Reuben's findings were favorable toward Celebrex, although these results have not been replicated by other legitimate researchers.[25] The articles in question were published in peer-reviewed journals (ten of them in *Anesthesia and Analgesia*), and the research was conducted under the auspices of the Baystate Medical Center in Springfield, MA, where, as in all hospitals, human subject research is governed by professional oversight. The consequence to Dr. Reuben of this massive medical fraud? As of May 2009, he was on indefinite medical leave.

With the notable exception of Madoff's sentence of 150 years in prison (and the even longer sentences awarded in 2000 to Sholam Weiss of 845 years and in 2008 to Norman Schmidt of 330 years),[26] there appear to be few penalties for violating the rules, even when those violations result in pain, illness, or death. Even Saul tried to avoid punishment at the hands of the Philistines by committing suicide before he could be captured. It is very difficult to imagine why we continue to believe that rules work in light of recurring examples such as these that they clearly do not.[27] Moral courage does not appear to be sufficiently common to guarantee good behavior and deter bad behavior. When the *risk* of being caught is small, and the *consequences* of being caught are negligible, a *moral hazard* is automatically established. The deadly trio leads in only one direction, to a repetition of the previous behavior. Then, if the risk and consequences have increased in small increments, when lawbreakers are ultimately caught, we are all shocked: How could they think they could get away with this?

Conclusion: A Values Deficit

It seems that our cultural expectations include acceptance of a "values deficit"—tolerance for moral failure due to our personal values limitations—as a legitimate mode of living. Our personal limitations are exacerbated by temptation, situational pressures, and a search for the easy way out. Moral courage demands that we balance our desires with restraint and seek not the easy way but the way we know is right. Although we may entertain choosing the easy way out, overcoming—instead of giving in to—temptation defines our status as "mighty" or as frauds.

The message from these stories is clear; let us rephrase the advice given by real estate agents: the three most important criteria for ethical behavior are Values, Values, Values.

Notes

1. Finkelstein and Silberman, 2006.
2. Biberfeld, 1978, 58.
3. Wiesel, 1981, 84.
4. Treviño and Youngblood, 1990.
5. Kidder, 2005.
6. Aristotle, 350 B.C.E.
7. PBS, 2009.
8. Dodd, 2007.
9. Arnold, 2007.
10. Malone, 2008; Piotroski and Srinivasan, 2008.
11. Rockness and Rockness, 2005.
12. Saporito, 2002.
13. Rockness and Rockness, 2005, 38.
14. Bragg, December 2002.
15. Schwartz and Ketz, 2006, 204.
16. Sims and Brinkmann, 2003, 253.
17. Jacobs, 2009.
18. See Jung (1964) for a discussion of the collective unconscious.
19. See Simon, 1991.
20. Ingram, 1995, 89.
21. Mallory, 1922, in Hornbein, 1998, 86.
22. Tomasello, 2009, in Wade, December 1, 2009.
23. Zhang and Jargon, 2009.
24. Martin, 2009, B2.
25. Borell, 2009; Kowalczyk, 2009.
26. Jones, 2009.
27. Michael, 2006.

References

Aristotle. 350 B.C.E. *Nicomachean ethics*. Book 3: 8–10, trans. W.D. Ross. www.constitution.org/ari/ethic_03.htm (accessed June 25, 2009).
Arnold, C. 2007. Economists brace for worsening subprime crisis. *All Things Considered*, August 7. At www.npr.org/templates/story/story.php?storyId=12561184 (accessed June 18, 2009).
Biberfeld, H. 1978. *David, king of Israel*. Jerusalem, Israel: Feldheim Publishers.

Borell, B. 2009. A medical Madoff: Anesthesiologist faked data in 21 studies. *Scientific American*, March 10. At www.scientificamerican.com/article.cfm?id=a-medical-madoff-anesthestesiologist-faked-data&page=3 (accessed June 22, 2009).

Bragg, R. 2002. Enron's collapse: Workers feel pain of layoffs and added sting of betrayal. *New York Times,* January 20, Section 1, p. 1.

Dodd, C. 2007. Senator Dodd: Create, sustain, preserve, and protect the American dream of home ownership. February 7. At http://dodd.senate.gov/?q = node/3731 (accessed June 18, 2009).

Finkelstein, I., and Silberman, N.A. 2006. *David and Solomon: In search of the Bible's sacred kings and the roots of the western tradition.* New York: Free Press.

Hornbein, T.F. 1998. *Everest: The west ridge.* Seattle: The Mountaineers.

Ingram, D. 1995. *Reason, history, and politics.* Albany, NY: SUNY Press.

InvestorWords.com. 2009. Moral hazard. At www.investorwords.com/3117/moral_hazard.html (accessed July 5, 2009).

Jacobs, T. 2009. Morals authority. *Miller-McCune,* May–June, 46–55.

Jones, A. 2009. Madoff's 150 year sentence: Long, but not longest. *Wall Street Journal*, June 29.

Jung, C.G. 1964. *Man and his symbols.* New York: Dell.

Kidder, R.M. 2005. *Moral courage.* New York: HarperCollins.

Kowalczyk, L. 2009. Doctor accused of faking studies. *Boston Globe*, March 11, B1.

Malone, M.S. 2008. Washington is killing Silicon Valley. *Wall Street Journal*, December 22, A19.

Martin, A. 2009. Troubled peanut company files for bankruptcy protection. *New York Times,* February 14, B2.

Michael, M.L. 2006. Business ethics: The law of rule. *Business Ethics Quarterly* 16(4), 475–504.

Piotroski, J.D., and Srinivasan, S. 2008. Regulation and bonding: The Sarbanes-Oxley Act and the flow of international listings. Working paper no. 11, January. Rock Center for Corporate Governance at Stanford University.

Public Broadcasting System (PBS). 2009. The Madoff affair: Timeline. *Frontline.* At www.pbs.org/wgbh/pages/frontline/madoff/cron/ (accessed June 18, 2009).

Rockness, H., and Rockness, J. 2005. Legislated ethics: From Enron to Sarbanes-Oxley, the impact on corporate America. *Journal of Business Ethics* 57, 31–54.

Saporito, B. 2002. How Fastow helped Enron fall. *Time*, February 10. At www.time.com/time/business/article/0,8599,201871,00.html (accessed June 22, 2009).

Schwartz, B.N., and Ketz, J.E. 2006. *Advances in accounting education.* Bingley, UK: Emerald Group.

Simon, H. 1991. Bounded rationality and organizational learning. *Organization Science* 2(1), 125–134.

Sims, R.R., and Brinkmann, J. 2003. Enron ethics (or: Culture matters more than codes). *Journal of Business Ethics* 45, 243–256.

Treviño, L.K., and Youngblood, S. 1990. Bad apples in bad barrels: A causal analysis of ethical decision-making behavior. *Journal of Applied Psychology* 75(4), 378–385.

Wade, N. 2009. We may be born with an urge to help. *New York Times*, December 1, D1.

Wiesel, E. 1981. *Five Biblical portraits.* Notre Dame: University of Notre Dame Press.

Zhang, J., and Jargon, J. 2009. Peanut Corp. e-mails cast harsh light on executive. *Wall Street Journal*, February 4, A4.

5

For the Greater Good

The Moral Courage of Whistleblowers

Stephen M. Kohn

Whistleblowing is no longer a uniquely American phenomenon. It has gone international.[1] It is on the agenda of governments on every continent of the globe. In 1999, the Council of Europe mandated whistleblower protections for every country in Europe.[2] Four years later, the United Nations approved a major Anti-Corruption Convention, signed by more than 130 nations (including the United States), that also created a mandate that nations throughout the world enact whistleblower protections.[3] These revolutionary provisions are the result of recognition that the success of anticorruption programs depends on employee whistleblowers.

Whistleblowing can have dramatic and powerful consequences. President Nixon resigned from office in large part due to the disclosures of one whistleblower.[4] President Clinton was impeached and found in contempt of court as the result of another whistleblower.[5] The disclosures of yet another whistleblower successfully challenged the legitimacy of the entire Vietnam War.[6] More recently, a Swiss banker exposed an illegal offshore tax scheme, managed at the time by the largest bank in the world: UBS. His disclosures have shaken the very foundations of bank secrecy in Switzerland, yielded billions of dollars in recovery to the U.S. Treasury, and, as of late 2009, resulted in more than 14,000 wealthy U.S. citizens' disclosing their secret offshore tax shelters, paying fines and back taxes, and facing legal penalties.[7]

The whistleblower who blew the lid off the Watergate scandal, "Deep Throat," was a high-ranking FBI official who risked his government career and reputation to expose grave threats to Americans' civil liberties. The Vietnam War whistleblower, Daniel Ellsberg, took even greater risks: He not only put his career on the line, he also risked his personal freedom. The government, wanting to conceal its misconduct in escalating the Vietnam War, considered his leaking of the Pentagon Papers a crime. After Ellsberg released the information to the *Washington Post* and the *New York Times*, he was indicted for improperly disclosing classified information and faced a long prison sentence.[8] These whistleblowers were deeply concerned about crimes committed by influential high-ranking officials. They cared about democracy and the rule of law. Their actions changed the public's perception of whistleblowers, demonstrated the power of employees who credibly exposed wrongdoing, and resulted in new laws that have revolutionized the employee-employer relationship in the context of fraud detection.

The story of whistleblowing goes beyond the benefits to society and organizations. It also entails the moral courage of whistleblowers, who typically take great risks and make personal and professional sacrifices.

The Benefits of Whistleblowing

A Definition of Whistleblowers

The National Whistleblower Center defines a whistleblower as:

- One whose loyalty is to the truth.
- One who exposes government or corporate misconduct, violations of environmental laws, threats to the public safety, or general employment actions that violate the law, risking his or her financial security and professional reputation in an effort to stop harmful actions on behalf of the public interest.

Because whistleblowers are current or former employees (including top-ranking officials) or contractors, they have access to inside information that is essential for keeping government and corporations honest. But whistleblowers do not just expose embarrassing national scandals to the newspapers. Far from it. Whistleblowers witness fraud, abuse, and other illegalities and report their observations to the appropriate authorities. Often they make their initial report to their manager or to an internal compliance officer or "hotline." However, if the issues they raise are not resolved, some whistleblowers will go further, reporting their information externally to the government.

The Role of Whistleblowers in Fraud Detection

There is solid evidence that whistleblowers' disclosures play a critical role in uncovering fraud. This evidence is not merely anecdotal. It comes from statistically valid surveys of the detection of fraud and from records generated as a result of the provisions of the False Claims Act.

Fraud is unlike other crimes. When someone is murdered, there usually is a body, which prompts an outcry for justice. If someone breaks into your home, no one objects to your calling the police. Street crime is not secret. But fraud is designed to escape detection. The essence of the wrongdoing is hidden. Bribes are not paid in public. If someone cheats on a government contract, who will find out? If a corporation lies to its shareholders, who would threaten their own jobs or the economic vitality of their employer to ensure that a higher dividend is paid? Moreover, in cases like the UBS bank scandal, entire industries are structured around hiding money to avoid taxes or conceal ill-gotten gain. Detection of governmental or corporate wrongdoing is completely distinct from detecting street crime.

How, then, is such wrongdoing discovered?

The PricewaterhouseCoopers Survey

Among the first organizations to study corporate fraud detection was the international corporate auditing firm PricewaterhouseCoopers (PwC). In 2007, PwC conducted a comprehensive survey of the chief executive officers, chief financial officers, and responsible compliance executives from more than 5,400 companies in forty countries. PwC issued the following findings:

- "Fraud remains one of the most problematic issues for business worldwide," but in order to detect and combat fraud, corporations "cannot rely on internal controls" to "detect and deter economic crimes."
- "[I]n virtually every region of the world, whistle-blowing is playing a role in uncovering the activities of wrongdoers. More and more companies are now promoting whistle-blowing policies as an integral part of their risk management programs."[9]

PwC reported that internal controls designed to detect fraud were insufficient; rather, 43 percent of corporate fraud was uncovered by the activities of whistleblowing tipsters. Based on their findings, PwC recommended that companies change their corporate culture and promote whistleblowing. They also recommended strict prohibitions against employee-whistleblower retaliation.

The Association of Certified Fraud Examiners Report

The Association of Certified Fraud Examiners (ACFE) obtained similar findings in a review of 959 cases of fraud.[10] In its 2008 report the ACFE underscored that insiders (i.e., whistleblowers) are essential for any effective antifraud program because "one of the primary characteristics of fraud is that it is clandestine, or hidden; almost all fraud involves the attempted concealment of the crime."[11] Furthermore, the ACFE report concluded that whistleblowers/tipsters uncover more fraud than internal corporate controls. Significantly, the ACFE found that whistleblowers/tipsters uncovered 46 percent of all frauds, a statistic remarkably similar to PwC's findings. Not surprisingly, the overwhelming majority of tipsters were internal employee whistleblowers. Like PwC, the ACFE recognized the contributions of employee whistleblowers and strongly endorsed changes in corporate culture that would encourage individuals to blow the whistle on illegal and/or unethical behavior in their organizations.

Data from False Claims Act Cases

The PwC and ACFE reports provide statistical confirmation of the critical role whistleblowers play in the detection of fraud. The contributions of whistleblowers to rooting out misconduct can also be demonstrated on a dollar-by-dollar basis. There is one major whistleblower law in the United States that not only protects employees from being fired, but also rewards them for exposing fraud in government contracting. Under the False Claims Act (31 U.S.C. § 3730), whistleblowers who risk their careers to expose corruption in government contracting are entitled to a percentage-reward based on the amount of money recovered from the dishonest government vendor.

Here is how the False Claims Act works: Assume a company is awarded a contract to build a bridge. As part of that contract the company is paid $10 million for high-grade cement. To cut corners and increase its profit, the company instead buys the lowest quality of cement. A whistleblower detects this and reports the fraud to the government. After investigation, if the whistleblower is vindicated, the company must pay back to the United States *treble damages* (i.e., three times the amount of the fraud). In this case, the company could owe the United States $30 million. The company is prohibited from firing the whistleblower, whom the government pays between 15 and 30 percent of the amount recovered from the contractor.[12]

Unlike other whistleblower laws, whose benefits are based on anecdotal evidence, this law requires the government to quantify the contributions of the whistleblower objectively. Whenever investigating and prosecuting fraud in government contracting, the United States must divide the cases into two categories: fraud uncovered by government investigators or other sources and fraud disclosed by whistleblowers under the False Claims Act. These statistics must be kept carefully, as the government is obligated to pay rewards from the monies obtained under the whistleblower provisions of the False Claims Act.

The results are staggering. They completely vindicate the findings of PwC and ACFE. The majority of monies the Department of Justice's Civil Fraud Division collected from fraudulent contracts and repaid into the Treasury resulted from whistleblowing. Here are the numbers: Between October 1, 1987 (the year after the law was amended to permit whistleblower recoveries), and September 30, 2009, the U.S. Civil Fraud Division recovered a total of $24.056 billion from fraudulent government contractors. Whistleblower complaints were responsible for $15.658 billion of the recoveries. In other words, under one whistleblower law alone, United States taxpayers were able to recover more than $15 billion in repayments.[13] These monies came mostly from large contractors or grant recipients. Many of the smaller companies found guilty of defrauding the government were bankrupted. Some of the cheats went to prison. Furthermore, the $15 billion number does not quantify the massive future savings to the taxpayers by companies that have reformed their contracting practices. As part of most False Claims Act settlements, the company must agree to a comprehensive compliance program. Given the costs and potential criminal implications, most companies do not want to lose two False Claims Act cases.

As can be seen, recoveries under the whistleblower program amount to approximately 65 percent of civil fraud recoveries from government contractors. These numbers further corroborate the statistical results from the auditing firms. They demonstrate, to the dime, that whistleblowing works.

Beyond playing a critical role in the detection of fraud, whistleblowers have been instrumental in protecting the public interest. Although the government does not keep statistics on the utility of these other areas of whistleblowing, publicly available legal decisions document case after case in which whistleblowers have saved lives, protected the environment, and exposed public safety scandals.[14]

The Perils Whistleblowers Face

There is a striking gap between the power of whistleblowing to recover money and the weakness of protections for whistleblowers found at the grassroots level. Although the Council of Europe mandates whistleblower protections, only one nation in Europe—Great Britain—has enacted a compressive whistleblower protection law. And even in Great Britain, there are no whistleblower rewards programs such as the False Claims Act. Elsewhere internationally, the situation is even bleaker, as the United Nations mandate to protect whistleblowers has been all but ignored. International banking and development organizations like the World Bank, the International Monetary Fund, and the United Nations itself, which could enforce strong standards against fraud in developing countries, have no effective programs to protect or reward whistleblowers who expose contract abuses. Even in the United States, the nation that has taken the lead in whistleblower protections, there are numerous loopholes and gaps in protection. For example, the rewards programs are currently limited to government contracting and tax fraud. Employees who expose securities fraud, environmental hazards, or safety violations are not entitled to any reward, no matter how much money civil or criminal penalties generate or how much money shareholders may recover. Indeed, many areas of the U.S. economy are still without any effective national legislation protecting whistleblowers. Most notable among these are national security employees, health-care providers, and most of the financial services and securities industry.

Deep-rooted cultural prejudices against whistleblowing still exist, even in the most developed industrial societies. No one likes a snitch. Corporations demand loyalty. In every advanced democracy in the world, whistleblowers are regularly fired and ostracized. In some nations their lives are threatened, or worse. The hostility against whistleblowers can be so blatantly dangerous that the U.S. Court of Appeals for the Ninth Circuit, in a landmark ruling, found that whistleblowers whose lives are in danger can be granted political asylum in the United States.[15]

Some cases of whistleblowing have been popularized in award-winning Hollywood movies, such as *Silkwood*,[16] documenting the life and tragic death of nuclear whistleblower Karen Silkwood, portrayed by Meryl Streep; and *The Insider*,[17] starring Russell Crowe as Jeffrey Wigand, who exposed the tobacco industry's practice of using additives to make cigarettes more addictive. Most whistleblowers work out of the spotlight at ordinary jobs but, like Silkwood and Wigand, suffer significant retaliation for trying to do the right thing.[18] If the government is serious about detecting and preventing fraud, waste, and abuse and ensuring public safety, it must enact laws that protect, encourage, and reward whistleblowers.[19]

The Moral Courage of Whistleblowers as a Trigger of Change: The Case of FBI Supervisory Special Agent Frederic Whitehurst

How can the gap between (1) the objective documentation that whistleblowers are absolutely essential to ensure safety and prevent fraud and abuse and (2) the cultural hostility toward whistleblowers ever be bridged? What will impel national leaders to enact whistleblower protections powerful enough to safeguard employees who want to serve the public good?

The answer begins with the whistleblowers themselves. American whistleblowers encounter retaliation, but they are better off than their counterparts elsewhere. Neither ideological nor intellectual arguments resulted in the enactment of the more than fifty whistleblower laws that now make the United States the envy of worldwide anticorruption advocates. Instead, moral courage triggered change. There is power in the act of an employee who, often against his or her own self-interest, goes forward to challenge major misconduct within his or her own company.

A case in point is the creation of whistleblower rights within the Federal Bureau of Investigation. In January 1993, the FBI was a secretive national police agency. The bureau had successfully avoided any external oversight for years. The scandals arising from the FBI's illegal surveillance of civil rights leader Martin Luther King and its years of abuses violating the civil liberties of American citizens never succeeded in obtaining any systemic reforms. The FBI remained a closed institution, governed by the motto, "Thou Shall Not Embarrass the Bureau."

But the closed system started to crack on February 26, 1993. On that day, the World Trade Center in New York City was bombed. Terrorists drove explosive-laden cars into the Trade Center's subterranean parking area and set off powerful explosions—killing six and injuring 1,042 people. At the time, this bombing incident was viewed as the worst international terrorist attack on U.S. soil. The FBI was immediately called to investigate.

What Agent Whitehurst Knew

The initial crime scene was secured by Supervisory Special Agent Frederic Whitehurst, then the FBI's top explosive expert. A three-tour combat veteran of the Vietnam War, Whitehurst was an agent's agent—dedicated, courageous, and willing to "walk through walls" to solve a crime. But Agent Whitehurst was more than just a cop. He had earned a doctorate in chemistry from Duke University and had done postdoctoral work at Texas A&M. Agent Whitehurst was a scientist—committed to the integrity and honesty of his profession.

In response to the World Trade Center bombing, the desire to convict terrorists collided with the search for truth. There was massive pressure to find those responsible for the bombing and to convict them of their crime. The prosecutors and agents responsible for the case wanted to win. They wanted to use forensic scientific evidence to pin the case on the suspects they had arrested.

At the time, the FBI crime lab was the premier forensic crime laboratory in the world. Its results went unchallenged in most court cases. To win a case for a prosecutor it was usually enough for an FBI forensic examiner to take the stand and link material evidence to a suspect. The lab's reputation was such that most examiners were not even cross-examined in criminal cases.

However, Whitehurst knew the dirty secret of the lab. He knew that the FBI laboratory was managed not by experienced scientists but by FBI officials trained only in criminal investigation. The laboratory had never been headed by a scientist. Worse, basic protocols designed to prevent and detect contamination of evidence were not in place. Persons unschooled in science or technology operated sophisticated scientific instruments. Whitehurst had firsthand knowledge that some of the examiners in the lab were committing forensic fraud by improperly altering lab reports to meet the needs of prosecutors and producing false evidence for them to use in court.

Agent Whitehurst Learned He Had No Rights

As a scientist and patriotic American citizen, Whitehurst dedicated himself to stopping these practices. When he witnessed forensic misconduct in the World Trade Center case, he decided he could no longer remain silent—it was time to blow the whistle on the FBI to the outside world. Criminal defendants and the public needed to know what was going on behind the closed doors of the FBI. The lab needed to change—but the lab's top managers ignored Whitehurst's repeated pleas. When Whitehurst told a prosecutor in the U.S. Attorney's Office about the problems in the lab and said he would tell the truth in court, the FBI retaliated by suspending him for two weeks. What could he do?

Whitehurst was told that FBI agents had no right to blow the whistle. They worked on top-secret cases. Public discussion of open criminal matters was strictly prohibited. Because of the sensitivity of their jobs, FBI agents were excluded from coverage under the federal employee Whistleblower Protection Act of 1989. The message was clear: Shut up or be fired—and if you are fired, your career in law enforcement will be over and you will lose your pension. When Whitehurst contacted an attorney, the Department of Justice warned him that he could be fired for telling his counsel what was wrong at the crime lab.

Agent Whitehurst Persevered

But shortly before the World Trade Center bombing, Whitehurst had attended ethics training sponsored by the Justice Department. At that training, he had seen, for the first time, a copy of a presidential executive order governing all federal employees. This order, E.O. 12731 of 1990, states: "Public service is a trust requiring employees to place loyalty to the Constitution, the laws, and ethical principles above private gain. . . . Employees shall disclose waste, fraud, abuse, and corruption to appropriate authorities."

Whitehurst believed in and made a personal decision to follow the dictates of that executive order, regardless of where his action would lead him. He made the decision to contact what he considered the "appropriate authority" for reporting waste, fraud, and abuse in the FBI crime lab. Because he had already exhausted his attempts to inform his managers and the U.S. Attorney's Office, he turned to Congress.

Things started to escalate when the FBI learned that Whitehurst had written a letter to a U.S. senator. The FBI's Office of Professional Responsibility (OPR) opened an investigation of Whitehurst. His alleged crime: sending a letter to the Senate Judiciary Committee alleging misconduct in the crime lab. The OPR unit of the FBI had a reputation for harassing employees. OPR agents ordered Whitehurst to sit for an interview without the assistance of counsel. Then they drafted a confession and demanded that Whitehurst sign it. Whitehurst asked if he could talk to attorneys before signing the statement. He was told he could not because the statement was part of an open investigation and contained so-called "confidential" information. Only *after* he signed it could the document be cleared for review by his personal counsel. Whitehurst asked what would happen if he refused to sign the confession. He was told, in no uncertain terms, that signing the statement was a "direct order" and that failure to sign would constitute insubordination. In the FBI, insubordination is a very serious offense that leads to termination. Whitehurst asked if he could call his attorneys and seek their advice about whether to sign the statement. The OPR agents relented and allowed him to make his phone call. Based on recommendation of counsel, Whitehurst refused to sign.

Whitehurst's refusal to sign the OPR statement was unprecedented and launched a five-year odyssey to fix the crime lab and establish rights for FBI agents. Word of his actions reached the Justice Department press corps. The investigatory antics of OPR were legendary within the bureau and among professional journalists who closely followed that institution. OPR was one of the primary units of the bureau designed to intimidate agents and enforce bureau secrecy and loyalty. All the reporters who heard about the agent who had refused to sign his statement wanted to meet him; they soon would.

After OPR's threats against Whitehurst, a lawsuit was immediately filed asserting his rights under the First Amendment to petition Congress, to hire and communicate to attorneys of his choosing, and to engage in freedom of speech protected under the U.S. Constitution. Under an obscure (and rarely used) law, the president of the United States was also sued for a writ of mandamus asserting that the president had the duty to protect whistleblower rights for FBI agents. As the news media learned that an FBI agent was alleging violations of law at the crime lab and asserting his constitutional rights as a government worker, interest in interviewing him and hearing his concerns escalated. The ABC News show *Prime Time Live* started shooting a program and demanded from the FBI the right to interview the FBI whistleblower. Journalists had learned that Whitehurst had testified in court about problems with the FBI crime lab related to the World Trade Center bombing; they had obtained the court transcript and were hot on Whitehurst's trail.

Initially, the FBI prohibited Whitehurst from any contact with the news media. But that did not slow down ABC's highly skilled team of investigative reporters. They were able to dig up the substance of many of Whitehurst's concerns, including those related to contamination, the falsification of laboratory reports, and specific misconduct related to the World Trade Center bombing. The pressure built on the FBI to permit an interview with Whitehurst. Barring him from the press looked like a cover-up and censorship. Ultimately, ABC chief investigative correspondent Brian Ross and his producer, Vic Walters, were able to put together a powerful show, even without access to Whitehurst. On the night it aired, the FBI finally relented, and permitted Whitehurst to speak live, on air, to the reporters.[20] He was able to confirm the allegations. Perhaps most surprising for the U.S. public to learn was that the world-renowned FBI crime lab was unaccredited.

Everything changed. For the first time, the American people could see and judge for themselves a credible FBI whistleblower presenting scientific evidence that gross misconduct had compromised court cases. The implications were clear. Bad science could put people in prison for life. It could cause the execution of an innocent person. In the past, juries had believed the testimony from FBI crime lab examiners. But thousands of convictions were thrown into doubt overnight, creating uproar. Within weeks, the attorney general of the United States announced that she was assembling a prestigious independent panel of experts to review the scientific practices at the FBI crime lab, and that the Justice Department's inspector general would lead an investigation. The FBI had to concur in this result. Outside oversight—for the first time in the bureau's seventy-year history—was coming.

What Whitehurst Endured

At each step of the way, the FBI retaliated against Whitehurst, trying to force him to stop his exposures. In 1993, they first used intimidation—that is, the OPR investigation, to try to get Whitehurst to back down. That did not work. In 1995, Whitehurst was removed from his highly skilled position as the bureau's premier explosives expert and reassigned as a trainee in paint chip analysis. In 1997, as he continued to blow the whistle, he was suspended from work and threatened with discharge. That still did not stop Whitehurst.

The outcry against the retaliation was profound. Senator Charles Grassley, well known for his support of whistleblowers, took to the floor of the U.S. Senate. He warned the FBI that there would be endless "oversight wars" if Whitehurst was fired. *Washington Post* cartoonist Herb Block used humor to expose the absurdity of the FBI's retaliation. Every major news station— from Larry King to the *Today Show*—followed the story. The Court issued one of the largest Freedom of Information Act disclosure orders in U.S. history—requiring the release of documentation concerning potential FBI abuses in hundreds of criminal cases, as well as FBI records documenting the retaliation against Whitehurst. While the Court was on the verge of ruling on Whitehurst's First Amendment and writ of mandamus lawsuits, the FBI and Justice Department folded.

Reforms Within the FBI

On April 28, 1997, President William Clinton signed the Memorandum of the President establishing whistleblower rights for FBI agents.[21] For the first time in U.S. history, the FBI was subject to external oversight. Under the presidential order and the attorney general rules that followed, all FBI employees would have the right to blow the whistle to the Department of Justice Office of Inspector General, among other DOJ and FBI officials. The FBI's prior monopoly on investigating itself came to an end. The inspector general was authorized not only to protect whistleblowers, but also to investigate FBI wrongdoing. Agents gained the right to demand an administrative hearing concerning any retaliatory actions. Whitehurst had won his case. In 1998, the FBI and Justice Department settled his claims for well over $1.5 million.

But money had never been the motivation for Whitehurst, who had staked his career on exposing the truth about the crime lab and achieving systemic reforms. By the time the FBI settled the case, Whitehurst's scientific concerns were also vindicated. His allegations of misconduct were documented. Forensic misconduct was found to have harmed other nationally high-profile cases, in addition to the World Trade Center bombing, including the Oklahoma City bombing, the O.J. Simpson murder trial, the impeachment of a federal judge, airline bombings, and numerous other convictions.[22] Executions were stayed, and some who had been wrongfully convicted were freed from prison.

Whitehurst achieved his goal of scientific reforms at the laboratory. FBI supervisors and examiners tainted by the scandal were removed from the laboratory. Sizable efforts were undertaken to clean up the contamination and ensure that proper scientific standards were met. A special task force was established to review past cases that may have been corrupted by forensic fraud, and tens of thousands of FBI case files were released to Whitehurst for his independent review. The FBI agreed to more than fifty substantive reforms within its laboratory, and a well-respected scientist was appointed as the new director. Finally, the FBI agreed that its lab would have to become accredited. It commenced the long and difficult process of submitting its program to outside scientific review.

In the process of reforming the crime lab and obtaining rights for FBI employees, Whitehurst did far more. His case played out, for five years, on the national landscape. Numerous newspapers and television and radio stations covered the story of his moral courage, his allegations, his retaliation, and, eventually, his vindication. The public learned from Whitehurst's example of the benefits and dangers of whistleblowing.

Whistleblowers, the Founding Fathers, and the First Amendment

Throughout his case, Whitehurst relied upon the protections offered every American under the First Amendment of the U.S. Constitution. That cherished provision of the Bill of Rights broadly protects freedom of speech and the right to petition government leaders for a "redress of grievances." Whistleblowing is core speech protected under that Amendment. When employees blow the whistle on misconduct and demand government reforms, they are acting in the best tradition of American democracy.

It is not surprising that the heart of the Bill of Rights provides protection for whistleblowers. As former Supreme Court Justice Louis Brandeis recognized in his famous 1927 concurring opinion in *Whitney v. California*, those who drafted, endorsed, and enacted the First Amendment were "courageous, self-reliant men, with confidence in the power of free and fearless reasoning." As Justice Brandeis further explained:

> Those who won our independence . . . valued liberty both as an end and as a means. They believed liberty to be the secret of happiness and courage to be the secret of liberty. They believed that freedom to think as you will and to speak as you think are means indispensable to the discovery and spread of political truth . . . and that this should be a fundamental principle of the American government. . . . Those who won our independence by revolution were not cowards. They did not fear political change. They did not exalt order at the cost of liberty.[23]

How do we know that the Founding Fathers were thinking of protecting "whistleblowers" when they enacted the First Amendment? At the very birth of the United States, one of the laws the Continental Congress enacted reads like a modern-day whistleblower law. On July 30, 1778, the Revolutionary

Congress urged the American people to expose misconduct and blow the whistle on wrongdoing. That law, passed by the Founding Fathers of the United States at the height of the Revolutionary War, used words remarkably similar in both language and intent to those in the executive order Whitehurst relied upon in 1992, when he commenced his whistleblowing: "Resolved, that it is the duty of all persons in the service of the United States as well as others the inhabitants thereof, to give the earliest information to Congress or other proper authority of any misconduct, frauds or misdemeanors committed by any officers or persons in the Services of these States, which may come to their knowledge."[24]

Whitehurst was clearly following in the tradition of freedom of speech that our Founding Fathers worshiped. He saw it as his duty to provide information about gross misconduct to "Congress" and "other proper authority." He disclosed "misconduct . . . and fraud . . . committed by . . . persons in the [s]ervices" of the government. Whitehurst's whistleblowing followed a tradition as old as the United States. The First Amendment was unquestionably designed to protect the morally courageous—including those who expose misconduct within the most powerful institutions of government or commerce.

Conclusion

The objective evidence shows that whistleblowing works. Consequently, protecting employees who disclose waste, fraud, abuse, and unsafe conditions is absolutely key for any successful anticorruption program—whether a corporation or a government agency manages that program.

The moral courage of whistleblowers is historic and enduring. The individuals who risk their own personal well-being to serve the public interest need protection. The victims of fraud and other injustices, too, need systems that encourage and reward employees who step forward to expose misconduct.

In sum, there needs to be change. Change in corporate attitudes toward compliance and fraud detection. Change in government attitudes toward ethics and oversight. Change in public perceptions of dissent and loyalty. Change in workplace attitudes that tolerate or accommodate corruption.

With the right laws in place, with enough employees willing to demonstrate the courage of their convictions, real change is possible. Employees have the ability to detect and expose frauds, safety violations, or other criminal acts committed by and in their organizations. They can drive the campaign to limit or stop corrupt practices in the government agencies and corporations in which they work. They can make change happen, from the bottom up.[25] But without strong and effective legal protections, whistleblowing will remain marginalized in most industries, and the morally courageous employees who risk their careers to serve the greater good will continue to suffer retaliation.

Notes

1. Kohn, 2009.

2. Council of Europe's Civil Law on Corruption (Article 9), 1999. Available at http://www.whistleblowers.org (accessed March 5, 2009).

3. Other international conventions that mandate or endorse whistleblower protection include the United Nations Convention against Corruption (Article 33), the Inter-American Convention Against Corruption (Article 3), the African Union Convention on Preventing and Combating Corruption (Article 5), the Anti-Corruption Action Plan for Asia and the Pacific (Pillar 3), and the Southern African Development Community Protocol Against Corruption (Article 4).

4. See Bernstein and Woodward, 1974; Woodward, 2005.

5. See CNN's *Larry King Live* interview with Linda Tripp, aired December 1, 2003.

6. See Ellsberg, 2002; *The most dangerous man*, 2009.

7. *U.S. v. Birkenfeld*, 08–60099-cr-Zloch (Sentencing Transcript), August 21, 2009. Available at http://www.whistleblowers.org (accessed March 5, 2009).

8. Because the Nixon administration ordered "plumbers" (i.e., operatives hired to "plug the leaks") to break into Mr. Ellsberg's psychiatrist's office illegally to obtain information to smear Ellsberg, all charges against him were dropped.

9. For more information about the survey, see PricewaterhouseCoopers, 2007.

10. ACFE, which provides antifraud training and education worldwide, works to reduce the incidence of fraud and white-collar crime and assists its nearly 50,000 members in fraud detection and deterrence; see ACFE, 2010.

11. ACFE, 2008, 4, 23.

12. Kohn, 2000.

13. U.S. Department of Justice, Civil Division, Fraud Statistics Overview (Oct. 1, 1987–Sept. 30, 2009). At http://www.justice.gov/civil/frauds/fcastats.pdf (accessed September 30, 2010).

14. *Winters v. Houston Chronicle Pub. Co.,* 795 S.W.2d 723, 727–33 (Tex. 1990) (concurring opinion of Judge Doggett); see also Greenberg, 2009; and Lacayo and Ripley, 2002.

15. *Grava v. INS*, 205 F.3d 1177 (9th Cir. 2000).

16. *Silkwood,* 1983.

17. *The Insider,* 1999.

18. See Alford, 2001; Glazer and Glazer, 1989, 1999; Miethe, 1999.

19. See Transparency International, 2009.

20. This *Prime Time Live* story can be viewed at www.whistleblowers.org (accessed March 5, 2009).

21. 62 Federal Regulation 23123 (April 28, 1997).

22. See Kelly and Wearne, 1998, for detailed accounts of forensic misconduct in these cases.

23. *Whitney v. California*, 274 U.S. 357 (1927) (concurring opinion of Justice Brandeis).

24. Library of Congress, Journals of the Continental Congress, vol. 11, 732 (Resolution dated July 30, 1778).

25. In chapter 13 of this book, Comer and Baker explore how the collective efforts of the members of a morally courageous coalition can effect bottom-up change that makes their organization more ethical.

References

Alford, C.F. 2001. *Whistleblowers: Broken lives and organizational power.* Ithaca, NY: Cornell University Press.

Association of Certified Fraud Examiners (ACFE). 2008. Report to the nation on occupational fraud & abuse. At http://whistleblowers.nonprofitsoapbox.com/storage/whistleblowers/documents/acfefraudreport.pdf.

———. 2010. About the ACFE. At www.acfe.com/about/about.asp.

Bernstein, C., and Woodward, B. 1974. *All the president's men.* New York: Simon and Schuster.

Comer, D.R., and Baker, S.D. 2011. I defy with a little help from my friends: Raising an organization's ethical bar through a morally courageous coalition. In *Moral courage in organizations: Doing the right thing at work,* ed. D.R. Comer and G. Vega, 171–187. Armonk, NY: M.E. Sharpe.

Ellsberg, D. 2002. *Secrets: A memoir of Vietnam and the Pentagon Papers.* New York: Viking Press.

Glazer, M.P., and Glazer, P.M. 1989. *The whistleblowers: Exposing corruption in government and industry.* New York: Basic Books.

———. 1999. On the trail of courageous behavior. *Sociological Inquiry* 69(2), 276–295.

Greenberg, M. 2009. *Perspectives of chief ethics and compliance officers on the detection and prevention of corporate misdeeds.* Santa Monica, CA: Rand Corporation.

The Insider. 1999. Directed by Michael Mann. Touchstone Pictures.

Kelly, J.F., and Wearne, P.K. 1998. *Tainting evidence: Inside the scandals at the FBI crime lab.* New York: Free Press.

Kohn, S.M. 2000. *Concepts and procedures in whistleblower law.* Westport, CT: Quorum Books.

———. 2009. Reporting corruption: Whistleblower protection and the public interest. Washington, D.C., National Whistleblower Center. Paper delivered at the International Anti-Corruption Day forum sponsored by the U.S. Embassy in Latvia, December 9.

Lacayo, R., and Ripley, A. 2002. Persons of the year 2002. *Time* 160(27) (December 30), 30–33.

Miethe, T.D. 1999. *Whistleblowing at work: Tough choices in exposing fraud, waste, and abuse on the job.* Boulder, CO: Westview.

The most dangerous man in America: Daniel Ellsberg and the Pentagon Papers. 2009. Directed by Judith Ehrlich and Rick Goldsmith. Independent Television Service.

PricewaterhouseCoopers. 2007. Economic crime: People, culture and controls. The 4th biennial Global Economic Crime Survey. At www.whistleblowers.org/storage/whistleblowers/documents/pwc_survey.pdf (accessed March 5, 2009).

Silkwood. 1983. Directed by Mike Nichols. 20th Century Fox.

Transparency International. 2009. Recommended draft principles for whistleblowing legislation. November. At www.transparency.cz/pdf/TI_Recommended_draft_principles_for_whistleblowing_legislation_Nov_09.pdf (accessed March 5, 2009).

Woodward, B. 2005. *The secret man: The story of Watergate's Deep Throat.* New York: Simon and Schuster.

6

Faith and Moral Courage

Why a Sense of Calling Matters

G. Jeffrey MacDonald

Linda James knows how to stand up to pressure at work. A nurse in the cardiology department of Boston's Brigham & Women's Hospital, she works every day with patients who may need heart transplants. She discusses risks and potential benefits of undergoing one of medicine's most complex and high-stakes procedures.[1] Her words for nervous patients and family members invariably shape what turns out to be the decision of a lifetime. She feels pressure—not only in the families' lounge area, but also in the staff room where a medical team meets to consider individual cases.

When the team gathers, James says, members routinely voice strong opinions about whether a patient ought to receive a transplant. A chorus of "no" tends to ring out, for instance, when an elderly patient has osteoporosis and diabetes, because such a patient likely would not survive the ordeal. But in those cases as in others, James pushes back against high-ranking fellow professionals who are unaccustomed to pushback. She believes patients can and must make informed decisions—without clinicians making choices for them. From this conviction, she routinely summons moral courage to defy a group of high-powered colleagues and insist that the final decision be left in the hands of the few ordinary people who have the most at stake. Taking this approach can be risky, James admits. A family could potentially make a disastrous decision that would forever haunt her conscience as well as theirs. Perturbed colleagues may at times question her professional judgment. Still, she sticks to her guns.

One factor explains why James takes these unpopular but principled stands: faith. An observant Roman Catholic, she believes that God has blessed her with a job that allows for daily exercise of what she calls her gift for caregiving. She is confident that the same providential God will guide each transplant prospect to the right decision. And she expects God to see her through any scorn she may endure from peers along the way. "If you have this gift, sometimes you burden yourself with more things that you can do and you find yourself praying for strength because it's not always pleasant," James says. "But the gift encompasses your whole life . . . so wherever there's a calling for you to use those gifts, you become involved."

What is the relationship between faith and moral courage in the workplace? To date, research has not specifically considered whether religious people are more or less likely than others to act courageously on the job. However, evidence suggests that religious beliefs do influence how even the most highly trained of professionals do their jobs. For example, a 2007 article in *The New England Journal of Medicine* reported that physicians with strong religious convictions were more likely than their nonreligious colleagues to see a role for personal morality in medical practice. Religiously observant physicians were more likely than their nonobservant counterparts to say they have a right to express moral qualms about certain procedures, such as abortion or contraception, when counseling a patient on her options. They also said physicians do not have to disclose all available options to a patient.[2] Thus, it seems faith can and does at times factor into workplace conduct. It may even motivate courage, because physicians put their reputations at risk when they offer controversial counseling on moral grounds.

Despite a limited supply of hard data on the topic, faith and moral courage in the workplace do seem to be connected. Inspired moral courage does not depend on adherence to a particular faith tradition. Instead, for those motivated by faith, courage seems to stem from a style of spirituality that transcends sectarian categories. What matters most is whether a person feels a strong sense of calling to a particular professional field, organization, or industry. When a person feels called to lead a life that includes a certain type of work, then he or she may be especially aware of work's moral dimensions—and may be more likely to take personal risks when necessary to preserve high moral standards. "The nature of a calling . . . lends itself to believing very deeply in what you're doing as an individual and being connected to an organization that you believe is impactful and making the world a better place," says Monica Worline, adding, "It makes sense to me . . . that people who're working out of a sense of calling would potentially act more courageously because they have a deeper internalization of the mission" than employees who do not feel a calling.[3]

What's Different About a Calling

That religion might play a role in inspiring courage in day-to-day life comes as no surprise to theologians or religious leaders. All three Abrahamic traditions

(Judaism, Christianity, and Islam) ascribe heroic status to martyrs—that is, to figures who stood for religious principle despite palpable risks and died in the process. Because these faiths have traditionally taught followers to expect costly consequences, it seems logical that workers would sometimes forgo lucrative opportunities—or blow the whistle on unethical practices—in the name of being faithful to a just deity.

"A schoolteacher who really feels called to teach is far more likely to take risks and to stretch themselves to display acts of moral courage because they care about their kids" in their classroom, says Paul Sangree, a United Church of Christ minister who teaches a course on callings at Andover Newton Theological School in Newton, Massachusetts. "They will go to extraordinary lengths to make a difference in their lives because that's what they're called to do—versus someone who teaches because they get summers off and have time with their own kids and it fits their family schedule."[4]

Simply having a strong religious faith may not be enough to compel principled sacrifice at work, according to Al Erisman. A former Boeing executive, Erisman is now Executive-in-Residence at Seattle Pacific University's Center for Integrity in Business, where he is the cofounder and editor of *Ethix*. Erisman has conducted dozens of interviews with corporate executives on the subject of ethical leadership. He finds that some staunch believers tend to downplay the importance of earthly affairs because their religious traditions emphasize that justice is ultimately God's—not humans'—to mete out. Certain fundamentalist sects expect justice to arrive soon in the form of Armageddon. Believers of this ilk may find no compelling reason to come clean about a fudged expense report, for instance, if doing so would have no bearing on their status before a God who is solely concerned with right belief. Thus, a belief system that puts no premium on calling, or vocation, to make a difference in the world offers little impetus for sacrifice.

Erisman also sees courage to be in short supply when believers practice what he calls a "compartmentalized" spirituality.[5] This refers to a life that draws a sharp line between religious and secular spheres. Business is understood in this framework as a zone where all decisions are economic. This mindset makes religious values irrelevant in the workplace, where financial concerns ostensibly trump all others. Classic examples of this type of thinking would include former Enron CEO and Sunday school teacher Kenneth Lay as well as Richard Scrushy, founder of HealthSouth Corporation and an active member of his Alabama congregation. Both oversaw famously scandalous practices. In 2006, Lay was convicted of fraud and conspiracy in a scheme that led to Enron's downfall and cost investors billions. Courts sentenced Scrushy to serve nearly seven years in prison for bribery and to pay $2.9 billion to investors for his leading role in an accounting fraud scheme.[6] But neither Lay nor Scrushy indicated that he felt like a hypocrite. In the apparent absence of a strong sense of calling, they could tell themselves that faith should not interfere with business decisions. In this approach to spirituality, courage may be amiss because a sacrificial act in business is not presumed to be pleasing to God. It would merely be a hindrance to a company's profit-making mission.

To explore how religious callings inspire moral courage, one needs to consider a calling's core elements. A calling is commonly defined as the nexus where a person's deepest passion meets the world's greatest need. It does not necessarily have to be attributed to God or another deity, although it often is. A person who feels called has a sense that God (or a higher power of some other kind) has ordained a purpose for his or her life. Because the divine has a stake in such a person's career, he or she may take principled risks with confidence in three assumptions: (1) God will provide; (2) worldly affairs have an ultimate significance; and (3) integrity—both personal and organizational—is worthy of personal costs.

Awareness of Providence

People with a sense of calling tend to have a twin sense that God provides to meet the need of the faithful. After all, if God furnishes a mission for one to fulfill at work, then God is already a provider of purpose—and will surely keep providing while this ordained mission is pursued. That is how it works in the Bible for such figures as Moses and Jeremiah, neither of whom has the gift of eloquence until God calls him to be a prophet. Then, by providence, they have all the linguistic skills they need in abundance. Such a sense of a provisional and hands-on God helps people with a sense of calling to take bold stands even at the risk of personal cost.

Those with a sense of calling sometimes feel compelled to stand up for principle—even when doing so seems to jeopardize their near-term business interests. Consider Donald Flow, CEO of Flow Automotive Group in Winston-Salem, North Carolina, who says that he feels as called by God to sell cars as any pastor would feel called to preach. Flow has done well for himself. His family business encompasses a network of thirty dealerships. Yet as an evangelical Christian, he also worries about practicing justice on the job. For that reason, he has made some moves that strike Erisman as morally courageous. For example, Flow ran the risk of alienating well-heeled customers by raising the prices they pay for new cars in order to cut what he saw as fairer deals with low-income buyers.

"We did a study and found that the people who typically paid the least for the cars were the most able to pay," Flow said in a 2004 interview with *Ethix*. "Those least able to pay paid the most. For me, it was wrong to take advantage of the least able, a clear violation of the biblical mandate in the book of Proverbs. We went back and restructured our business. Our profit structure has to be much tighter around the mean, and we have to communicate enough value that a person will pay us a fair return."[7] Flow overhauled his firm's business model with confidence that, while he might lose a few customers along the way, he would not go out of business and would ultimately prosper by doing what was right. That conviction stemmed from his sense of providence: God would not let His faithful servant perish. Indeed, profitability and customer loyalty have flourished, he says, as he has tried to make Flow Automotive Group's dealerships into venues for practicing Christian moral principles. "I am talking about living out the implications of what I believe," Flow tells *Ethix*. "This is reflected in how we treat people, what our practices are, and what we think is important. This is where my drive comes from."

Having a strong sense of providence, whether understood theistically or not, may actually be essential for moral courage to manifest on the job, according to Rushworth Kidder. Kidder, founding president of the Center for Global Ethics in Rockland, Maine, defines moral courage as "the willing endurance of significant danger for the sake of principle."[8] In his view, moral courage manifests through trust that those who pursue values such as honesty, fairness, and compassion will be vindicated, even if they suffer a bit in the short term. "Trust would say that no matter what I'm seeing around me, there is some sense of goodness," Kidder says. "And it just may be that if I can just push through this [trying situation], that principle of goodness is going to carry me through."

Faith in a providential God is not essential for moral courage, but it serves as a useful foundation, explains Kidder. Many major religions assume the universe to be guided by a benevolent force. If a benevolent force is indeed at work, then employees who refuse to mislead clients or to practice deceitful accounting can trust that they will not be forsaken in their sacrificial acts. A benevolent hand will see them through, even if an angry boss or disappointed client makes their lives difficult for a while. Conversely, a person with no confidence in a benevolent force will likely calculate that the costs associated with a principled stand are not worth the risks. Kidder says the cynic, who, by definition, contemptuously dismisses the idea of goodness, is unfit for senior leadership. "In the end, the cynic will have nothing in which he can trust," Kidder says, "and will therefore not be morally courageous when he most needs to be."

Emphasizing This World, Not the Next One

People with a sense of calling and a habit of courage tend also to be aware of high stakes in their day-to-day lives. According to Erisman, they reject any spirituality that emphasizes an afterworld whose affairs are more important than those of this world. They also downplay notions of a divine justice that is entirely separate from one carried out by human hands. God cares about human-made outcomes in the worldviews of these workers, Erisman says, and that compels them in many cases to accept personal costs en route to fulfilling larger, long-term goals. "Those people who hold to a fairly narrow view of faith—who regard their faith as having an otherworldly focus and believe that what happens here is just temporary—don't seem to really understand what it is to act with moral courage," Erisman says. "They view what they're doing now as a tool to something else, whereas people with a broader grasp of what their faith is about seem to demonstrate moral courage right where they are."[9]

This latter, earthier approach to spirituality resonates with Jeff Smith of Winnetka, a suburb of Chicago. Smith is a middle-aged evangelical Christian and a business development specialist for firms that manage financial assets for institutions. He regards his career as a God-given calling to help clients make prudent use of resources entrusted to them. To be sure, he strives to earn a good living to support his wife and three children. But he is also aware that having a calling means that worldly affairs matter to God—and therefore sometimes require personal sacrifice. He believes that he must uphold high principles lest he fail to bear authentic witness to God's ways. Thus, he sometimes must take steps that will potentially hurt his family's bottom line, at least in the short term. "My family is watching me, just like the other employees in the firm are watching me," Smith says. "People are watching how I behave, how I react to situations, what my decisions are, and they're adding it all up. I have a witness for Christ in the workplace and at home. I need to live up to that."[10]

At work, Smith has at times felt torn between what seems morally right and what his superiors expect. In one case, he had recently won a big account to have his firm manage a $250 million pension fund for Missouri teachers. But soon after the deal closed, the highly acclaimed fund manager in charge of investing these assets left Smith's company. Smith's superiors wanted him to keep mum about the star manager's departure because the teachers might pull their assets if they thought the risk had increased. But Smith, recalling his sense of Christ as a bold truth teller, took his bosses to task for proposing a less-than-forthright course of action. His sense of calling had brought him to put his job at risk for a moral principle.

After some tense conversations, Smith prevailed. His superiors came to see that honesty would bode well for the firm's long-term reputation, and they authorized Smith to disclose the fund manager's departure. It was a costly decision for both Smith and his employer. The teachers promptly switched to another investment firm. The $250 million account was gone, as was Smith's lucrative commission. But his bosses did not resent him. On the contrary, they worked to restore his lost commission over several years.

Smith felt vindicated, even though he had been mentally prepared to find another job if necessary. For him, being called by God had come to mean taking a very real risk precisely because a trust-based relationship with a client hung in the balance. Because the integrity of human affairs matters enormously to God, he reasoned, he would sometimes have to be a courageous risk-taker in defense of principle. "If I call myself a Christian, I need to live up to the principles that Jesus sets out in the Bible," Smith says. "That's not easy, but with His help in my life, I endeavor to do that."

A sense of calling to manifest noble outcomes, even at high personal cost, does not always stem from a close personal relationship with God. Sometimes a person will feel called or compelled by duty to a human community. This was the case for Mary Fisher Lee, a social worker who waged a landmark campaign for a smoke-free workplace in the late 1970s.

Then employed by the Massachusetts Department of Public Welfare, Lee (a nonsmoker) worked in a windowless office with twenty colleagues, including several smokers. At the time, she says, her boss laughed off her request for a nonsmoking workspace as "silly." Coworkers teased her for being annoyed and sickened by their smoke. But she found outside support, not in the local Catholic parish where she played the organ, but among family members and physicians who assured her that she had a valid complaint. She filed suit against the state despite personal risks involved in doing so. "I got the courage . . . from the doctors," Lee says. "Most people would be afraid and say, 'You can't go to court over something like this.' But I have two daughters who are lawyers, a son-in-law who's a judge, and a son-in-law who's a doctor. Everybody knew how right I was. It just took somebody to have the gumption to do it."[11]

Bullying on the job intensified, Lee says, as the suit went forward and after CBS's *60 Minutes* news program featured her story. Coworkers called her names, such as "smelly underwear," because she had told a reporter how her undergarments would reek of smoke after a day of work. Her boss, she says, berated her for causing trouble in the workplace. Her state employees union "did absolutely nothing," she says, to address the alleged abuse. In court, her adversaries tried to portray her as "maladjusted," she says. The ordeal had made her into a pariah and inflicted emotional wounds.

Despite obstacles, Lee drew strength from her sense of calling. She felt a duty to deliver what she knew in her heart to be morally right—that is, a workplace where no one is subjected to the health risks of secondhand smoke. She wanted to make a difference not only for herself, but also for others who might not have the strength to fight such a battle on their own. Thus, she refused to quit either her job or her suit. In 1982, Lee won a restraining order that separated smokers from nonsmokers on the job. The ruling set the stage for three decades of regulations, which came to create smoke-free bars, restaurants, and other public spaces. Her moral courage had paid off.

Looking back, Lee does not frame her experience as one of embracing a personal mission from God. In fact, she felt unsupported by priests and churchgoers at her parish during her highly public ordeal. "It was a subject they didn't touch on," she recalls. But her moral courage traces nonetheless to a type of spirituality—call it humanistic, perhaps—that involves a calling and a compulsion to advance a particular change in worldly circumstances. Like Smith, she has a sense that worldly affairs need to be managed in a just manner and that the onus rests with individuals to turn principles into practices—even, sometimes, at great personal cost.

Lee represents the phenomenon of morally courageous workers who feel compelled by necessity to defend a trampled principle. This dynamic resonates across generational and religious lines. Maryam Abdi, a Muslim immigrant from Somalia who now lives in Eden Prairie, Minnesota, was just sixteen years old in 2008 when she took a stand for religious freedom—namely, for her right to wear a *hijab*, or Islamic head scarf, at work. When she applied for a cashier's job at an Old Country Buffet in Fridley, Minnesota, a manager allegedly said her hijab would constitute a violation of the restaurant's dress code. "I knew it was unfair," Abdi says, "but they said [the head scarf] wasn't the uniform, so I thought, 'Maybe they're right.' I didn't know what to do about it."[12]

Abdi thought about giving up, but instead drew strength from her Somali community to raise questions as a matter of seeking justice. Another Somali teen, she says, encouraged her to contact a local chapter of the Council on American-Islamic Relations (CAIR), a Muslim advocacy and civil rights organization. With CAIR's help, Abdi challenged the manager's assessment of the situation and reapplied for the job. Within a few days, she was working at Old Country Buffet in her hijab. She admits that the process, which played out in the glare of Minneapolis news media coverage, made her nervous. She worried about a potential backlash from coworkers, whom she feared might resent her for apparently being difficult or demanding special privileges. Showing up for the first day of work required courage. But she says she found the work environment very welcoming and cordial. In hindsight, she feels the risks and worries were worthwhile, especially because they might inspire others in her community of Somali-American Muslims to claim their rights as well. "Now a lot of Muslim girls out there know they can take a stand for their religion and their head scarves," Abdi says.

A similar sense of compulsion to pursue what is right comes through in research on whistleblowers, that is, employees who expose wrongful workplace practices despite risks of retribution. C. Fred Alford identified in interviews with twenty whistleblowers a pattern of thinking in terms of duty. "It's simply that some people can't help themselves," Alford says. "When they see something [corrupt], they feel indignant and outraged. The outrage is not just for the public, but also for themselves. They've been cast into a den of thieves and are expected to become another thief. They're expected to corrupt themselves like everybody around them. Their moral purity has been tarnished, and they're angry."[13]

The whistleblowers Alford interviewed were not motivated by a sense of faith or a God-given mission. But they were compelled by a sense of obligation to change systems that corrupt all who work within them. This further reinforces the idea that a certain type of spirituality, focused pragmatically on earthly outcomes, may have a greater effect on morally courageous behavior than adherence to any particular religious tradition. As long as one feels duty bound to change circumstances for the better, he or she may be a good candidate for taking the personal risks that mark a courageous minority in the workforce.

Survey responses from thousands of employees at twenty-two federal agencies likewise suggest that a desire to make a tangible difference in others' lives drives people to act with moral courage.[14] Marcia Miceli, Janet Near, and Terry Dworkin, who analyzed these data, neither sought nor found a correlation between whistleblowing and religiosity (or with any other personality characteristics, for that matter). However, workers were much more likely to speak up about ethical problems when they felt higher-ups would listen and make changes. In other words, whistleblowers weren't cynical: they believed they could make a difference in material ways for colleagues and future generations of federal employees. They were willing to incur personal costs—but only if the payoffs for their institutions stood a good chance to be prompt and profound. "They blow the whistle if: the wrongdoing they have observed is serious; they feel that telling somebody about it will actually make a difference; and they feel they're going to get some support in the organization for doing that," Near says.[15]

Aligned Missions, Personal and Organizational

Together, awareness of providence and concern for worldly outcomes seem to galvanize morally courageous behavior in those who feel called (either in religious or nonreligious terms). Appreciation for an abiding goodness in the universe helps instill confidence; duty insists that they do what is necessary, even when that may involve incurrence of personal costs. But calling becomes even more empowering, it seems, when workers regard their employer as every bit as called as they are. Then the stakes involve not just personal duty but also the integrity of an institution—bigger than any one person called to lofty purposes. When personal and organizational callings are married, then individuals seem to recognize especially high stakes in ethical dilemmas and show a willingness to incur costs for principle if necessary.

Individuals with a strong sense of personal calling sometimes make it a point to work with organizations that share a similar sense. Consider, for instance, the career of Ralph Nesson, a Reform Jew from the Boston suburbs who found his calling in the Ozark Mountains. An active member of his Little Rock–area synagogue, Nesson understands his life as both an adventure and an opportunity to "do mitzvah"—that is, to perform good deeds. He pursues both in his role as executive director of the Arkansas Single Parent Scholarship Fund (ASPSF). The organization is a nonprofit that helps Arkansas single parents (mostly mothers) break cycles of poverty by covering costs associated with postsecondary education.

Even after twenty years at ASPSF, Nesson still needs to muster moral courage on a regular basis. Some of the directors at ASPSF's sixty-seven local chapters relish their role as gatekeepers, he says. When they discourage potentially good students from applying, Nesson has to choose between smooth politicking and confrontation with some important figures in the local education scene. Because his own sense of calling is integrated with that of his organization, he does not hesitate to put his congenial personality aside and stand up to a local bigwig who is being an obstructionist.

"Sometimes you get to a point where a board president, a leader, would be driving people away and destroying what you're trying to create," Nesson says. "That is the junction at which my job is to face that person . . . and say, 'I know you have the best interests of your county at heart, but look at what's going on here. . . . Maybe it's time for you to take a break and let somebody else lead.' People put a lot of ego into these civic positions, and they *don't like it* when a stranger comes along and says, 'You're really not doing this right.' It's one of the most difficult parts of my job, but sometimes confrontation is necessary if you want to right the ship."[16]

Nesson's willingness to ignite the ire of local civic leaders when necessary grows out of his Jewish upbringing, he says. As a child, he attended synagogue and Hebrew school. He also observed his father, who dutifully provided for his family as a retail merchant but never seemed especially satisfied in his career. Nesson consequently passed up business opportunities in order to work in VISTA Corps and at a community mental health clinic. Both work environments seemed committed to doing mitzvah, in his view. He later relocated with his wife to Arkansas, where they lived largely off the land and he worked in the antipoverty Community Action network for more than a decade before founding ASPSF. As the arc of his career shows, his quest to fulfill a personal sense of mission kept him involved with one mission-driven organization after another. It also led him to practice a habit of personal risk-taking as he continually moved from safe employment situations to less certain ones, where he could more effectively do mitzvah. Over time, moral courage at work became a sort of second nature.

"If you're really intent on doing a mitzvah, a good deed, sometimes it's painful to have to do things that hurt people's feelings or drive people away," Nesson says. "But in the long run, that's the only way that things are going to get better. And if you don't do [the hard thing], then you look yourself in the mirror and say, 'I failed. I knew what had to be done, I knew it would take courage and composure, but I didn't do it. I failed, and as a result, the community is going to fail.'"

People may be especially willing to take a moral stand when they believe deeply in their organization's mission. Cynthia Pury has found that the main driver for courageous action among college students is not high tolerance for risk. More important is a person's commitment to particular outcomes, including, but not limited to, those associated with a sense of calling. Although she has not tested the relative impact of commitment and risk-tolerance in work environments, she expects her findings to apply there as well. "The goal that the person is trying to pursue," she says, "turns out to be much more important for the person taking the courageous action than their ability to withstand risk."[17]

For workers with a sense of calling, life inside an organization with no principled sense of mission can quickly become unbearable. That happened to Jeff Smith when he worked for an employer that did not share his values, a Midwestern company with major institutional accounts. The City of Detroit, one of Smith's clients, was considering options for how to invest $80 million. Going with a privately managed account could have saved the city about $200,000 per year, Smith recalls. However, the broker involved in the deal stood to earn an extra $5 million if the city were to deploy its funds in a more expensive mutual fund. Smith's superiors urged him to stay mum about the less expensive option because the broker was an important business partner whom they wanted to keep happy. Smith protested at first, but eventually relented. He did not tell the client about what he saw as Detroit's best option. But his conscience weighed on him for practicing what he regards in hindsight as a sin of omission. Not wanting to face such pressure again, he left within months for a job at another firm. "I would like to be able to do what I do in a way that promotes the firm [that employs me] and doesn't compromise my Christian principles," Smith explains.[18]

Toward a Future Where Workplace Callings Get Noticed

Having a sense of calling is not necessarily a ticket to moral behavior in the workplace. Like any powerful force, it is capable of doing harm as well as good. Someone prone to delusions, for instance, could theoretically feel called to sabotage certain functions of an organization or even to harm coworkers. Thus, it is important not to extol callings as positive motivational forces under all circumstances. To say they function best when accompanied by a solid moral compass would be more accurate.

Caveats notwithstanding, callings may be more integral to motivating displays of moral courage than observers have generally recognized. Managers routinely screen for skill sets and attitudes. But most secular organizations do not take the time to probe whether employees or job candidates feel a sense of calling or accountability to a higher authority. In overlooking this area, employers may be turning a blind eye to one of the most important factors for predicting whether a worker takes responsibility for an error, say, or declines a bribe. Perhaps organizations will explore in the years ahead how to identify people with a true sense of vocation or even how to help employees see their work as vocation. Even so, realism demands acknowledgment of the fact that some organizations will always prefer to hire docile employees instead of individuals disposed to making waves.

More research is needed to clarify the relationships between spirituality or religious faith and propensities for displaying moral courage. Surveys investigating the beliefs and spiritual practices of people who have taken brave risks for the sake of principle would help illuminate these connections. Meanwhile, people with a strong sense of calling will likely continue to distinguish themselves from coworkers who profess similar beliefs but do not feel that God, or a higher power of some other kind, has given them a personal mission to fulfill in the workforce. The mysteries of spirituality may have more light to shed in the years to come.

Notes

1. From the author's June 2009 telephone interview with Linda James.
2. Curlin et al., 2007.
3. From the author's January 2009 telephone interview with Monica Worline, a professor of organization and management at Emory University's Goizueta Business School.
4. From the author's March 2009 telephone interview with Paul Sangree, pastor of Bethany Congregational Church in Foxboro, Massachusetts.
5. From the author's January 2009 interview with Al Erisman.
6. Davidson and Beasley, 2009.
7. Erisman, 2004.

8. The quotes in this section come from the author's January 2009 telephone interview with Rushworth Kidder; see also Kidder, 2005.

9. From the author's January 2009 telephone interview with Al Erisman.

10. The quotes in this section come from the author's July 2009 telephone interview with Jeff Smith.

11. The quotes in this section come from the author's May 2009 telephone interview with Mary Fisher Lee.

12. The quotes in this section come from the author's January 2009 telephone interview with Maryam Abdi.

13. From the author's January 2009 telephone interview with C. Fred Alford, professor of government at the University of Maryland; see also Alford, 2001.

14. For details on the research, see Miceli, Near, and Dworkin, 2008; see also Kohn, in chapter 5 of this book.

15. From the author's January 2009 telephone interview with Janet P. Near, professor of management at Indiana University's Kelley School of Business.

16. The quotes in this section come from the author's May 2009 telephone interview with Ralph Nesson.

17. From the author's January 2009 telephone interview with Cynthia Pury, a psychology professor at Clemson University.

18. From the author's July 2009 telephone interview with Jeff Smith.

References

Alford, C.F. 2001. *Whistleblowers: Broken lives and organizational power.* Ithaca: Cornell University Press.

Curlin, F.A., Lawrence, R.E., Chin, M.H., and Lantos, J.D. 2007. Religion, conscience and controversial clinical practices. *New England Journal of Medicine* 356(6), 593–600.

Davidson, L.V., and Beasley, D. 2009. HealthSouth's Scrushy liable in $2.88 billion fraud. Bloomberg.com, June 18. www.bloomberg.com/apps/news?pid=2060110 3&sid=a89tFKR4OevM.

Erisman, A. 2004. Don Flow: Ethics at Flow Automotive. *Ethix* 34 (March/April). http://blog.spu.edu/ethix/2004/03/01/ethics-at-flow-automotive (accessed November 8, 2000).

Kidder, R.M. 2005. *Moral courage.* New York: HarperCollins.

Kohn, S.M. 2011. For the greater good: The moral courage of whistleblowers. In *Moral courage in organizations: Doing the right thing at work,* ed. D.R. Comer and G. Vega, 60–74. Armonk, NY: M.E. Sharpe.

Miceli, M.P., Near, J.P., and Dworkin, T.M. 2008. *Whistleblowing in organizations.* New York: Routledge.

7

The Social Entrepreneur

Combining Head and Heart to Find Innovative Solutions to Local Problems

ROLAND E. KIDWELL

I love to work with kids. I love to fish.
I just knew that kids needed to go fishing.

—Joey Puettman, Executive Director, Joey's
FlyFishing Foundation Inc., Sheridan, Wyoming

Economic development is directly tied to housing.
If there is no affordable housing, then it doesn't matter
how many job opportunities there are, particularly
with young families who want to set down roots.

—Marie Lowe, Executive Director,
Sheridan Housing Action Committee

I've always been a social entrepreneur and didn't
know it until a couple of years ago. . . . My folks know
we have to make a profit. . . . Money feeds the mission.

—Jeffrey Holsinger, President and CEO,
Wyoming/Montana Volunteers of America

Heart of the West

Nestled against the Big Horn Mountains, Sheridan, Wyoming, a city of about 16,700 people in the least populated state in the nation, is described in tourist brochures and Web sites as the "West at its Best." Kevin Drumm, who served as president of the local community college from August 2004 until January 2010, finds "Heart of the West" to be another appropriate nickname for Sheridan. He believes doing social good via nonprofits is the "dominant organizational model" of Sheridan, which has an inordinate proportion of social entrepreneurs and social enterprises for a community of its size.[1]

It is perhaps curious that a small city where Buffalo Bill Cody once auditioned acts for his Wild West show attracts and sustains a variety of people who wish to explore and recognize social problems and then organize to provide innovative solutions to those problems. Why does tiny Sheridan seem to have more than its share of social entrepreneurs—individuals who adopt a mission to create and sustain social value, recognize and pursue new opportunities to serve the mission, engage in continuous innovation, act boldly without being limited by currently available resources, and exhibit a high level of accountability to those they serve?[2] Why does Sheridan, at least in terms of social entrepreneurism, seemingly contradict the "clustering force" idea that large cities and mega-regions drive the world forward in terms of creative skills and talents that offer clear social and economic advantages to their inhabitants?[3]

Although detailed answers to such questions deserve more rigorous study than this chapter can offer, one key element supporting social ventures and the courage to be a social entrepreneur appears to be Sheridan itself, a place the local residents describe as a caring and giving community and a place of significant creativity among the inhabitants. Sheridan was established in 1882 by John Loucks and named after Loucks's Civil War cavalry commander, General Philip Sheridan.[4] The town grew from 281 people in the 1890 census to more than 9,000 by 1920 to about 16,700 in 2007.[5] Founded near the old Bozeman Trail to the Montana goldfields, the area has seen armed conflicts with the native population, frontier forts, cattle drives, and, more recently, ranches, coal mining, telecommuters, and seasonal residents.

Sheridan's pioneering spirit continues, Drumm said, and in terms of social ventures translates into the more modern-day outcome of "How do I follow my passion for doing something pioneering and be able to pay my personal bills as well?" He points out that the question is not much different from what the original pioneers faced. Many people whose ancestors homesteaded the area are still in Sheridan. In addition, Sheridan was home to the nation's first dude ranch, and many others have since sprung up. Dude ranching represents a different kind of original spirit; thus, pioneering "something" has been very much part of Sheridan's culture since its inception.[6]

The values of Sheridan as a place of social good were forged by Whitney Benefits Inc., started in 1927 as the first educational foundation in Wyoming.[7] Described as Sheridan's international man of mystery, Edward A. Whitney, whose estate funded Whitney Benefits, lived frugally, never married, and left little record of his personal life.[8] After education and travels in various

European countries and elsewhere in the States, Whitney arrived in Sheridan in 1885, possibly to cope with his chronic lung disease by living in a dry Western climate. He purchased Loucks's store, founded the town's first bank, and was eventually elected mayor. After several travels around the world and further contributions to the community, Whitney died of pulmonary problems in 1917 at age seventy-four. Ten years later, following the instructions of his will, trustees of his estate established Whitney Benefits, which has gone on to provide more than $20 million in no-interest loans to 5,000 local college students in the last eighty years. The foundation has also financially supported Sheridan College, the Sheridan YMCA, a local park, an ice rink, and a community building.[9] Whitney Benefits inspired other philanthropic enterprises based in the area, providing added funds for social ventures focused on a variety of missions. "While raising start-up funds for any nonprofit is never easy, there is much more of a base in Sheridan, especially of foundations, than most anywhere in the nation per capita. If you've got a good idea, there are several well-heeled foundations and individual philanthropists who at the very least will listen to a pitch,"[10] explains Drumm.

Thus, geographer Richard Florida's clustering-force argument, although aimed at large cities and mega-regions, seems relevant to the success of social entrepreneurship in Sheridan: "When people—especially talented and creative ones—come together, ideas flow more freely, and as a result individual and aggregate talents increase exponentially: the end result amounts to much more than the sum of the parts."[11]

The three examples of social entrepreneurship examined here represent in part a movement away from philanthropic charity toward sustained efforts at community improvement. These efforts can ultimately result in social enterprise, that is, the use of earned income strategies to pursue a financial, social, and environmental bottom line, either as a social sector business or as part of a revenue stream that includes charitable contributions and government subsidies.[12] Each venture is guided by social entrepreneurs motivated by the idea of doing right in their community, either by founding an organization to address a perceived social ill or by growing an existing organization into a key solver of social problems in the community. By examining these ventures, we can gather insights as to how social entrepreneurs find the moral courage to start and sustain new social organizations.

About five years ago, Joey Puettman, a former schoolteacher and current mental health worker, realized his key goal to give kids a chance to do what many in Wyoming take for granted: go fly-fishing on the bountiful streams in the Sheridan area. To that end, Puettman incorporated a nonprofit organization, set up a board, developed a business plan, received a donated building in which to give lessons, and embarked on his social venture. He operates two-day fly-fishing camps for children ages nine to eighteen.[13]

Marie Lowe was selling real estate in Sheridan when she uncovered a problem in assisting her customers: lack of affordable housing for working people in low- to middle-income brackets. She planned six months ahead and eventually quit her job to found Sheridan Housing Action Committee (SHAC), which focuses on providing affordable housing for working families. Using a combination of education, financing, and building, SHAC has helped fifty-seven families become homeowners in Sheridan.[14]

Jeff Holsinger wanted to grow an existing social organization, the local Volunteers of America affiliate, into a sustainable enterprise that would rely on diverse sources of funding and revenue and could weather the vagaries of charitable giving and government funding. Based on a social enterprise business model, the VOA Wyoming-Montana affiliate has grown from a $1-million- to a $12-million-a-year operation with forty-three different sources of revenue since Holsinger became CEO seven years ago.[15]

This chapter next describes the general characteristics of social entrepreneurs and how these relate specifically to moral courage in the starting and sustaining of new social ventures. Then, the activities of the three Sheridan social entrepreneurs are detailed, followed by insights into the different ways they serve as exemplars of moral courage—the willingness to do the right thing even when it is not convenient to do so.

Characteristics of the Social Entrepreneur: The Intersection with Moral Courage

As is evident in these thumbnail descriptions of three social organizations, there are multiple approaches and definitions that may apply when one attempts to examine the concept of social entrepreneurship. Before detailing each venture and its impact on the community, it is useful to discuss the general elements of social entrepreneurship and social enterprise and what motivates individuals to get involved.

Social entrepreneurs tackle important social problems and unsatisfied human needs by developing and relentlessly pursuing innovative approaches untried by private, public, and nonprofit sectors; by operating very close to the problem at a local level; by moving quickly, unfettered by stifling bureaucracy; and by applying business savvy that assists in problem resolution.[16] "Social entrepreneurs, operating outside of the constraints of government, significantly enhance our ability to find and implement effective solutions to social problems,"[17] writes Dees. Typologies of social entrepreneurs have centered on the concepts of entrepreneurial drive (passion versus business), desired return (return on investment versus social return on investment), venture mission, and primary market impact.[18]

David Bornstein identifies six key characteristics of the social entrepreneur.[19] He observes that social entrepreneurs are willing and able to make corrections on their own, willing to share credit for their successes, willing to break free of established structures to try something new, willing to build networks across disciplines, and willing to work quietly without fanfare. The sixth characteristic of social entrepreneurs is their strong ethical impetus, which propels them to act with moral courage. The ethical quality of the motivation that leads social entrepreneurs to act involves the nature of their vision and desire to make the community where they live better than it is. Combined with passion about the venture, care about the people affected by it, and reinforcement through successful results, the moral courage of the social entrepreneur comes to the fore.

John Wood, a Microsoft executive, was on a backpacking trip in Nepal when he discovered that the Nepalese schools suffered from a lack of books for their students. Wood formed a nonprofit to deliver books to Nepalese schools; the organization evolved into Room to Read, which partners with local communities in several countries to build libraries and schools and provide educational opportunities to female students.[20]

Wood faced a great deal of inner turmoil before making a courageous leap from the high salary and perks of the corporate world to an uncertain social venture. Whereas his position at Microsoft offered stability and pride in working for a leading-edge company, providing books for Nepal offered more—a chance to make a difference in the world: "Did it really matter how many copies of Windows we sold in Taiwan this month when millions of children were without access to books? How could I get fired up about our electronic-commerce initiative in Hong Kong, or antipiracy efforts in China, when seven of 10 kids in Nepal faced lifelong illiteracy?" Wood writes.[21] His three-week trip to Nepal touched his heart and spurred him to action; in particular, he was inspired by the headmaster of a rural school who suggested, "Perhaps, sir, you will someday come back with books."[22] On his return from Nepal, Wood sent a plea for books to people on his e-mail list. A huge positive response coupled with his family's support bolstered his moral courage to start a new social venture.

The founders of p:ear (Program: Education, Art, Recreation), a highly regarded nonprofit organization in Portland, Oregon, sought to provide homeless youths with a number of educational and growth activities such as working in a gallery alongside established artists who were engaged in creating, displaying, and selling their art. The three founders started the organization in 2001, after being laid off from the Salvation Army; they went without a salary for two years. "The main motivation for me in beginning p:ear was a deep passion to continue working with these kids in an environment that inspired hope and change," cofounder Beth Burns said.[23]

Although the p:ear founders did not have to deal with the decision to quit steady jobs to pursue their passion, moving from a relatively comfortable position in the private sector to an uncertain one as a social entrepreneur can be a tough challenge. Yet, many social entrepreneurs are so passionate about what they are doing that they make the leap; to them it may be less an issue of dealing with their own personal risk than being comfortable with the ambiguity of beginning a new social venture, developing a plan, and looking for key financial and in-kind support. The examples from Sheridan illustrate social entrepreneurs' passion to make a difference and capability to handle a situation fraught with uncertainty; they also indicate that as a venture grows, developing alternative income sources to turn the venture into a sustainable enterprise requires additional doses of courage.

Joey's FlyFishing Foundation: An Embryonic Social Venture Takes Its First Steps

A few years ago, a colleague asked Joey Puettman what he wanted to do with his life. The answer became Joey's FlyFishing Foundation. In his mid-twenties, Puettman made the decision to pursue his dream while fly-fishing on the Big Horn River. The mission is simple: take children fly-fishing near Sheridan. Puettman works during the school year as a children's counselor for Northern Wyoming Mental Health; he has also worked as a fly-fishing guide. Putting elements of his expertise together gave birth to a social venture. He drew up his initial business plan on a napkin and then invested $3.85 in a blue binder to hold his revised business plan and a white binder to contain the program elements.

Puettman explains that there are many social programs, but that he found a niche by combining their approaches. For example, Big Brothers/Big Sisters offers one-on-one experiences for adults and children that probably do not involve fly-fishing. The local YMCA recreation program takes fifteen to twenty kids on a fishing program. Joey's FlyFishing takes about five children and adult volunteers on a two-day, four-hour program that combines one-on-one contact with the fly-fishing experience. Puettman's contact with local ranchers has resulted in his camp's access to some of the best-kept water in the area.

On the first day of the program, Puettman focuses on teaching the kids about aquatic habitat and instructing them in how to tie flies and put together lanyards to secure their equipment. Once they have mastered these elements, the second morning is spent fishing in a nearby stream. The children selected for the program are referred by local schools and counseling programs. Puettman asks caseworkers and therapists the basic question, "Do you have four or five kids who would benefit from this fly-fishing experience?" Boys and girls of various ages have participated in the program.

The focus can be to help children with attention-deficit/hyperactivity disorder (ADHD), whose fishing experience brings together the five senses and creates an anchored focus on an activity; children with obsessive-compulsive disorder, who need to establish an alternative routine such as fishing to help deal with their issues; or children who just never have the opportunity to get out and fish. Puettman does not engage in diagnosis; instead, those with proper training refer children to the program, letting parents or guardians know the child has received a "scholarship" to Joey's FlyFishing.

Originally from Casper, Wyoming, Puettman studied elementary education at the University of North Dakota. His background includes stints as a waiter, schoolteacher, and wrestling coach. In Sheridan, which he calls "the biggest small town," he has put together a board of directors that includes a city planner, a school counselor, a marketing/advertising person, and a Wyoming game and fish investigator. He spends three to five hours a day networking, to raise both funds and awareness. Thus far, the foundation has subsisted through grants, in-kind donations, and fund-raisers. Eventually, Puettman hopes to contract with local schools and agencies to take kids into the program.

Initially, Puettman worked out of a local outdoors store while preparing the kids for the fishing experience. But in the spring of 2009, his accountant donated to the foundation a downtown building, which Puettman, AmeriCorps, and other volunteers spruced up and converted into the headquarters for a year-round program. Puettman plans eventually to leave his other job so that he can devote all of his time to the foundation. In the winter months, November to April, kids who are not playing sports or engaging in other extracurricular activities now have a safe place to hang out where they can build fishing rods.

Circumstance seemed to provide a motivation for Puettman to take action on what had been a long-term dream and vision. He believes that if he had not started the organization when he did, he might not have gotten another chance: "Do it while you're young. I didn't want to be forty years old and think, 'God, I wish I'd started that fishing camp for kids.'"

Sheridan Housing Action Committee: A Social Venture Grows in the Community

Since its founding in late 2004, the goal of Sheridan Housing Action Committee (SHAC) has been to provide affordable housing for working families. Marie Lowe, SHAC's founder and executive director, says SHAC facilitates affordable housing by establishing partnerships between the city and private developers, building houses and setting up infrastructure for housing developments, providing home buyer education and financial counseling to more than 200 families, and engaging the community in its activities.

Lowe notes that the average renter has only $4,050 in net worth, whereas the average homeowner has $254,000. SHAC's prospective clients include office workers, employees at local businesses, city and county employees, military personnel, nurses, police officers, and teachers. SHAC provides affordable housing in the $150,000 range, whereas the local median market home prices range from $270,000 to $300,000. The organization's focus is on individuals at a higher income level than those who would qualify for help by other housing groups such as Habitat for Humanity, which focuses on people with very low incomes. SHAC clients are usually young working families with small children; however, SHAC has assisted other demographics, including the elderly.

Since November 2007, SHAC has built seven houses and sold them to its clients, but has used a variety of methods to help almost sixty families become homeowners. "We don't compete with the free market for construction," Lowe said. "We don't take a profit; we pay ourselves a project management fee when we sell a house." Actual building is only a small part of SHAC's activity, but provides a third of its operating revenue. SHAC has also worked with builders to establish three affordable housing developments in the community. One of its first projects was a community build, at which locals came together to donate materials and labor for a new home. Sale of the home at a relatively low price generated money for a revolving loan fund that was used for future projects.

Lowe's family background in the construction industry and her ownership of a real estate company elsewhere in Wyoming gave her the knowledge for forming SHAC. A variety of local people with housing expertise have also helped, including Kyle Williams, an entrepreneur who founded Big Horn Granite & Marble, a custom manufacturer of countertops, and who also serves as SHAC board president. Others involved in SHAC specialize in banking, new private-sector ventures, or planning and economic development for the city or are members of the local Big Horn Homebuilders Association. Lowe developed a group of mentors who can answer questions about the challenges her organization faces; she regards relationships of this type as key to the growth and sustainability of any social venture.

After seeing the lack of affordable housing in Sheridan while she was working as a real estate agent, Lowe spent two years doing research on housing before starting the organization. The combination of passion, comfort with doing something new, understanding of key issues, and having a supportive community network helped her muster the moral courage to quit her job. "I've always been an entrepreneur and self-employed. You just have to go for it. My avocation became my vocation." After deciding SHAC would be an "action" committee, she placed a high priority on hiring an executive director to move it forward. "The most important thing is you believe in what you are doing. It's great to be excited and love what you're doing every day."

Volunteers of America: Social Entrepreneurship Becomes Social Enterprise

Jeff Holsinger and his staff have built the Wyoming/Montana Volunteers of America affiliate into a model of what some social ventures might become once they recognize how to turn initial passion into sustainable sources of income. Yet, this type of growth requires the moral courage to take risks.

The VOA is a faith-based nonprofit organization that consists of local affiliates operating in 44 states and more than 400 communities. The organization—founded by social reformers Ballington and Maud Booth, the son and daughter-in-law of Salvation Army founder William Booth—focuses on helping those in need rebuild their lives and reach their full potential through a variety of human service programs that include housing and health care. "Since 1896, our ministry of service has supported and empowered America's most vulnerable groups, including at-risk youth, the frail elderly, men and women returning from prison, homeless individuals and families, people with disabilities, and those recovering from addictions,"[24] reports the VOA's website.

Jeff Holsinger, president and CEO of the Sheridan-based affiliate, views his organization as fully in the "entrepreneurship mode." Holsinger, who has a twenty-five-year career in nonprofit organizations, says that the affiliate has become more self-aware and focused as a social and entrepreneurial enterprise in the last couple of years. Heath Steel, the affiliate's executive vice president of operations and entrepreneurial guru, says, "I believe the Volunteers of America has been a socially entrepreneurial company for the last 113 years,"[25] starting at the grassroots by going into prisons, providing ministry and meals, and taking on social issues such as addiction. In the process, VOA has built models that allow it to become sustainable, a new behavior based on old practices.

"You have other nonprofits that get so fixated on the mission and the emotion tied to it that they don't have good business principles that they operate from," Jeff said. Such organizations are driven by donor support or limited contracts, and thus at the mercy of changing environments: when donations go down and contracts end, the sustainability of the organization and the services it provides are under serious threat.

Holsinger and Steel believe the answer lies in aggressive entrepreneurial behavior and social enterprise, diversifying into a variety of activities that produce income that goes back into the social venture and strategically merging with other nonprofits. Delegating decision making and encouraging an entrepreneurial culture, VOA moves quickly to address a variety of needs in the community. These include affordable housing for seniors and veterans, group homes for those (including veterans) battling drug and alcohol addiction, a homeless shelter in Sheridan, youth homes, day care, specialized foster care, transitional living facilities, community-based adult correctional services, occupational drug testing, and supervision of the county's in-school suspension program. "As long as we're serving people in the context of our mission, we can serve them in any capacity," Holsinger said.

Steel, a fourth-generation Wyoming native, has a background in agriculture, a private-sector building company, and a nonprofit therapeutic equine riding program, which he closed down several years ago due to funding issues before he moved to the VOA. "The American farmer and rancher is the original innovator," he said. Steel has brought several innovative approaches to the organization, based on expanding programs originally designed to serve VOA clients and employees. Some of these programs include drug testing, which was originally set up for VOA employees but has taken on several private-sector contracts; a commercial kitchen that was first focused on VOA group facilities but now is able to provide catering services to the community; and snow removal, which expanded beyond VOA facility driveways and parking lots to take on private work. "It's all about sustainability and diversification of our dollar," Holsinger said. In the growth of Wyoming/Montana VOA to a $12-million-a-year organization, employment has jumped from 30 to 140 employees, but administrative overhead has stayed at 12 percent of revenues.

At one point, VOA supplied meals for the local jail, while a private out-of-state contract provider took three months to gear up. The VOA commercial kitchen was serving 100 meals three times a day within a week. Establishing that service as a permanent contract would bring in $250,000 a year, money that could be used for other areas of service. Holsinger and Steel see this prospect partly as diversification but also as a protective move, citing the recent example of a private for-profit company challenging the nonprofit Meals on Wheels in Denver; the private company provides a slightly more expensive meal, using real silverware rather than plastic knives and forks.

VOA in Sheridan is geared to focus on growth and opportunity while delivering quality programs in a variety of human service areas. Its leaders view a culture of teamwork, managed risk taking, learning, and innovation as the means to survive and thrive in difficult times. Working with an active board of directors that has established a five-year strategic plan, Holsinger and Steel believe the organization's approach allows it to anticipate changes in the environment and provide solutions in the community. Their plans include a major capital campaign, new fund-raising strategies, and a new headquarters campus that will house several group facilities.

Sheridan Social Entrepreneurship and Moral Courage

"I think that anyone who strikes out on their own to address a social issue exhibits moral courage by doing so and continues to exhibit it for as long as they remain dedicated to that cause for their livelihood or for a substantial portion of their daily activities," says former Sheridan College president Kevin Drumm.[26] Yet, beyond the startup and growth of a new social venture, different situations result in the need for additional doses of moral courage when doing what is right might not be financially or personally convenient.

For Joey Puettman, who has gone heavily into debt to get the fly-fishing venture off the ground, the next step entails leaving his full-time job to devote all of his energies to the foundation. Puettman recently moved to a part-time counselor position as the renovations to his downtown headquarters building were finished to accommodate year-round activities such as building fishing rods; the foundation served a record 150 children in 2009. Meanwhile, he continues to deal with raising money and coordinating volunteers. His largest issues are managing the debt he has already incurred in launching this social venture and getting people to invest their time. Leading an organization in its infancy, Joey must worry about basic fund-raising and organizing his programs before seeking alternative sources of income.

With a more established organization, Marie Lowe has problems other than giving time, talent, and treasure to SHAC. For example, she encountered negative community response to a proposed ten-home development in one of Sheridan's neighborhoods. People in the neighborhood had a NIMBY (not in my back yard) reaction. They agreed that affordable housing for working families was a great idea, but they did not want the development near their homes—unless there was a concrete block wall around it. Lowe could not accede to such a demand, which could have hurt the dignity of the working families she has tried so hard to help. The neighborhood organized a petition drive to city council, which voted to yank its support of a $250,000 federal grant to assist in buying land and providing infrastructure to the new development. Yet, Lowe bravely moved on, despite the devastating result, which indicated that obstacles still present themselves to SHAC's ideals, even in Sheridan. "We worked eight months on the project. It was a big blow," she said. "It was three steps forward, one step back. I thought we were over that."

Another issue that involves moral courage as an organization grows is the challenge for the social entrepreneur to keep focused on the venture's aims while satisfying its funders. Regular contributors to an organization may want more say in its operations. "So, how do you stand up to your funders while not jeopardizing their support?" Kevin Drumm asks. This is a constant question for social entrepreneurs. To address it, the VOA's leaders have exhibited a different type of courage, one that deals with the potential balance between head and heart, staying true to the mission while being entrepreneurially aggressive. In some cases, the leaders of social ventures with a sound mission but insufficient funding must be brave enough to shut down, as Steel's equine center did, or to merge with larger organizations with greater resources.

Jeff Holsinger says social entrepreneurs making the transition from private- or public-sector employment must ask the question, "How am I going to make a living off this?" One big challenge is to sustain the organization and the individuals operating it over the long term by operating as a sound business. But does this focus on business practices lead the players to forget why they are providing the services in the first place?

The VOA leaders see this as a question of balance and willingness to revise the mission. Recently, VOA revisited and redefined its mission. The leadership planned to build an apartment complex and rent to the public with priority for veterans. A board committee noted that the apartment complex was not a program and therefore did not fit with VOA's mission to run programs to help people. Plans to pursue the complex were dropped at a cost of $20,000 already invested in preliminary steps. "It was a learning experience," Holsinger said. The board and its executives are attempting to revise the mission statement, as the current one did not provide enough information on what not to do. In the process, the board reworked the affiliate's strategic plan.

Challenges for VOA and its social enterprise mission are similar to those of any fast-growing organization: establishing functional areas such as human resources and grant writing as well as staying up-to-date with all of the core competencies (corrections, substance abuse treatment, youth issues) provided to the 700–800 people the organization serves each day. A key element is "ensuring that the quality of what we say we're doing, we're actually doing," Steel said. The VOA in Sheridan has made significant progress in connecting innovation, quick movement, and response to local social needs. For many social entrepreneurs, driven by their passion, "the head work and the heart work conflict with each other," Steel said. "At the end of the day, not-for-profit, for-profit, or charity is a business, and that's the part that gets left out."

Interestingly, as the social venture grows into a social enterprise, the values of the successful social entrepreneur remain consistent, but the challenges that require morally courageous actions by the leadership require broader consideration of varying situations. The examples of these three social entrepreneurs indicate the changing requirements of passion and risk taking that present themselves at different stages of organizational growth. They also underscore the importance of community values to the success of social entrepreneurship.

Notes

1. Drumm, 2009a.
2. Dees, Emerson, and Economy, 2001.
3. Florida, 2008.
4. Popovich, 2004.
5. Economic Analysis Division, 2008.
6. Drumm, 2009b.
7. Whitney Benefits, 2009a.
8. Whitney Benefits, 2009b.
9. Ibid.
10. Drumm, 2009b.
11. Florida, 2008, 66.
12. Institute for Social Entrepreneurs, 2009.
13. Puettman, 2009.
14. Lowe, 2009.
15. Holsinger, 2009.
16. See Bornstein, 2004; Dees, 2007; Seelos and Mair, 2005.
17. Dees, 2007, 24–25.
18. See Neck, Brush, and Allen, 2009; Vega and Kidwell, 2007.
19. Bornstein, 2004.
20. Wood, 2006.
21. Ibid., 36.
22. Ibid., 10.
23. Short and Palmer, 2008, 122.
24. Volunteers of America, 2009.
25. Steel, 2009.
26. Drumm, 2009b.

References

Bornstein, D. 2004. *How to change the world: Social entrepreneurs and the power of new ideas.* Oxford: Oxford University Press.
Dees, J.G. 2007. Taking social entrepreneurship seriously. *Society* 44(3), 24–31.
Dees, J.G., Emerson, J., and Economy, P. 2001. *Enterprising nonprofits: A toolkit for social entrepreneurs.* New York: John Wiley & Sons.
Drumm, K. 2009a. Opening remarks, "Sheridan Wyoming: Mecca of social entrepreneurialism." Teaching Creativity Panel Discussion, Laramie, Wyoming, February 26.
———. 2009b. Personal correspondence, June 22.
Economic Analysis Division. 2008. Wyoming incorporated place population estimates: April 1, 2000 to July 1, 2007. July 10. http://eadiv.state.wy.us/pop/SUB-07EST.htm (accessed June 3, 2009).
Florida, R. 2008. *Who's your city? How the creative economy is making where to live the most important decision of your life.* New York: Basic Books.

Holsinger, J. 2009. Personal interview, Sheridan, WY. May 21.

Institute for Social Entrepreneurs. 2009. Social enterprise terminology. http://socialent. org/Social_Enterprise_Terminology.htm (accessed June 3, 2009).

Lowe, M. 2009. Personal interview, Sheridan, WY. May 21.

Neck, H., Brush, C., and Allen, E. 2009. The landscape of social entrepreneurship. *Business Horizons* 52(1), 13–19.

Popovich, C.W. 2004. *Sheridan, Wyoming, and area historical sites.* Sheridan, WY: C.W. Popovich.

Puettman, J. 2009. Personal interview, Sheridan, WY. May 22.

Seelos, C., and Mair, J. 2005. Social entrepreneurship: Creating new business models to serve the poor. *Business Horizons* 48(3), 241–246.

Short, J.C., and Palmer, T.B. 2008. Bridging the gap between service-learning and social entrepreneurship: An interview with the founders of p:ear. *Journal of Applied Management and Entrepreneurship* 12(4), 121–128.

Steel, H. 2009. Personal interview, Sheridan, WY. May 21.

Vega, G., and Kidwell, R.E. 2007. Toward a typology of new venture creators: Similarities and contrasts between business and social entrepreneurs. *New England Journal of Entrepreneurship* 10(2), 15–28.

Volunteers of America. 2009. http://www.voa.org/About-Us.aspx (accessed June 8, 2009).

Whitney Benefits. 2009a. About Whitney. www.whitneybenefits.org/AboutWhitney. htm (accessed June 3, 2009).

———. 2009b. Edward A. Whitney: Sheridan's first and foremost benefactor. www. whitneybenefits.org/history/EAW.pdf (accessed June 3, 2009).

Wood, J. 2006. *Leaving Microsoft to change the world: An entrepreneur's odyssey to educate the world's children.* New York: Harper-Collins.

8

NGO Leaders on the Edge

The Moral Courage to
Fight for Human Rights

JUDITH WHITE

This chapter presents profiles of three morally courageous individuals who lead organizations working to develop civil society and democracy in Burma. Civil society includes formal and informal groups that operate outside the formal economic and political arenas for the purpose of developing civility, citizen participation, and community for society's common good. Among these groups are nongovernmental, religious, educational, political, and voluntary organizations. Nongovernmental organizations, or NGOs, may be large and international, like the Red Cross, or small and local, like the organizations discussed here. The morally courageous leaders I discuss work under difficult and sometimes dangerous circumstances that may put them, their colleagues, and their program participants at risk.

Moral courage is different from physical courage because it involves the willingness to uphold moral principles in the face of opposition and possible harm to oneself and others. It includes a tacit acknowledgment of one's vulnerability as a human being, subject to others' power. Physical courage involves the willingness to suffer physical harm, but by itself does not require acting on a set of moral principles.[1] The three individuals I profile represent a larger group of more than fifty leaders of small, local NGOs working primarily outside Burma on the borders with Thailand, India, China, Bangladesh, and Malaysia. Most of these organizations offer capacity-building programs, designed to increase the knowledge, skills, and abilities of their members, and thereby enhance the effectiveness of their organizations. These training and development programs focus on leadership, literacy, human rights education, women's empowerment, foreign affairs training, teacher training in critical reading and writing, HIV/AIDS education, socially engaged Buddhism for monks and nuns, advocacy, environmental rights, and assistance for political prisoners. Funding for these NGOs comes from individuals, foundations, and some Western governments that are interested in promoting democracy. I interviewed these and other leaders in Burma and Thailand to understand the foundations of their moral courage in their fight for justice. My interest in moral courage in the pro-democracy movement began in 1997, when I interviewed Aung San Suu Kyi, leader of the opposition pro-democracy party, at her home in Burma.

Historical, Political, and Cultural Backdrop

Burma gained independence from Britain in 1948, had a few years of democratic rule, and since 1962 has been ruled by a military dictatorship. Although Burma's military government renamed the country Myanmar in 1989, Burma is the name used by pro-democracy activists across the world. The government denies such fundamental human rights as speech, association, press, religion, access to information, jobs, physical safety, and voluntary labor. Burma is approximately 93 percent Buddhist; the rest of its people are Christian or Muslim. The country has more than sixteen ethnic groups, which tend to live in specific regions, but not every region is named for an ethnic group. The largest ethnic group is Burman; other large ones are the Shan, who primarily live in Shan State, and the Karen, the largest Christian ethnic minority in Burma, who live in Kayin State. In the past forty years ethnic conflicts have intensified between minority groups and the Burman regime. Amnesty International, Human Rights Watch, and the U.S. Department of State consider Burma's military-ruled government, which uses torture, killings, systematic rape, forced labor, and destruction of villages to control its people, one of the world's worst violators of human rights. The government has no legislative branch, and the judiciary is controlled by the military, which rules by force and decree. In 2007, the army violently attacked and in some cases killed monks and civilians because they were peacefully demonstrating for lower gas prices and freedom of association and speech. Throughout Burmese history, monks have been the moral standard-bearers of the country; therefore, when they were beaten, disrobed, imprisoned, tortured, or killed, the people's minimal trust of the government was lost.[2]

Burma, a country of approximately 60 million people, has natural resources including timber, petroleum, natural gas, copper, precious gems, sugar, tin, limestone, lead, and coal. In the early part of the twentieth century Burma was the rice bowl of Asia, but today most of the population lives on less than one dollar a day. China, Burma's largest trading partner, supplies most of the military hardware the Burmese army uses against its own people. Since the pro-democracy demonstrations in 1988, more than 1.5 million people have fled Burma to live illegally in Thailand, and another 120,000 live in refugee camps on the Burma-Thai border. Two million people live in (internally) displaced-persons camps inside Burma. Bangkok and the Thai border cities of Chaing Mai and Mae Sot are centers of Burmese NGO activity, with as many as forty local NGOs there and on the borders with India, Bangladesh, and China. The Burmese military intelligence has agents, provocateurs, and informants throughout Thailand to thwart the Burmese pro-democracy movement there. Intercity buses are stopped to check for illegal Burmese. Some NGOs have been broken into and had their offices torn apart. Much of a refugee camp was destroyed after it was twice set on fire. Many believe that the Burmese military perpetrated this violence while the Thai police looked the other way.

The military government's inadequate and delayed response to the catastrophic Cyclone Nargis in May 2008 underscores Burma's current political, social, and economic crises. Some monks and civilians who provided humanitarian aid immediately after the cyclone have been imprisoned. Aung San Suu Kyi, the Nobel Peace Laureate and leader of the main opposition party, the National League for Democracy, has been under house arrest for fourteen of the past twenty years. As of this writing more than 2,100 political prisoners remain in prison without due process. They receive minimal food and medical care and suffer routine beatings and torture.

Profiles

The following three individuals demonstrate moral courage in their daily lives because their moral principles are an integral part of their identities. While pursuing a moral vision of a better society for their country, they take legal, physical, social, and financial risks and make sacrifices of home and family, education and career, money, and legal status. Despite these risks and sacrifices, they persevere and remain optimistic.

Nang Charm Tong, Member of the Shan Women's Action Network and Director of the School for Shan State Nationalities Youth

Charm Tong, born in Shan State in 1981, is one of the youngest, most courageous, and internationally recognized leaders of Burma's pro-democracy movement in Thailand. At seventeen, she was a delegate to the United Nations Commission on Human Rights, representing Shan women who had been systematically beaten and raped by the Burmese junta since 1988. Charm Tong has not attended college, but she has received human rights awards in Europe, Asia, and the United States; testified at the United Nations Commission of Human Rights and people's forums of the Association of Southeast Asian Nations (ASEAN); and been the honored speaker at various international forums.

Charm Tong appears young and unassuming, but she is relentless in her struggle to support men and women whom the Burmese military dictatorship has repressed and attacked. In 1999, Charm cofounded, together with more than forty women on the Thai-Burma border, the Shan Women's Action Network, or SWAN, which published a report demonstrating that the Burmese army condoned rape as a "weapon of war."[3] The group defied the Burmese government by organizing members to collect information to document the systematic rape and violence against Shan women inside Burma. In an attempt to refute the report and attack Charm Tong and SWAN, Burma's state-run newspaper, *New Light of Myanmar*, published an article and a photograph of Charm with the caption, "License to Lie." Her response is, "But so what? We want real freedom. We ourselves are traumatized when we hear the stories of violence; for the women, to tell their stories, to break the silence, is very painful, but it is very important to break the silence."

In 1987, when Charm Tong was six years old, her parents brought her to a Catholic orphanage on the Thai-Burma border because of the lurking danger in Burma. Charm credits Teacher Mary, the director of the orphanage, for providing a positive role model of leadership and hard work. Charm observed how Teacher Mary, overcoming hardships and challenges, procured food and financial resources for the orphanage and maintained good relationships with the community. While still learning English herself, Charm Tong taught the language to the smaller children. At seventeen, Charm Tong left the orphanage and interned with the Shan Human Rights Foundation in Thailand, gathering information and writing stories, in an effort to help the Shan. From there she interned at Altsean-Burma, an NGO that provides capacity building and leadership training for women from Burma and advocates for human rights and democracy in Burma. As Charm developed leadership skills and learned about conflicts, human rights struggles, and war beyond Burma, she recognized "that we are not alone; there is so much support for what we are doing."

Today Charm Tong focuses on the needs of the Shan refugees and migrant workers and advocates for social and political change in Burma. SWAN provides programs for women's health, housing, education, women's empowerment, documentation, crisis support, and income generation for Shan women and their children. Its mission is to promote "gender equity and justice for Shan women in the struggle for social and political change in Burma through community-based actions, research, and advocacy." SWAN runs nine schools for basic literacy; seven nurseries; three community-based health clinics; training programs on leadership, gender equity, and human rights; a one-year internship program; and two crisis-support centers.

As a member of the SWAN advocacy team, Charm Tong goes abroad to remind donors, diplomats, politicians, and the United Nations of the current struggles of women of Burma. Every day SWAN deals with "crises, with difficult situations of trauma and violence," where people are oppressed and abused. Charm Tong told me, "Just last week a woman was gang-raped in Shan State by the military. This happens almost every week. Our work makes a difference in women's lives, and one indicator is that the regime is not happy with SWAN." Charm Tong is committed to ensuring that SWAN is a democratic, participative, and inclusive organization. Its nonhierarchical organizational structure empowers individuals and emphasizes teamwork. Yet, Charm Tong is modest about her own role in SWAN, emphasizing that leaders are always responsible to the women participants they serve.

> When we travel, we are responsible to take the voices of the people on the ground, our participants, to the UN, to the other governments and other people we speak to. We are also responsible to bring the information from the UN, and other places, back to the people on the ground. We consult with people on the ground, they support us when we go and do international work. You have to practice what you preach; you have to walk the talk. If we preach equality, participation, inclusiveness, and democracy, then we have to practice it in our organization. We don't want a "struggle within the struggle."

Charm Tong and her colleagues advocate successfully for gender equity, freedom, and democracy in Burma, demonstrating through their programs that Burmese women can be self-sufficient and competent. In addition to being a founding member of SWAN, which cofounded the Women's League of Burma, she and other refugee youth from Shan State started the School for Shan State Nationalities Youth (SSSNY) in 2001, to empower young men and women from Shan State who are current or future leaders in their community-based organizations. In the nine-month program they study social justice, democracy, HIV/AIDS education, English language, human rights, leadership, and advocacy.

As director of the school, Charm's responsibilities include fund-raising, reviewing curriculum, and teaching. She is pleased with the school's progress and the quality of the program and reports that students and staff alike have learned about group dynamics and team facilitation. On reflecting upon herself as a morally courageous leader, Charm Tong says her strength and dedication come from the collective work with other women, working as part of a larger group, within a larger movement. She says her identity is as a woman activist, an ethnic Shan, a Burma activist, and a fighter for justice.

Myo Min, Founder and Director, Human Rights Educational Institute of Burma

Myo Min is the first openly gay man working in the Burmese pro-democracy movement and one of the few gay men to advocate explicitly for lesbian, gay, bisexual, and transgender (LGBT) rights in the human rights movement. He has received international awards for his work on human rights for Burma and LGBT rights in general. He received the 1999 Felipa De Souza award from the International Gay and Lesbian Human Rights Commission and the Honor of Courage award from the San Francisco City Board. As an advocate for human rights, he has contributed to drafting the future constitution of Burma.

Myo Min was born in 1966. While he was in high school, government officials twice voted him as an outstanding leader for his skills at first aid and his ability to organize community youth activities. During the 1988 national demonstrations for democracy, Myo Min was a university student and a leader in the student-led demonstrations. He first witnessed bloodshed when his close friend, portrayed by the government as a "destructive element," was killed by government troops. That murder was the catalyst for Myo Min to join the All Burma Students Democratic Front army (ABSDF), to fight the military offensive in Burma.

At the time, ABSDF, the first all-student army anywhere in the world, had only 5,000 men, fighting in the jungles against the State Law and Order Council (SLORC), now called the State Peace and Development Commission. Initially, gays were closeted in the ABSDF, and being gay was punishable by five years in the students' army prison. In the ABSDF, and while growing up, Myo Min was denied his human rights; in his words, he was not given "the space to maintain my dignity to be myself." Over time, in the army, Myo Min came out as a gay man, "but because I am a strong person, they didn't give me too much trouble." Nevertheless, he had to work twice as hard to overcome discrimination and have his ideas recognized: "I speak for all LGBT; why should I have to hide who I am?" While serving in the army as a foreign affairs officer, he fell in love with a lieutenant commander. His lover, who was attacked for being gay, was later killed in combat. Myo Min quit the army after two years. Years later he provided human rights and gay rights training for the ABSDF, which eventually abolished its antigay policy.

After attending Columbia University's Human Rights Advocate Program in 1993, Myo Min worked in Bangkok at the National Council of the Union of Burma (NCUB), which represents exiled political and armed groups, to develop a democratically elected federal government in Burma. He documented human rights violations in Burma and worked on foreign affairs, seeking support for Burma's 1990 democratically elected government from other governments and international groups like the United Nations Human Rights Council. Myo Min influenced the NCUB to develop LGBT programs for Burmese migrants.

At NCUB Myo Min felt determined to "teach human rights and social analysis, to teach the Burmese people, whether in refugee camps, schools, families, or community-based organizations, to take action, not just learn for the sake of learning but to do something with the new knowledge." In 2000, he began teaching in the refugee camps and getting requests for human rights education and training. Soon thereafter, he and four colleagues founded the Human Rights Education Institute for Burma (HREIB), based in Thailand. Myo Min became the executive director, and by 2007, HREIB had staff working on the borders in Thailand, Burma, China, India, Bangladesh, and Malaysia. Its mission is "to empower people through human rights education to engage in social transformation and promote a culture of human rights for all."

Myo Min asserts that HREIB's five programs—general human rights, children's rights against recruitment as soldiers and trafficking, women's rights and gender, transitional justice, and community organizing—are building a culture of human rights, respect, diversity, and freedom. He says, "It takes a lot of work to educate people and get them to change their attitudes and behavior in regards to class, ethnic minorities, violence against women, and sexual orientation." He tells participants in his programs that he knows suffering because he has felt oppression, suppression, and discrimination as a gay man. Inside Burma it is too risky to refer to "human rights"; program leaders and participants avoid using this term and refer instead to women's issues, literacy, diversity of religion, and community development. Gays and people in general "need courage to overcome the pressures on the individual from society. Society puts you in a box, and when you speak out for LGBT rights you are outside of the box," he said.

Some of Myo Min's courage to work for human rights and democracy comes from seeing communities working together, seeing people "go out and pass on their knowledge and get others to act." Myo Min, who has no children of his own, has a close bond with program participants, colleagues, and staff: "My work is my life; my colleagues are like my family." Myo Min says that his approach is "interfaith," because no particular religion guides his work. For the long term, "We want to go home to Burma. . . . I'm satisfied and proud of my work, but I don't let pride get in the way of continuing to work hard." The success he has seen in his work gives him hope for eventual democracy in Burma.

Harn, Founder of Alternative Education for Social Engagement

Harn was born in Shan State and completed high school in 1996. His father, after retiring from the Shan resistance army, became a community-appointed schoolteacher. As Harn was growing up in rural areas of Shan State, he witnessed brutal civil war, which sparked his interest in rebel groups and nonviolence. Because universities were closed when he graduated from high school, he went to Bangkok to work as a front-desk clerk at a small hotel. Next, he interned for a year with the Asia Forum for Human Rights and Development in Bangkok, and then spent two years with the Nationalities Youth Development Program (NYDP), working in Bangladesh, India, and Thailand with ethnically and religiously diverse youth who were fleeing war and oppression in Burma. While at NYDP, he attended a training program in facilitation and nonviolence with Quakers in Philadelphia. Harn says his inspiration for civil society in Burma comes in part from studying the civil society movements in Eastern Europe, the Philippines, and Indonesia.

Harn is the director of Alternative Education for Social Engagement (AESE), a small NGO inside Burma he founded with some friends in 2003 to build civil society in Burma using three strategies: (1) capacity building for adults; (2) alternative media; and (3) progressive education for children. AESE works mostly in Shan State with young adults, women's groups, and community and religious/spiritual leaders. AESE provides training workshops, contemplative practices, and study trips with the aim of promoting collective initiatives for personal and social transformation. Workshop participants learn community building, Buddhist social analysis, socially engaged Buddhism, leadership, and social change through democratic and other nonviolent means.

AESE teaches alternative educational practices for lay and spiritual teachers working in monasteries, churches, and community schools. The approach incorporates the ideas of Montessori, Waldorf, Reggio Emilia, and Howard Gardner. AESE publishes Shan-language print and video journals on civic participation, sustainable development, and progressive education. Because successive military regimes have permitted only Burmese, not ethnic languages, to be used in public arenas, these alternative media are complementary forms of education that help the Shan reclaim their own culture, language, and literature.

Harn offers training and development in social engagement to Buddhist monks and nuns. He teaches them about Buddhist activists (such as the Dalai Lama, Ambedkar in India, and A.T. Ariyaratne in Sri Lanka) and takes them on exposure and study trips to Sri Lanka and Thailand so they can learn from other activist monks and nuns. He wants them to see how they could use their power as teachers and spiritual leaders to develop civil society in Burma. Buddhist monks and nuns traditionally participate actively in social, cultural, and political life as teachers, community leaders, and medical doctors. But since the last century, Burma's secularized structure has kept them from these roles, which Harn is encouraging them to resume. For example, monks and nuns led the 2007 demonstrations, and many provided relief aid to victims of Cyclone Nargis in 2008.

Reflecting on AESE's programs, Harn compares the progress to bending a tree, inasmuch as the changes will be slow. He claims that the women feel more effective in their organizations because it is easier for them to work together. Some monks and nuns are setting up kindergartens, primary schools, microfinance programs, and other community development programs. In the future, Harn wants "to enable people to resume their traditional roles as social, cultural, and community leaders—to stand up for their rights and move towards a more progressive and holistic educational approach for the collective spiritual development."

Harn is keenly aware that the work he does is considered subversive inside Burma. When we met inside a hotel in Burma, he did not want to be seen talking with a Westerner, which would have drawn the attention of the military intelligence and police. He was taking additional precautions to keep a low profile because of recent arrests of activists at that time in Shan State. AESE, which does not have official status anywhere, is vulnerable to the Thai and Burmese police. Harn is both an activist and a scholar. He has written a book in Burmese and is working on the English translation.[4] He serves on the executive committee of the International Network of Engaged Buddhists, a global network of scholars, practitioners, intellectuals, and activists.

Concerning religion he says, "We are Buddhist because our families are, but only in the last five years have I begun to understand Buddhism in a way where factors other than our personal actions affect the world." He and his colleagues are committed to both personal and professional growth, including annual retreats for "inner and outer transformation." Harn acknowledges few outward signs of change inside Burma, but stays hopeful and courageous:

> Yes, there is a time for disappointment; it is natural, but the teachings of the Buddha help me go forward. My hope stems from the Buddhist notion of impermanence. Nothing stays the same forever. Things change all the time. The situation in Burma will change for sure, but I cannot say with certainty in which direction. I often liken our works to planting trees. It takes time and patience to see the trees growing to their full. Yet, the small changes that we make are also one of our sources of hope, which enable us to keep on working. We have just worked for a few years, and so it is not realistic for us to expect too much so soon. . . . We want change now but cannot get it now.

Harn believes that change depends on factors beyond his group's control, such as the cultural and religious beliefs of the Burmese people. He says the Burmese would mistake the popular beliefs of a mixture of animism, Hinduism, and Buddhism for true Buddhism. Some rely on their understanding of karma as the predestined outcome of some wrongdoing in their previous life to explain why they do not actively oppose injustice or oppression. But for Harm, this is a misinterpretation of karma as the law of cause and effect. He thinks if they could understand karma as intentional actions of one's own choosing with concomitant consequences, they would be compelled to act for their own welfare and liberation. He demonstrates his commitment to a free and democratic Burma through his leadership in AESE; his writing and political critique of the cultural, religious, and ideological issues in this struggle; and his personal intellectual and spiritual development.

Themes

One of the several leaders I interviewed told me, "My friends and I felt a sense of urgency. We had to do something, so we sold t-shirts to raise money for food and medical supplies for people fleeing the violence and devastation in their homes and villages. We thought it would be over in a few weeks, and here we are twenty years later." Despite death threats, office raids, and family sacrifices, she supports and trains other activists developing their own groups, assisting them to organize, write grants, speak to the press, and lead community-based organizations. Indeed, two major themes emerge from talking with these activist leaders: (1) risk and sacrifice and (2) moral vision and goals. Some of the circumstances of these leaders' lives are quite different, but all take risks and endure sacrifice and hold a moral vision of a democratic society in their home in Burma.

Risk and Sacrifice

These leaders take risks in several spheres of their lives. Being dependent on donors is risky. Funding for their organizations is uncertain in part because some donors will fund political groups, whereas others will support only humanitarian work. For the leaders and their program participants, the distinction is not always clear, but many donors consider most of these small NGOs political rather than strictly humanitarian. When funding is precarious, these NGO leaders' own source of financial support, limited as it is, is threatened. Their compensation is like a small stipend. Without family support, they sometimes live in the very modestly appointed offices where they work. These leaders take risks when they go back and forth between Burma and its borders with Thailand, India, Bangladesh, China, and Malaysia to lead programs, meet with participants, and make contacts. Without legal status outside of Burma, they risk harassment, arrest, and possibly prison sentences in Burma. Along the borders, immigration officials frequently check for illegal Burmese. In Thailand, just meeting with Westerners can jeopardize them, their staff, and the Burmese participants in their programs. One leader received a death threat, and at least two organizations had their offices broken into and computers confiscated. One man, while completing an Ed.D. in the United Kingdom, was asked by the British Broadcasting Corporation Radio (broadcast inside Burma) for his views on the educational system in Burma. He was frank in his critique and paid a heavy price for it: the military ransacked his mother's house in Burma as they looked for his papers and correspondence, and he is not allowed to return to Burma.

Inherent in risk is the possibility of sacrifice, and the leaders of this movement for democracy and human rights made sacrifices in their lives even before working in their respective organizations. They have sacrificed their careers, education, finances, physical safety, legal status, and relationships with family. One activist's fiancée broke off their engagement because she did not want to wait for someone who risked being arrested and imprisoned for years. Another lost a lover during a violent conflict with the regime. Several had to leave the country, leaving behind their families. Some had opportunities to resettle comfortably in a Western country, but stayed to work for human rights.

Moral Vision and Goals

All of the individuals I interviewed have a vision of a free and democratic Burma where people enjoy basic civil liberties and have opportunities for education, health care, and adequate nutrition and where all ethnic groups can work together to rebuild their country. They maintain optimism, and they persevere in spite of the odds. Although Western politicians, scholars, and diplomats are almost uniformly pessimistic about the future of Burma, these NGO leaders see that other movements for democracy around the world have taken many years to realize their goals. Their role models include such leaders of social political and social change as Nelson Mandela, Vaclav Havel, the Dalai Lama, and Gandhi. They are especially inspired by the moral strength of Aung San Suu Kyi as she waits under house arrest to lead their country. Each of these leaders has a moral vision of a democratic homeland. Each can identify a source of motivation and optimism that helps her or him continue to fight for the rights of the Burmese people. For the leader of an organization that assists political prisoners and their families, what keeps him going is "[the] faces of those who died and of those who are still in prison, and thinking of the number of years of their sentence, how much longer they will be in prison." Another is not optimistic in the short run but believes her programs, and the entire movement across the world, make a difference. She helps opposition groups "keep their voice" and coordinate their efforts during this protracted transition period. She says she has a moral mandate to continue working so that all who are in exile will be allowed to return home.

Moral Courage: Risk and Sacrifice for a Principled Vision

The NGO leaders struggling for democracy and human rights for Burma teach us that individuals can respond to daunting external circumstances by summoning up the inner strength to take risks and make sacrifices in the pursuit of a moral vision. These leaders work at the grassroots level, from the bottom up, as they teach, train, and empower people who have endured physical, emotional, psychological, and financial hardships. They tell us that moral courage as an abstract concept is not relevant to them; instead, they enact it daily and help others to develop the same inner strength to maintain moral principles and envision a path of action as they see themselves and their circumstances in a new light.

These morally courageous leaders are committed to principles, values, and a vision of a better Burma they may not see in their lifetime. Every day they make sacrifices and overcome dangers for what seems to others an almost hopeless challenge. Moral courage requires the ability to endure hardship, while holding true to one's principles. The leaders of this movement work patiently for a new social and political reality, even though they cannot predict the outcomes of their efforts. They started without knowing what the future would bring, with only the hope for a democratic society, an empowered electorate, and freedom from oppression.

The situation in Burma and the circumstances of their fellow Burmese are so compelling that despite difficulty and uncertainty, they devote their lives to attempting to midwife political and social change in Burma. These and other NGO leaders exemplify the essence of moral courage as they strive optimistically and persistently to develop civil society in Burma in the face of a brutal dictatorship. Their lives, and the lives of those with whom they work, are filled with constant risks and sacrifices; and they know there is no guarantee that they will live to see the fruition of their long-term goals. Nevertheless, they soldier on, working to empower women, children, teachers, political prisoners, community leaders, and Buddhist monks and nuns.

Implications and Conclusions

The leaders of these pro-democracy and human rights groups demonstrate that moral courage is the everyday enactment of principles such as integrity, honesty, compassion, service, generosity, caring, fairness, and respect. Those who strive to be morally courageous in organizations—that is, to act in accordance with their principles at the workplace—need to have a clear vision of their moral goal.

These leaders teach us that anyone interested in doing the right thing when others are doing something else needs to be prepared to take risks and make personal and professional sacrifices. Their examples show us that those who act with moral courage can eventually achieve their goals but cannot give up when results do not come immediately. Because they may have to exert protracted effort, it is important for them to cultivate patience and persistence. An additional lesson we can glean from the leaders discussed here relates to their assertion that moral courage is not an abstract concept they contemplate, but something they do intuitively. Perhaps they are telling us that we act with moral courage when we do what feels right in our guts, in our hearts. Yet, by articulating our moral principles, we validate and reinforce them, giving ourselves the strength to follow them.

These history-making leaders in Southeast Asia are on the cusp of political and social change. With hope and dedication, they are working for a free and democratic Burma that they may not see in their own lifetimes. They do not think specifically in terms of moral courage, but they demonstrate it every day and help others to develop this same inner strength to endure hardship in order to see a better life for their children and children's children. Their morally courageous deeds inspire individuals in any organization to take the high ground.

Notes

1. Kidder, 2005, explains that moral courage is the willingness to uphold virtues and principles, despite the possible harm to one's physical or emotional well-being, reputation, financial stability, or self-esteem. Courage that is moral embodies the values of honesty, respect, responsibility, fairness, and compassion.

2. These demonstrations were part of the "Saffron Revolution," named by pro-democracy activists who see the Velvet Revolution, a bloodless overthrow of the communist regime in Czechoslovakia in 1989, as a model for social and political change. Saffron refers to the yellow robes of Burmese monks.

3. The report, "License to Rape: The Burmese Military Regime's Use of Sexual Violence in the Ongoing War in Shan State," documents the Burmese military's rape and violence of 625 Shan girls and women between 1999 and 2001. Tragically, one-quarter of these victims died as a result of the sexual violence against them.

4. The book, *In Search of Civil Society and Its Relevancy to Burma's Crisis,* has not yet been published.

Reference

Kidder, R.M. 2005. *Moral courage.* New York: HarperCollins.

Part III

The Skills and Information That Enable Moral Courage

9

Giving Voice to Values

Building Moral Competence

Mary C. Gentile

Several years ago, after nearly two decades of work in the arena of business ethics and management education and development, I must have heard almost every possible reason for why the "right thing" to do in the workplace was neither clear nor financially feasible. I began to wonder, ironically, whether it was even ethical to teach about business ethics to business students and business practitioners if it was not possible to act on those lessons. Was this just an empty exercise in political correctness—a practice that allowed us to check off the box that says, "We introduced and discussed codes of conduct and responsible business behavior"—and if it was such an exercise, was I contributing to an increase in cynicism and spending my professional career engaged in a sham?

As is often the way with such things, this personal crisis of confidence was the seedbed for developing the approach to voicing and acting on our values in the workplace that I share here.[1] Through a combination of fortunate coincidences as well as focused attention, I set out to gather stories of times when managers and business leaders had found effective ways to voice and act on their values, and to try to figure out what had enabled that behavior. My goal was not to generate hypotheses to prove or disprove. Rather, I wanted to understand this phenomenon from the inside out, from the perspective of the individuals who had done the acting and voicing, and from a listening position open to possibility (rather than from a stance of so-called objective skepticism) so as to understand what they believed had enabled them to do so, and what they believed had disabled them in other situations. The ideas discussed in the following pages are informed by a wealth of research in psychology, sociology, and management studies, but the lessons are practical, and the intent is to offer actionable guidelines to any individuals who want to voice and act on their values in the workplace.

Shifting the Frame

One of the first and most important lessons I drew from the stories of voicing values is that the way we frame our ethical challenges has a great deal to do with how we perceive our ability and confidence and willingness to act on them. I have come to believe that moral competence may be the entrée or the way in to moral courage. That is, if we believe that we have the skills and the arguments or scripts to voice and act upon our values, the quest for Herculean stores of courage becomes less relevant. Rather than exerting energy in op-position to the pressures upon us, we can allow ourselves to act in harmony with a well-developed, well-rehearsed position.

There is something oddly counterproductive about the way we often frame ethical challenges and try to encourage ethical behavior by trying to scare ourselves straight with a focus on the negative examples, the cautionary tales, and the costs of transgression. Think of the innumerable invocations of the names Enron and WorldCom, for example. And when we are not trying to scare ourselves with the stories of costs incurred, we are talking about how difficult it is to voice our values and how we need to resist the ubiquitous pressures and be proof against the risks of standing up for what we believe is right. These scare tactics and this appeal to the daunting levels of courage required to enact our values can discourage and de-skill us. However, a focus on naming the skills needed to voice and act upon our values, and then on providing opportunities to practice them, can make whatever stores of moral courage we possess more easily accessible to us.

This emphasis upon reframing challenges in ways that are more conducive to values-driven behavior as well as naming and building the necessary skills is a missing piece in the way we tend to approach ethics. Too often we focus upon whether individuals (including ourselves) are ethical or unethical—or good or bad—people. As we review the stories of individuals who have found ways to voice their values, however, it becomes abundantly clear that these individuals have both enacted their values at some points in their careers and failed to do so at others. They were not all good nor all bad, not all coura-geous nor all cowardly.

But we know this already, do we not? We know this from our own experi-ences. And that is why the often heard appeal for better ways to assess the ethics of potential job candidates in order to weed out the so-called bad apples in an organization can miss the point. That is, there are certainly some folks who may have a less developed sense of ethics than others. But if we look closely at the most egregious cases of ethical transgression in business, we see that they are not about just a few bad people. They are often about a few folks who influence or intimidate the many into going along with some unsavory course of action; or perhaps even more often about individuals who, although often guided by ethics in their careers, at some point take a wrong turn in a certain situation and then are unable or unwilling to find their way out of it. That is, they are stories about all of us. And what is needed is not simply a better screening mechanism, but rather better preparation and practice so that we can avoid the influence of the former and can ourselves avoid becoming the latter, on some occasions in our lives.

So once we have released ourselves from the assumption that ethical business conduct requires a superhuman level of courage, and once we have recognized that it is about training and preparation for all of us, rather than about some sort of ethical radar that enables us to detect and eject the dangerous few, then we can turn to naming, developing, and practicing the perspectives, frames, and skills we will need. The following pages will outline some of the most common challenges to moral competence, as well as the most helpful responses to these challenges and the critical recognitions and abilities that enable values-driven behaviors in the workplace.

The Challenge of Preemptive Rationalizations

Discussions of ethical behavior in business often move quickly to the argument that it is not always easy or even possible to determine just what the right thing to do may actually be in a particular situation. Such discussions lead quickly to the comment that the truly difficult ethical issues are not situations of right versus wrong, but of right versus right or even wrong versus wrong. And others will argue that this ambiguity dictates that what people need to prepare for ethical action are a greater awareness of the kinds of ethical conflicts they may encounter in the workplace and a set of reasoning tools for more rigorous analysis to make decisions.

Admittedly, because a rapidly changing business context can lead to unanticipated situations, some preparatory efforts to raise awareness are useful; and admittedly again, there are indeed situations where reasonable people of goodwill may disagree about what the right course of action may be, and ethical analysis can be extremely helpful and necessary in such instances. However, these two concerns, valid as they are, can too often morph into what I call "preemptive rationalizations." That is, when we assume that ethical behavior in a certain situation is too difficult or even impossible, we often then skip over the effort to frame an ethical response and move directly to the generation of reasons why it is not actually wrong after all, or at least why we are not certain that it is, or perhaps why any other course of action is just as bad, and so on. In other words, the assumption that voicing and enacting our values is not feasible triggers a defensive process of self-justification that, in fact, means that we never do the hard work of problem solving that we might with a non-ethics-based challenge.

An effective way to address this tendency toward preemptive rationalization is the practice of "normalization." That is, the explicit recognition and naming of the fact that ethical challenges are a normal part of any business activity that they are inescapable and that they are vulnerable to the same problem-solving techniques and practices that we would apply to any other business problem. Rather than a stress reaction of denial or freezing, we can take the time to reflect upon and name the kinds of ethical challenges that are typical in our particular industry and business function. And then we can reflect in advance upon the various strategies that may be available to us, or that we may have seen others use, to address them.

This process does not ensure that these challenges will be easy to deal with, but it does require that we look them in the eye, squarely, and it can mean that we will recognize that they are often not one-time events. Certain kinds of challenges are likely to recur in certain fields, and without a willingness to admit and accept that fact, we will often be motivated, consciously or unconsciously, *not* to see that they are going to surface again and therefore to be more likely to punt on our ethics, telling ourselves that it is "just this once."

In addition, this process mitigates the sense of urgency or time pressure that can often lead us to take the path of (short-term) least resistance. And by naming the challenge as predictable and unexceptional, we can also position our response as a process of ongoing problem solving rather than an immediate go/no-go kind of choice. For example, a problem-solving approach allows individuals to identify and focus upon incentive systems that encourage distortions in sales reporting rather than focusing on labeling and dismissing colleagues who react to these incentives as simply unethical. In this way, we are required neither to vilify and therefore alienate our colleagues, nor to come up with the elusive and often just plain nonexistent silver bullet for addressing a values conflict. Instead, we can talk openly about the challenge and work on building a careful coalition-based process to address it.

The Twin Challenges of Cynicism and Naïveté

Just as my previously mentioned crisis of faith led me to wonder if ethical action was in fact even possible in a business context, often our biggest obstacle is doubt as to whether anyone ever does voice and enact their values in the workplace, whether our organizational and industry setting allows it, and whether we ourselves are capable of it. The flip side of this sense of discouragement or cynicism is a Pollyanna-like naïveté that can set us up for disillusionment or simply poorly executed efforts to enact our values because we underestimated the difficulties.

The most powerful talisman against this Janus-faced obstacle is recognition of choice. That is, by intentionally looking for, recognizing, and collecting examples and stories of times when we ourselves have voiced and acted on our values and when business people around us have voiced and acted on theirs, we recognize that such choice is in fact possible. Also important to recognize are the times when we ourselves and those around us have failed to do so. The latter examples may be easier to spot, at least for those around us. We need only to read the business section of the newspapers. The former stories—the positive examples—may sometimes be more challenging to find, but once we start to look, they are there.

In fact, one of the most powerful skill-building exercises I have developed is called "A Tale of Two Stories." This exercise asks us to remember a time when we have been directed or invited to do something in the workplace that conflicted with our values—and we found a way to voice and act on those values anyway. We then answer a set of questions about what motivated us, what enabled us to voice our values and what made it difficult, and how we feel about the outcome. Then we are invited to remember another time when we have been directed to do something that conflicted with our values—but we failed to voice and enact those values. We then can answer the same set of questions about motivation, about what disabled us from voicing our values, and how we feel now about this second situation.

This exercise has been used now in many, many business education and leadership development contexts, and the lessons are powerful. First of all, participants recognize that we all have acted on our values in some circumstances and failed to do so in others. Thus, none of us is always and only good or bad, and we all have the capacity for both choices. Second, we recognize that there is a predictable set of contextual as well as individual factors that can enable or disable values-driven behavior. Some of these are pretty widely shared: for example, most of us find it more difficult to act on our values if the individual pressuring us to violate them is our boss or a close friend. Similarly, most of us find it easier if we have allies who feel the same way that we do. On the other hand, some enablers or disablers are more specific to one individual or another. For example, some folks are more comfortable with public debate than others and therefore will be more comfortable with that form of voice, as opposed to writing a memo or setting up a private conversation, off-line, to discuss the situation.

There are two particular skill-building features of this exercise. First, we reframe these situations as genuine choices we are capable of making—as opposed to falling prey to crippling discouragement on the one hand or over-simplistic naïveté that can diminish our skillfulness on the other. Second, we can begin to create a profile of the kinds of features we need to look for or create in the organizations where we work, as well as our own personal strengths and challenges, so that we can recognize the degrees of freedom we have to frame values conflicts in ways that take advantage of our own and our organization's strengths and that avoid or neutralize our own and our organization's weaknesses as much as possible—which leads us to the next challenge and response in our toolkit.

The Challenge of Self-Doubt

Sometimes the greatest disabler to voicing and enacting our values is our own doubt about our personal capabilities: we question whether we are too timid to stand up to our boss or colleagues or whether we are too career-oriented to risk retaliation or whether we think well enough on our feet to address the challenges we face or whether we are too junior in the organization to have the credibility to resist the situation at hand. The most effective tool we have found to address this barrier is our concerted effort to understand and name our own personal profile—that is, our preferred communication styles, comfort levels with risk, preferences for autonomous or cooperative activity, personal career motivations, and sense of purpose—and then the conscious effort to frame ethical challenges in a way that plays to our strengths and natural preferences.

So, for example, if I see myself as risk averse, I can frame the values conflict I confront in such a way that the decision to voice my values is the safer option, focusing on the risks of not doing so rather than the risks of speaking up. On the other hand, if I enjoy living on the edge, I can frame the choice to voice my values as the nervier option. In fact, when I interviewed folks about times when they did, in fact, act on their values, I found this to be the case. The individuals who viewed themselves as timid framed their decision as cautious; the individuals who viewed themselves as bold or self-confident viewed their decisions as such. This observation is in line with the lessons of strengths-based psychology:[2] that is, that we will be better able to exercise our ethical muscle by framing choices in ways that play to our strengths than by preaching to a fearful person to be brave or to a real risk-taker to be more conservative.

The Challenge of Relativism

Another major challenge to our intention to voice and enact our values is the concern that we may be parochial and that our own values may not be shared by our target audiences. Although there are indeed cultural differences in behavioral styles, comfort levels, and even values, there still are a small number of foundational values that are widely shared across cultures and time periods.[3] The key things to remember here are that: (1) there are indeed shared values to which we can appeal in most circumstances; and (2) they form a very short list (values like honesty, respect, humanity, or compassion)! That is, we should not assume that there is no common ground between different people, nor should we assume that all ground is common.

Therefore, in addition to examining our own motivations, to ensure that core values are truly at stake, we should think about how to frame our reactions and arguments so they appeal to such widely shared values. Rather than expecting others to see things exactly as we do, we need to help them to find and see our shared goals. For example, a respect for diversity in the workplace does not require that everyone agree with or view all religions as equally true, but it does require that we treat all of our work colleagues with personal respect, regardless of their religion. And it will be much more feasible and effective for any one of us, as a manager in such a workplace, to appeal to this shared value—a commitment to human respect—than to argue that every religion is equal.

The Challenge of Reasons and Rationalizations

One of the most powerful tools to increase the frequency and effectiveness of our efforts to voice and enact our values is the practice of reframing ethical challenges and pre-scripting our responses. This is because the explanations—I call them "Reasons and Rationalizations"—that we hear (or assert ourselves) for not acting on our values tend to be predictable, to fall into some commonly recognized categories, and to be vulnerable to argument. By naming and examining them, and working to craft or pre-script our responses to them, we make it easier and more likely that we will be prepared and able to respond in the moment, when these challenges arise.[4] Four of the most commonly heard of these "reasons and rationalizations" are:

- Appeals to expected or standard practice: "Everyone does this, so it's really standard practice. It's even expected."
- Appeals to materiality: "The impact of this action is not material. It doesn't really hurt anyone."
- Appeals to the locus of responsibility: "This is not my responsibility; I'm just following orders here."
- Appeals to loyalty: "I know this isn't quite fair to the customer, but I don't want to hurt my reports/team/boss/company."

What has been most compelling about the stories of folks who have found ways to voice their values is that the arguments they have offered in response to such reasons and rationalizations are often not stunningly original. They are usually just a statement of an alternate view of the argument at hand, a view that is often left unstated or assumed to be inadequate in the workplace. In other words, we often seem to demand a degree of unassailable logic and demonstration of ultimate benefit from our arguments *for* values-driven positions that we do not demand from the commonly heard reasons for *not* acting on our values. Yet this tendency has not daunted the individuals who have voiced their values. They simply state the other side.

So, for example, in response to the statement that a particular behavior "happens all the time," they may ask why, then, there is an internal policy, or an external regulation or law, against it. Or they may offer examples that they have collected of times when it did not occur. Such examples are most powerful when they are drawn from the same organization, but can be effective when taken from competitors as well.

Appeals to materiality can be countered by explaining that size does not always matter when it comes to some infractions—fraud is fraud, for example, as one Harvard business professor pointed out to me—or that from an organizational and managerial perspective, such choices can create a fertile environment for greater transgressions.[5]

The appeal to responsibility is an interesting one. Individuals at lower levels within an organization will often explain that they will be better able to enact their values when they are more senior, with more credibility, organizational power, and experience. However, CEOs and other high-level executives will often explain that it would be easier to enact their personal values if they were more junior in the organization, with less at stake—for the organization as well as its employees—and less complex decisions to make. So we might conclude that it is hopeless no matter where we are situated in the organization, except that there are people at all levels who did, somehow, find ways to act and voice their values. It simply seems that they needed to understand the differing constraints and appeal to the different degrees of freedom that they had, given their positions. More junior folks, for example, would sometimes position their arguments as questions, identifying themselves as newcomers to the firm or the industry and asking for clarification. In this way, they seemed less arrogant and accusing but were able to identify the ethical conflict nonetheless. And more senior executives would sometimes frame their values-based choices in inspirational terms and as a challenge, neither denying the potential costs nor, on the other hand, downplaying the very real benefits of such decisions.

Or in response to the appeal to loyalty, individuals may argue their position from an appeal to another loyalty. For example, one woman we interviewed said that when a friend asked her to leak proprietary information to him, appealing to their long-standing relationship, she replied that she felt a similar loyalty to her other colleagues and her employer and named the conflict of loyalty. He was not happy with this response, but it effectively neutralized the charge that she was disloyal.

The trick here is not that these arguments are so difficult to identify but rather that our reflecting upon them and practicing them in advance make them more accessible to us when we need them, and our recognizing that the arguments for unethical behavior are just as vulnerable to debate (if not more so) as the argument for values-based choices emboldens us to use them.

In addition to practicing our responses to these "reasons and rationalizations," an extremely valuable tool for voicing our values is insight into decision-making biases.[6] But there is an interesting twist that we have discovered. That is, often when folks point out such biases—the false consensus effect (the tendency to believe that others will think as we do), for example, or the tendency to protect "sunk costs" by "throwing good money after bad," or the "social consensus" effect, described below—they do so with an eye to exhorting us to look out for these tendencies and to try to make ourselves less vulnerable to them. Yet, although such awareness may make us more cognizant of these biases in the people we are dealing with, it is less likely that we will be able to recognize and reverse such biases in the (often unconscious) application of them in our own decision making.[7]

Here, however, let me suggest a different way to use and benefit from these insights about observed biases in decision making. If we know that people are more likely to be confident in their position and to act upon it if they believe their relevant peers agree with them ("social consensus" effect), then perhaps we can spend some time thinking about how to build a group of peers who would support our values-based arguments and/or to make them more visible, more evident to the individuals we are trying to persuade. That is, construct a different "social consensus" for them.[8]

Or if we know that people tend to discount the less immediate and less concrete implications of their actions, then we can strengthen our arguments by gathering stories that emphasize the tangible aspects of longer-term impacts or that identify nearer-term implications that people's decision-making calculus often overlooks. In fact, this example supports another tendency reflected in the stories of folks who voiced their values successfully: they define and appeal to broad definitions of purpose. That is, if you define your professional purpose on a particular day in terms of closing the deal at hand, cutting costs this quarter, or maximizing share price at close of trading, you will have fewer arguments upon which to draw than if you define your purpose as serving your clients well, building a solid product pipeline, or providing a strong and sustainable return to investors.

The point is, we can apply the entire set of educational, argumentation, and persuasion tools that we would employ in any other discussion or negotiation to our efforts to voice our values. Too often, on the contrary, when the subject turns to ethics, we feel that somehow we must stand up, immediately and with passion, to make a righteous speech. It seems somehow less ethical to make the same kind of reasoned and compelling presentation when it comes to ethics that we might use in another situation. So, in fact, we are damned if we do and damned if we don't. That is, if we do not have unassailable arguments, we sometimes assume we had best not even try to voice our values; and if we do have persuasive arguments, we sometimes assume that it is inappropriate to use them in the service of values-based positions, that such positions should stand on their moral merit alone.

Often people want to voice their values but fail to do so due to the reality or the assumption that others will not agree with them. Pre-scripting compelling arguments that can make it easier for folks to understand the real stakes and implications of a particular decision is a valuable and appropriate way to proceed . . . and in fact, why wouldn't we use all our best skills in the service of our ethics? The point here is not to manipulate or trick others into values-based positions, but rather to enable them to make a conscious decision because the preemptive rationalizations will have been unmasked and defused, and the decision-making tendencies and biases that work against such decisions will have been set up against an equally or even more compelling counterperspective.

But now the question becomes: how do we make it more likely that we will actually use some of these skills and arguments?

The Challenge of Hesitation and Inaction

Some have commented that the approach described here is too analytical and reasoning-based to respond to the emotional realities and challenges of voicing and enacting our values. They will point out that we often freeze when we encounter such conflicts, or that the moment passes before we can muster our thoughts, or that we just do not feel confident (or courageous) enough to "speak truth to power."

One of the formative influences in forging the *Giving Voice to Values* approach was some research on altruism and moral courage that I read many years ago.[9] Individuals who had placed themselves at risk to aid others who were threatened during the Holocaust were interviewed to find any common threads in their backgrounds. One such commonality was that these "rescuers" reported that at an earlier point in their lives, they had had the experience of having rehearsed their answer to what-if scenarios—hypothetical moral challenges—out loud, in response to and in the presence of a respected elder (a parent, a teacher, a mentor, etc.). This pre-scripting operates on both a cognitive and an experiential level.

From a cognitive perspective, familiarizing ourselves with the arguments that we are likely to hear in defense of morally questionable activities and the possible responses to them makes us more likely to be able to call them up in the heat of the moment. But experientially, having actually practiced saying these things, out loud in front of peers, who stand in as proxies for the intended workplace audiences, can make us more physically comfortable with voicing values in real time. I drew this insight—oddly enough—by extrapolating from a self-defense class I took a number of years ago. The instructors spoke of "muscle memory" and explained that if we were to practice delivering, full force, the defensive kicks and blows we were learning in simulated attacks with padded confederates posing as assailants, we would be more likely to access those movements in future times of stress.[10]

So, finally, one of the strongest methods we can employ to build the skills and increase the likelihood that we will effectively voice our values is to practice: not only to anticipate and pre-script our arguments but to practice voicing them to others. Additionally, it can be helpful to anticipate and de-bunk some of the stories we tell ourselves that can scare us out of doing so. For example, we all have heard, or said, "I wanted to say something but it all happened so fast . . . and then the moment was over. It was too late." And, of course, there are times when the decision is made and acted upon in a single meeting. More often, however, decisions are made, and then action plans are constructed.

One senior manager told me a story about a meeting with her CEO and a set of other senior managers wherein a decision that violated her values was proposed and agreed upon. She wanted to resist but could not muster her arguments quickly and persuasively enough. However, she took the time after the meeting to think through the decision, to confirm that she felt strongly enough that it was wrong, and to construct as strong a set of coun-terarguments as she could. She also reflected upon her own strengths (i.e., she was most comfortable communicating in writing) and the tendencies of her target audience (i.e., analogies and stories had persuaded him in the past to change his mind). She tried to play to both realities. She wrote out her arguments in a careful memo and used an illustration of the point she was trying to make. She then called him and explained that she felt strongly that there were some other points he should hear before acting on the decision, and asked for a meeting the next day. She arrived at the meeting with her written memo in hand and her oral story prepared, and between the two, she was able to change the CEO's mind.

The point here is not that we can always change our boss's mind nor that this manager's techniques would work for all of us. Rather the point is that it's not over until it's over: do not assume that you cannot revisit a decision. Play to your strengths, but do not ignore what you know about the tendencies and preferences of your audience either. And practice your voice!

Conclusion

Practicing our voice is probably the single most important thing we can do to build the moral competence that enables moral courage. We can practice reflecting upon the barriers to action and voice that we experience when we encounter values conflicts. Now that we know that the rationalizations for unethical action are predictable and vulnerable to debate, we can practice constructing counterarguments that build upon our knowledge of reasoning and decision-making biases. And we can practice the self-awareness that enables us to recognize when a conflict is framed in a way that plays to our insecurities and to reframe it to play to our personal strengths. Most crucially, we can practice actually voicing out loud and in front of peers—stand-ins or proxies for the very colleagues or bosses we will need to persuade or challenge in our later careers—the scripts that we have created to express our values.

The more we prepare and rehearse these scripts, the more likely they are to become our default positions. We become more fluent with them, more at ease expressing them. We begin to notice and collect examples of times when others voice their values, and by so doing, we begin to feel that this action is just as possible as any other. Gradually, we realize that this comfort and competence with values scripts is the pathway to acting with moral courage. Ultimately, such moral competence makes moral courage a much less daunting aspiration.

Notes

1. The ideas shared in this essay are drawn from the *Giving Voice to Values* curriculum, an approach I developed with the assistance and support of the Aspen Institute as incubator and founding partner, along with the Yale School of Management, and with ongoing support from Babson College. For more information, see www.givingvoicetovalues.org and Gentile, 2010a.

2. Cameron, Dutton, and Quinn, 2003.

3. Donaldson and Dunfee, 1999; Kidder, 2005; Seligman, 2002.

4. Gentile, 2010b.

5. As Comer and Vega discuss in chapter 3 of this book, abandoning our values in circumstances of low moral intensity (i.e., low materiality) may desensitize us

to the point that we eventually behave unethically even in situations of substantial moral impact.

    6. Messick and Bazerman, 1996; Prentice, 2004.

    7. Bazerman, Loewenstein, and Moore, 2002; Messick and Bazerman, 1996.

    8. Comer and Baker, in chapter 13 of this book, provide suggestions for building a morally courageous coalition with peers.

    9. Huneke, 1985; London, 1970.

    10. See also Damasio, 1994.

References

Bazerman, M.H., Loewenstein, G., and Moore, D.A. 2002. Why good accountants do bad audits. *Harvard Business Review* 80(11), 96–102.

Cameron, K.S., Dutton, J.E., and Quinn, R.E., eds. 2003. *Positive organizational scholarship.* San Francisco: Berrett-Koehler.

Comer, D.R., and Baker, S.D. 2011. I defy with a little help from my friends: Raising an organization's ethical bar through a morally courageous coalition. In *Moral courage in organizations: Doing the right thing at work,* ed. D.R. Comer and G. Vega, 171–187. Armonk, NY: M.E. Sharpe.

Comer, D.R., and Vega, G. 2011. The personal ethical threshold. In *Moral courage in organizations: Doing the right thing at work,* ed. D.R. Comer and G. Vega, 25–44. Armonk, NY: M.E. Sharpe.

Damasio, A.R. 1994. *Descartes' error: Emotion, reason and the human brain.* New York: Grosset/Putnam.

Donaldson, T., and Dunfee, T.W. 1999. *Ties that bind: A social contracts approach to business ethics.* Boston: Harvard Business School Press.

Gentile, M.C. 2010a. *Giving voice to values.* New Haven, CT: Yale University Press.

———. 2010b. Keeping your colleagues honest. *Harvard Business Review* 88(2), 114–117.

Huneke, D.H. 1985. *The Moses of Rovno.* New York: Dodd, Mead.

Kidder, R.M. 2005. *Moral courage.* New York: HarperCollins.

London, P. 1970. The rescuers: Motivational hypotheses about Christians who saved Jews from the Nazis. In *Altruism and helping behavior: Social psychological studies of some antecedents and consequences,* ed. J.R. Macaulay and L. Berkowitz, 241–250. New York: Academic Press.

Messick, D.M., and Bazerman, M.H. 1996. Ethical leadership and the psychology of decision-making. *Sloan Management Review* 37(2), 9–22.

Prentice, R. 2004. Teaching ethics, heuristics, and biases. *Journal of Business Ethics Education* 1(1), 57–74.

Seligman, M.E.P. 2002. *Authentic happiness: Using the new positive psychology to realize your potential for lasting fulfillment.* New York: Simon & Schuster.

10

Developing Professional Moral Courage

Leadership Lessons from Everyday Ethical Challenges in Today's Military

Leslie E. Sekerka, Justin D. McCarthy,
and Richard P. Bagozzi

In this chapter we examine professional moral courage in military officers' daily organizational lives. Although we focus on officers, the ethical situations they confront represent the challenges employees of any organization might experience. People in every type of organization and role encounter issues that range from rule bending to outright illegal behavior. Both government and private-sector employees face situations where peer pressure and the influence of social norms add complexity to the decision-making process. Employees perceive that their decisions may threaten their status, peer allegiance, or even career progression. These concerns may prohibit them from acting with moral strength and proceeding with right action.

News headlines evidence the propensity for unethical actions by corporate and government leaders alike, including Eliot Spitzer (former governor of New York), Andy Fastow and Jeff Skilling (former Enron executives), Michael Sears (former CFO of Boeing), and Randy "Duke" Cunningham (former California congressman), to name a few. Other ethics scandals, such as those at Abu Ghraib prison; Walter Reed Army Medical Center; Adelphia; and Friedman, Billings, Ramsey Group, as well as the rampant accounting fraud associated with the recent global economic recession, make it clear that all types of organizations are vulnerable to creating unethical contexts. Here, we see that social and performance pressures, arrogance, greed, and the lack of moral fortitude can influence good people to make poor choices, resist action, and make individual and collective unethical decisions. Situations can transform character, and ordinary people have the capacity to engage in acts of wrongdoing and even evil.[1]

Today's global employees face pressures to respond swiftly, improve efficiency, and achieve maximum effectiveness. Such pressures may, albeit unintentionally, influence managers and leaders to shortcut decision-making processes without giving sufficient attention to ethical considerations. For people to engage in moral action in the workplace, they must make decisions with moral fortitude. Their leaders must set the example by aiming for the moral high ground with practical knowledge and skill sets that can be readily applied.

Moral courage is necessary to ensure moral decision making and action. We view moral courage as a professional managerial competency that can be developed. We begin by defining professional moral courage and describing its component competencies. Then, we offer suggestions to leaders to support the enhancement of their employees' professional moral-courage competencies. Although we explore the ethical challenges of career officers in the military, our recommendations apply to members of all types of organizations.

Professional Moral Courage

The process of addressing an ethical challenge requires reasoning and behaving according to values in ways that go beyond self-interest.[2] Therefore, we contend that moral courage is necessary to engage in sustained ethical thinking and action as one undertakes work, especially when influential forces such as social norms make other alternatives seem reasonable or acceptable. We refer to this capability to do the right thing at work as professional moral courage (PMC).[3] Those with PMC do what they know they ought to do, even in the face of a moral challenge.[4] We conceptualize PMC as making the decision to engage in right action given the ethical standards of one's profession and then displaying the moral strength to pursue this path of action—despite its potential negative consequences, including unpleasant emotions, risk, difficulty, or threat to self. In short, personal needs become secondary to doing what is right.[5]

Members of the military profession have a special duty to act with PMC because they are given the authority to apply force on behalf of society.[6] Military professionals in the armed forces of the United States are required, by law, to follow certain explicit and implicit rules beyond what ordinary morality requires.[7] Their special status empowers military leaders to initiate actions that may constrain others' fundamental rights, and potentially cause death or destruction. This authority stems from the principles and values manifest in the Constitution, to which military leaders pledge their oath of allegiance. Former secretary of the navy Gordon England affirmed the association between the military, the Constitution, and PMC when he said, "At the end of the day, the military is the ethical standard the nation looks up to."[8] Military personnel are responsible for protecting the country's citizens and its borders and, in doing so, must also preserve and enact moral principles in their daily actions. According to military ethicist James Toner, any recent military scandal involving a moral failure has at its core a leadership failure.[9] He underscores the essential nature of leaders' living by their word and deed and claims that any program in ethics education invariably depends upon an organization's leaders. We argue that it is a leadership obligation to educate managers and employees on how to engage in exemplary moral conduct on a daily basis.

Practicing Professional Moral Courage

PMC is an essential component of leaders' and managers' behavior in their organizations. The ongoing display of unethical actions at every level of organizational life and across industries suggests, however, that PMC is often absent. Proactive concern about ethics led the U.S. Navy to institute the Ethics in Action Program.[10] This initiative began with an inquiry conducted with junior officers, with a goal to understand what serves to promote right action in the course of performing daily activities. These junior officers, as middle managers within their organization, face challenges that cross hierarchical boundaries and involve people who are both junior and senior to them. This puts them in a particularly uncomfortable role, sometimes described as being "caught in the middle."[11] During this period in their career they draw from their leaders' behaviors and their own experiences to begin to hone the skill sets they will be expected to demonstrate as they progress in rank. To identify the personal competencies that foster PMC, we asked thirty-five junior officers to describe ethical experiences that they have encountered and their responses to these encounters. Our interviews produced ninety-nine scenarios (each officer provided two or three situations), with typical situations related to rule bending to accomplish a task or to accommodate a senior officer's request, or to inappropriate use of funds or missing funds/resources (see Table 10.1).

These managers demonstrate PMC in their decision-making process by going beyond rule adherence to strive for a morally principled response—despite negative personal consequences. We now consider the skills that managers need to respond to an ethical challenge with PMC. We identified four personal governance practices that reflect the competencies involved in efforts to act with PMC: (1) emotional signaling; (2) reflective pause; (3) self-regulation;

Table 10.1

Ethical Situations Faced by Supply Corps Officers

Type of Ethical Situation*	Percentage of Total
Rule bending to accomplish a task	25.0
Combination**	13.9
Inappropriate use of funds or missing funds/ resources	12.0
Rule bending to accommodate senior officer's request	11.1
Inappropriate sexual activity	10.2
Stealing	7.4
Drug or alcohol abuse	6.5
Cheating/lying	5.6
Harassment (other than sexual)	4.6
Payoffs, bribery, or inducements	3.7

*Each officer provided two or three examples, producing a total of 99 scenarios.

**Some scenarios involve two or more ethical issues that combine to form a single problem (e.g., rule bending involving alcohol abuse). A scenario coded as "combination" is not counted elsewhere.

and (4) moral preparation. We provide representative quotations to illustrate and clarify our descriptions of each of these practices.

Emotional Signaling

Because emotions and cognition are intertwined, it is difficult to separate them.[12] Feelings contain important signals that influence the cerebral aspects of moral decision making.[13] Therefore, affect plays a critical role in either promoting or inhibiting the choice to engage in PMC. The emotions junior managers expressed most frequently were worry, loneliness, fear, shock or surprise, and hurt feelings (often stemming from a sense of betrayal). A common theme among those who ultimately demonstrated PMC is their initial experience of confusion, agitation, or helplessness, often accompanied by a sense of personal harm and some discomfort or distress.

But the individuals with PMC did not ignore, repress, or sublimate these emotions. Their emotional awareness did not block or thwart them but, on the contrary, enabled them. A manager described how he became aware of his emotions and then used them: "I felt hurt. My heart was beating fast. I went to go eat, to relax my mind. About two hours later I called my clerk in and said, 'Hey, let's go through it again.'" He added that by recognizing and letting his feelings play out, he was better equipped to move forward. The capacity to be fully aware of one's emotional response to ethical situations helps one to cope with and then to regulate the input of these emotions. Emotions that are welcomed, rather than dismissed as distractions or suppressed, can serve as cues that guide the ethical decision-making process.[14] Individuals who are open to their feelings can make more informed decisions by incorporating these important visceral reactions.

Reflective Pause

Whereas emotional signaling prompts an individual to pay attention to feelings about moral issues, a reflective pause enables a person to explore and interpret these feelings. The purposeful use of a reflective pause as part of one's strategy in decision making represents an ability to carve time from one's schedule, as needed, to take a self-imposed time-out for deliberation and insight. During this break individuals examine possible avenues for right action, often weighing the pros and cons of the circumstances and thinking about potential implications (i.e., reviewing past lessons, assessing present circumstances, and anticipating future repercussions). The display of prudential judgment that occurs during these self-directed periods of reflection appears to be an important component of PMC. It is as though the time-out helps people discern options and then garner and build informed momentum toward moral action. Individuals use this period to consider alternative options and their associated outcomes, as they work to gather additional information about the rules and other particulars regarding the situation at hand.

One participant explained how a time-out helped him move forward: "It was more reflecting on the situation. I guess [one] of the things in the past that started weighing on my mind was a sense of fairness—reading and following the rules. That's what I was thinking primarily about. Because of what he was doing, and what I had done. I had to think of it in terms of the present, because if I had waited too long, it would have been a done deal, and hard to undo." A reflective pause bolsters PMC by affording people an opportunity to collect their thoughts, generate options, and seek support during the initial stages of their decision-making effort. Taking time to reflect often alters, overrides, or postpones some initial reactions while also targeting responses for appropriate timing. Routine care in reflection may actually serve as a portal for all the personal governance practices, but it is especially important for self-regulation.

Self-Regulation

As we have described thus far, initial reactions to ethical challenges require the use of emotional signaling and reflection. But to pursue right action habitually and to manage and address tough moral decisions, individuals must also balance their reactions by considering their responsibilities along with their own personal desires. Managers in all organizations have a variety of goals. How they set and achieve these goals must be tempered with decisions about when and how to tackle the ethical challenges that emerge. They must discern whether to postpone a response or engage in immediate action. This ability to regulate one's initial reactions necessitates restraint coupled with an ability to move forward—despite expectations of negative impacts on oneself or others. It can be particularly difficult for managers to regulate their own behavior when peers or leaders are engaged in morally questionable activities or are asking them to condone or engage in such activities.

One participant in our interviews described a leader's behavior as starting out with small improprieties (inappropriate phone use), but eventually escalating to taking special trips to engage in an extramarital affair: "I didn't realize how a situation like that would snowball. And by ignoring it a little bit early [I] emboldened him to do more and more." He added, "We [the officer and two other officers on board] each had a little piece of the puzzle . . . and we couldn't understand the whole picture; we just saw a piece of the picture. But once we shared what we knew and composed the picture, at that point the problem was so far down the road that it was unsalvageable." In this case the manager eventually recognized that his delayed response contributed to the problem: "I think, in the future, once I get a piece of the picture and learn to trust that little voice in my head that says, 'Something doesn't smell right here,' then I need to do something about it right away, because it gets worse with time." Using emotional signals and reflection to understand what had happened, he added, "I think if I was faced with a situation again today, I would close the door, take off the rank, and I would have said, 'Knock if off.' But that's not easy to do, particularly if it's the first time you face a situation like that."

Self-regulation may mean knowing when to proceed as well as withholding the impulse to act immediately. Many of the managers who shared their stories with us expressed regret that they had not acted sooner. Their respect, appreciation, care for others involved, or sense of loyalty to their command served (at least initially) to inhibit action. But delayed action, they realized (in hindsight), only exacerbated the problem: "[The captain] was probably the most charismatic, dynamic, effective leader I've ever worked for, and he flushed it all away because of a character flaw, essentially. . . . I saw how big that snowball got as it rolled downhill."

PMC requires, and is further developed by, dealing with one's personal internal struggle. The self-regulatory process involves identifying and discriminating among competing values and establishing the timing of one's response. Such self-control has been regarded as the moral muscle—an inner directive to alter one's immediate responses and to redirect them toward the good of others.[15] In this light, self-regulation is the cornerstone of virtuous behavior. Although only a few individuals may be naturally predisposed to apply this competency, most of us have the potential to develop it. Learning to quiet one's immediate impulse to react to or to ignore an ethical problem and then to reflect upon and manage initial thoughts and feelings can begin a course of personal development marked by habits of moral strength.

Moral Preparation

The fourth component of PMC involves a preparatory thought process as to how one would—and would not—act when faced with an ethical challenge in the future. That is, individuals who act with professional moral courage appear to think through the consequences, both to themselves and others, before an event occurs. Their ongoing preparatory efforts, including a review of situations in which they have acted or failed to act and a consideration of their emotions and evaluations, enable them to do the right thing when they encounter a moral situation. People who continue to be aware of how emotions and situational factors can influence their reactions can then choose to respond in similar or different ways as familiar scenarios play out and new ones emerge. Their heightened level of moral preparedness for ethical challenges, often expressed by continued vigilance of "the moral line," helps them to deal with ethical issues while they are still manageable.

"At what point do I draw the line and say you've now crossed? I know now it would be much earlier in the process," commented a manager who realized he should have drawn the line sooner. We see that people with PMC have thought through positive and negative consequences of acting and not acting, recognized and managed their emotions, and developed a keen awareness of where the line is—before ethical problems become unwieldy. This rehearsal process helps prepare individuals to respond mindfully and effectively when problems occur. By working to locate their moral line above the rules and regulations, a misstep does not mean immediate infraction.

We also observe that moral preparation is likely intertwined with and potentially dependent upon the use of the other personal governance competencies. For example, emotional signaling, taking a reflective pause, and exercising self-regulation are typically precursors for the ability to proceed with right action. To establish an integrated approach that uses all four personal governance practices, managers must persistently self-monitor and reflect upon their motives. As such, moral agents remain nimble, looking both forward and backward. Those who proceed with PMC are able to ascertain lessons by considering current challenges and recalling past ones. Not only do they plan how they might prevent such issues from recurring, they also maintain a continuous improvement mindset, always considering how they will deal with similar or nuanced situations they may encounter in the future. Based upon the ethical experiences of the officers we interviewed, moral preparation in support of PMC necessitates sustained self-awareness, personal introspection, and the willingness to remain open to learning. Because every situation is unique, there is a constant need to respond to new ethical challenges. As a result, building the capacity for acting with PMC is a leadership requirement.

Leading with Professional Moral Courage

Rules and regulations are similar to locks on doors—they provide some protection, but alone cannot promote moral action or good deeds. A lack of ethical fortitude results in broken locks, kicked-in doors, and moral weakness. As in many other organizations, the moral climate within the military is driven from the top. Wavering leadership can compromise values. Therefore, leaders must consistently and proactively model exemplary behavior by applying the personal governance practices we have described as they build a climate that supports moral strength. When a child misbehaves, a parent who can pause in the heat of a problem to model for the child the ability to control his or her own temper demonstrates to the child the moral muscle of self-regulation. Likewise, a leader's display of emotional signaling, reflective pauses, and self-regulation provides visible signs of ongoing preparation for moral action and thereby models appropriate behavior for subordinates. Subordinates learn to avoid responding with knee-jerk reactions when they observe the benefits of establishing balance before imposing action.

Another component of modeling moral behavior is helping employees develop their capacity for emotional awareness by creating opportunities for them to explore their own feelings when facing ethical challenges. Leaders can also encourage subordinates to discuss ethical situations with one another. Open communication enables them to think through the potential consequences of their actions and feelings, and then to collaborate about when, where, and how they might engage in PMC. Explicit attention and sustained commitment to personal governance practices and transparency reinforce moral decision making.

Organizational leaders need to clarify where they draw the moral line and then to stay well above it, because their followers observe and adopt their (un)ethical behavior. As one manager suggested, "Open forums among both senior and junior personnel along with forums with just peers would be beneficial. . . . Junior officers learn from senior officers and their respective experiences." Indeed, as another manager stated, subordinates watch their superiors to see what really matters: "We still see the problems we do because senior folks make ethically incorrect decisions and get away with it, thus setting an example for the junior folks. We all nod our head affirmative and press the 'I believe' button on ethics, then turn around and see people making the wrong decisions and climbing the ladder to success." Leaders need to uphold their moral standards and to address any infractions. Rewarding people for decisions and performance that lack moral strength is dysfunctional and can corrode the entire organization. Even the appearance that a leader's behavior is less than exemplary can diminish subordinates' willingness to engage in moral action.

Leaders need to cultivate their own and their followers' PMC by sharing with their peers and subordinates the ethical situations they have encountered and encouraging dialogue about these situations. Setting aside time on a regular basis to discuss ethical concerns contributes to the development of norms about how to deal collectively with challenges—even before they emerge. In addition, by providing these explicit structured opportunities for ethical conversations, leaders demonstrate that they expect reflection and communication about ethics and promote comfort and facility with ongoing ethical discourse. Leaders need to remind themselves and others to check for emotional signals, set aside time for reflective consideration, and support the use of self-regulation to enhance moral preparation. Promoting PMC and ethical performance requires the constant vigilance and collective support of a trusting, transparent, and communicative environment. Creating such an environment, in which managers feel safe talking across levels about their ethical concerns, is not easy, especially in hierarchically driven organizations like the military. But our interviews with managers indicate that leaders who model PMC can foster ethical performance in their organizations.

Leaders must insist on ethics education that goes beyond compliance to provide opportunities that help people hone their skills. Conventional approaches to ethics training that merely convey rules, codes, and regulations and review reporting channels and requirements are typically too superficial to succeed.[16] Employees need to be engaged in professional development activities that help them to understand, value, and practice personal governance. Personal governance is indeed a practice. People can build the four competencies that support PMC if they understand their current capabilities and work on improving them. Leaders must encourage their people to exercise their personal governance practices and provide coaching and developmental feedback to promote the enhancement of skills.

People need to exercise the four PMC competencies simultaneously. Indeed, these component skills typically do not operate in isolation, and it makes little sense to teach them sequentially. Because multiple factors affect ethical decision making, moral action requires dexterity in personal governance. Emotions and cognition are intertwined, and employees need to experience how PMC comes from within—driven from an inner strength that provides the motivation and direction to face ethical challenges. We present the following recommendations for leaders:

- Model personal governance practices with consistency in front of peers and subordinates. Openly demonstrate emotional signaling, taking a reflective pause, exercising self-regulation, and engaging in moral preparation as means for dealing with ethical challenges.
- Establish an ongoing collaborative discussion across ranks about the ethical issues people face, thereby further promoting moral preparation. Use this discussion of ethical issues and situations as a catalyst for continuous development, showing how emotional signaling, reflective pause, self-regulation, and moral preparation can positively influence outcomes.
- Create a climate of openness that fosters the self-awareness and emotional expressiveness that individuals need to apply personal governance practices.
- Encourage people to support one other when engaging in personal governance practices and ethical decision making in daily task actions. Reward those who engage, and remind everyone that PMC is more often a developmental process than an end state.

Concluding Remarks

This chapter has described professional moral courage and its component competencies, as well as leaders' roles in weaving PMC into the fabric of their organizations. Although individual contributors must exercise moral competencies, leaders are responsible for setting the example and creating an environment that expects, supports, and nurtures moral strength. Therefore, leaders need to demonstrate emotional signaling, reflective pauses, self-regulation, and moral preparation as they simultaneously cultivate these practices throughout their organizations. In our final quote, a manager describes how moral strength at the top can produce PMC at every level: "It's the way [our senior leadership] conducted themselves with the crew—high expectations, very demanding, but at the same time respectful and professional. You didn't want to let them down. They were well focused and well organized. It was like a symphony orchestra. How that influenced moral behavior? Well, the C[ommanding]O[fficer] had a strong moral compass. I thrive in that; it makes me want to do the right thing, makes me want to be a part of that community, do right things for the people there."

Leaders, by modeling professional moral courage and maintaining a dialogue about ethical issues and concerns, can bolster the personal governance practices their managers need to proceed with right action. As Aristotle suggested, moral excellence comes about as a result of habit.[17] Thus, leaders and managers need to practice exercising PMC on a daily basis.

Notes

We wish to thank the United States Naval Supply Corps for their support. Assistance was provided by LCDR Rodney Blevins and Ms. Martha Shaw, who contributed to our data collection and analysis. Special appreciation is extended to the officers—their openness and candor made this chapter possible. The findings and opinions expressed in this chapter are those of the authors and do not necessarily represent the views of the U.S. Navy.

1. Zimbardo, 2007. Zimbardo's Stanford Prison Experiment first documented this phenomenon.

2. Maccoby, 2005.

3. Sekerka, Bagozzi, and Charnigo, 2009.

4. Solomon, 1998.

5. This depiction of PMC is consistent with the literature and has been validated in Sekerka, Bagozzi, and Charnigo, 2009.

6. Hartle, 1989.

7. Davenport, 1997.

8. England, 2005.

9. Toner, 2006.

10. The Ethics in Action Program is sponsored by the Supply Corps, approximately 3,500 officers who provide operational logistics and business management support to the U.S. Navy and other joint forces.

11. Jick and Rosegrant, 1990.

12. Forgas, 2003.

13. Sekerka and Bagozzi, 2007.

14. Mayer, Salovey, and Caruso, 2008.

15. Baumeister and Exline, 1999.

16. Fisher, 2003.

17. Aristotle [350 bc], 1999.

References

Aristotle [350 bc]. 1999. *Nicomachean ethics*, trans. T. Irwin. Indianapolis: Hackett.

Baumeister, R.F., and Exline, J.J. 1999. Virtue, personality, and social relations: Self-control as the moral muscle. *Journal of Personality* 67(6), 1165–1194.

Davenport, M.M. 1997. Moral constraints on the conduct of war. *Perspectives on the Professions* 16(2), 3–5. www.iit.edu/departments/csep/perspective/v16n2 perspective.pdf (accessed May 26, 2008).

England, G. 2005. Secretary of the Navy Address at the All Flag Officer Training Symposium. U.S. Naval Academy, Annapolis, MD, April 4.

Fisher, J. 2003. Surface and deep approaches to business ethics. *Leadership & Organizational Development Journal* 24(2), 96–101.

Forgas, J.P. 2003. *Handbook of affective sciences.* Oxford, UK: Oxford University Press.

Hartle, A.E. 1989. *Moral issues in military decision making.* Lawrence, KS: University Press of Kansas.

Jick, T.D., and Rosegrant, S. 1990. Three in the middle: The experience of making change at Micro Switch. Harvard Business School Case 491022. Boston, MA.

Maccoby, M. 2005. Creating moral organizations. *Research Technology Management* 48(1), 59–61.

Mayer, J.D., Salovey, P., and Caruso, D.R. 2008. Emotional intelligence: New ability or eclectic traits? *American Psychologist* 63(6), 503–517.

Sekerka, L.E., and Bagozzi, R.P. 2007. Moral courage in the workplace: Moving to and from the desire and decision to act. *Business Ethics: A European Review* 16(11), 132–142.

Sekerka, L.E., Bagozzi, R.P., and Charnigo, R. 2009. Facing ethical challenges in the workplace: Conceptualizing and measuring professional moral courage. *Journal of Business Ethics* 89(4), 565–579.

Solomon, R.C. 1998. The moral psychology of business: Care and compassion in the corporation. *Business Ethics Quarterly* 8(3), 515–534.

Toner, J.H. 2006. The merge, educating for "exemplary conduct." *Air & Space Power Journal* 20(1), 18–26.

Zimbardo, P. 2007. *The Lucifer effect: Understanding how good people turn evil.* New York: Random House.

11

Stand Up and Be Counted

Legal Protections for Those Who Act with Moral Courage

JUDITH W. SPAIN

> *First they came for the communists, and I did not speak out—because I was not a communist.*
> *Then they came for the socialists, and I did not speak out—because I was not a socialist. . . .*
> *Then they came for me—and there was no one left to speak out for me.*
>
> —Pastor Martin Niemöller[1]

Who *does* speak out for you? Over the past sixty years our legislators have enacted various federal and state employment and labor laws that provide far-reaching protection for you, as an employee, in all aspects of an employment relationship. Ranging from protection against discrimination to providing benefits in the face of medical emergency to prohibiting retaliation for exercising your legal rights, these statutes protect you from employers who are knowingly or unknowingly violating the laws. However, *you* must exercise these rights. It is the exercise of these rights that will challenge your moral courage.

In the workplace, faced with the threat of retaliation from your employer for standing up for your employment rights, do you have the courage to rise above your fears and assert your rights? And, if you do summon your courage, what specific legal protections exist to protect you and your family and provide you a safety net if reprisals do occur?

Join a typical working couple, David and Elaine, while they move through their lives and face a series of road bumps. They discover the strength of their moral convictions as well as the legal support and protection for their choices.

Introducing David and Elaine

David and Elaine, high school sweethearts, start their married life together. Elaine joins the human resource (HR) department of a company in the fashion industry with more than 1,500 employees. David starts working as a carpenter in a small manufacturing company with about 75 employees. Theirs is a mixed marriage—David is a conservative Democrat, and Elaine is a free-spending Republican—but it works for them. Life is good, and their future seems bright.

Their First Road Bump: Sexual Harassment

Elaine wants to pursue her education. She attends a few classes each year at the local university. Several years fly by, and graduation day is in sight. Her boss, Bob, a married man with children about the same age as Elaine, has strongly supported her educational pursuits, even encouraging her to use the company's flextime program to arrange her work and class schedule. One Thursday afternoon in mid-May, Elaine is sitting in her office celebrating the receipt of her semester grades as Bob walks by. He inquires as to the reason for the big smile on her face, and Elaine proudly informs him of her academic achievements. Bob promptly gives her a big bear hug and says, "Let us celebrate with a drink after work." Because David will be working late that evening anyway, Elaine agrees.

Over drinks that evening, Bob's hand grazes Elaine's knee. He quickly apologizes, but Elaine feels uncomfortable. At the end of the evening, Bob's lingering good-bye hug makes her even more uncomfortable. The next day at work, Bob stops by Elaine's office to schedule her annual review and evaluation meeting. After they have set a time, Bob suggests that they have drinks again sometime later in the week. Elaine quickly changes the subject, and the moment passes. Yet, Elaine spends the rest of the day in turmoil . . . worrying that clearly she must have allowed this situation to start getting out of hand, thinking about her yearly evaluation by Bob scheduled for next week, fretting about her long-term employability if she ever complained about this situation, and wondering how she could even report it, because Bob is the supervisor of her company's EEO office.

What Are Her Morally Courageous Options?

Life presents options. Elaine could, of course, simply ignore her discomfort around Bob and skillfully avoid any situation in which she could be cornered into accepting an invitation for after-hours drinks. Or, she could address the situation head-on—recognizing that her ability to function effectively in the workplace would likely be stifled by Bob's actions (now and in the future) and deciding that dealing with this situation now would be better than spending the rest of her working career hiding behind the water cooler to avoid Bob.

It will certainly require tremendous moral courage for Elaine to complain about this situation; but it is the right thing to do. Elaine is not looking out just for herself; rather, she is looking out for all other employees who could be subjected to the same type of inappropriate behavior from all the "Bobs" out there in the working world.

What Are the Legal Protections for These Actions?

Title VII of the Civil Rights Act of 1964 (Title VII) provides the broadest range of legal protection for Elaine.[2] Administered by the Equal Employment Opportunity Commission, this act prohibits employment discrimination based upon race, religion, color, national origin, and sex, including sexual harassment. Sexual harassment ranges from making an employee's job contingent upon compliance with a direct request for sexual favors (e.g., "Go to bed with me or you will lose your job") to workplace conditions that create a hostile working environment (such as posting nude photos, making inappropriate jokes at the lunchroom table, or patting a coworker's buttocks while the worker is leaning over the water cooler). In Elaine's case, both of these forms of harassment occurred; that is, Bob made a direct request (mentioning going out for drinks right after scheduling her annual evaluation) and created a sexually hostile working environment (hugging her and touching her knee).

If Elaine believes that Bob has violated her employment rights, she possesses multiple options to address the problem. She could confront Bob directly and attempt to work out the problem, file a discrimination complaint with her company, or file a federal or state employment discrimination claim. Elaine may choose not to confront Bob but to file a complaint with her company instead. If her company is a proactive employer, it would identify at least two individuals within the organization to whom employees could air their complaints in order to avoid scenarios such as this one. But because Bob is currently the only employee designated to handle such matters, Elaine can file a complaint directly with Bob's supervisor. Best practices for investigating this type of complaint dictate that a company conduct a confidential and expedient investigation, with frequent contacts with the complainant for updated status.

If Elaine chooses to file a complaint with the Equal Employment Opportunity Commission or applicable state fair employment practice agency, the agency will investigate and make a determination as to whether a violation of the law occurred. Elaine can avail herself of the option to file a federal or state complaint with the agency even if the company has also conducted a full investigation. Indeed, Elaine can ultimately file a lawsuit in federal or state court if she is not satisfied with the decision of the agency.

In the meantime, during any of these investigations (and arguably afterward) Elaine enjoys even more protection under Title VII. If she loses her job or suffers other adverse employment actions because of filing the employment discrimination claim, she can pursue a separate Title VII action against her employer for retaliation.[3] Just as Elaine's employer must treat her as if she had never filed an EEO complaint, Elaine should take care to continue working to the best of her ability. Despite her legal protections, Elaine will probably feel very vulnerable during this time. As she waits for a legal resolution, she will likely have to contend with snide comments from some coworkers and the "cold shoulder" from others. She will need to summon all of her moral conviction as she focuses on the target of having her complaints addressed in a transparent process.

In addition, the Civil Rights Act of 1991 may be applicable to Elaine's scenario.[4] This act provides Elaine the right to a jury trial and allows her to seek and recover emotional distress and punitive damages. These remedies, combined with remedies available under Title VII (lost wages, future wages, and possible reinstatement) could net Elaine sufficient compensation to offset any lost income caused by this road bump in life.

The Second Road Bump: Unequal Treatment for Medical Leave

Fast-forward a year. Elaine is still employed with the same company; Bob no longer works there (the company terminated him after the EEOC ruled that a violation had occurred) . . . and the next bump in life occurs. Elaine discovers she is pregnant. Both she and David are elated, but realistic. Because money is tight, Elaine will have to continue working until right before the baby is born and then return to work soon thereafter. The problem is Elaine's boss, Anne, a divorced woman who does not allow her personal life to interfere with her work life and insists that her employees do the same. Elaine has hidden her pregnancy from her boss, but as her pregnancy progresses, it will be more difficult to keep it a secret. Also, because Elaine works in the HR department and helps occasionally with payroll, she knows that the company has applied sick leave benefits differently for a male custodian whose three-week absence from work following his hernia operation was covered under sick leave, and a female custodian who had to use vacation leave for the six weeks she took after having a baby. It certainly does not improve Elaine's mood when David tells her that all the guys in his department were laughing at him when he said he was going to take time off from work to help with the baby.

What Are Their Morally Courageous Options?

Unless Elaine can successfully hide the pregnancy until delivery, deliver the baby during nonworking hours, and return to work the day after the birth, she is going to need to divulge the existence of her pregnancy and address in a practical way the myriad of issues surrounding a pregnancy leave. The "traditional" view of the female who should not work while pregnant is long past. Elaine has to deal with more challenging complications than this traditional view suggests, because she has a boss who will resent her pregnancy, will not appreciate that Elaine will need—and is entitled to—time off to recuperate, and will think less of her because she will not be able to stay late/come in early as a matter of course.

Elaine has to muster her courage to talk about her pregnancy to her boss. She needs to schedule an appointment with her boss, tell her the news, identify her expected due date, frankly discuss what work needs to be completed before she goes on leave, pragmatically address how work products could be handled while she is on leave, and start to plan for her transition back to work at the end of the leave. An open line of communication is the key.

Meanwhile, David should ignore his coworkers' old-fashioned ideas about fatherhood and, instead, exercise moral courage to do what he feels is right for his family. He is to be commended for planning to take time off to be with his newborn and to begin to forge a bond with the child. Indeed, the bond between a father and his child plays a very important role in the child's mental and physical development and overall well-being.[5] Although his coworkers may taunt him for being a "wimp," perhaps David will be the last one laughing when he reaps true fulfillment from fatherhood and stays married in a healthy and supportive working-couple relationship.

What Are the Legal Protections?

The Pregnancy Discrimination Act prohibits discrimination on the basis of pregnancy, birth, or related medical conditions.[6] Women affected by these conditions must be treated in the same manner as male or female employees with "similar" limitations, such as a kidney infection or hysterectomy. In this scenario, treating a female employee and a male employee differently simply because of their "types" of condition, even though both were entitled to sick leave and vacation leave, would violate the Pregnancy Discrimination Act. Thus, the employer should immediately cease treating males and females differently.

Under the Family Medical Leave Act (FMLA), workers who are employed by firms with fifty or more employees and have worked for the employer for at least twelve months are legally entitled to twelve weeks of unpaid leave for medical reasons, including pregnancy and birth of a child.[7] Elaine, with her four weeks accrued sick leave and three weeks accrued vacation leave, would be able to remain off work for up to twelve weeks (seven weeks paid and five weeks unpaid), just as if she had a heart attack, gallbladder surgery, or another medical condition. Elaine knows when her baby is due, and she needs to provide notice to her employer of when she is anticipating using FMLA leave. According to the provisions of the FMLA, an employer is required to keep an employee's job open for only twelve weeks. Therefore, Elaine must return to work at the end of her FMLA leave if she wants to keep her job. If David's company has at least fifty employees and he has worked there for at least twelve months, he is eligible for time off under the FMLA for the birth of his child.

The Third Road Bump: Military Leave Conflict

Fast forward again a few more years to another bump in life's travels. David has been working for approximately fifteen years and has consistently received excellent annual evaluations. Not a big talker but a hard worker, David is the "go-to" guy whenever a project needs doing and no one else can figure out how to do it. Upon turning eighteen, David enlisted in the National Guard. He believes firmly in his duty of loyalty to the United States, and Elaine strongly supported his decision. David has just received notification that his unit is going to be activated and that he can anticipate a four- to five-month stint of service. Although Elaine will miss David, she is proud of his patriotic loyalty. David worries that his boss, Ray, will not appreciate his loyalty. He dreads telling Ray that he will be leaving in one month, at the scheduled start of the huge construction project for which he is to be the carpenters' team leader. David knows that if Ray were to fire him, he would have no income and no insurance benefits—and that by the time he filed a complaint alleging a violation of the applicable law, he would have lost his house due to foreclosure. David's courage of his convictions is stressed to the utmost.

What Are His Morally Courageous Options?

Thank you, David, on behalf of our country for making this commitment. Employer—are you willing to make the same type of commitment? David's employer has an opportunity to step forward and do the morally right thing—that is, encourage his participation in the National Guard and Reserve, recognize and publicize his dedication, and work to facilitate the employee's transition from military to civilian work life.

What Are the Legal Protections for This Action?

The Uniformed Services Employment and Reemployment Rights Act of 1994 (USERRA) is a federal law providing protection for persons who serve or have served in the Armed Forces, Reserves, National Guard, or other "uniformed services."[8] The law applies to all public and private employers, regardless of size.

Upon David's return from military service, his employer must provide prompt reinstatement (typically within two weeks after David applies for it) into the same position that he had when he left. USERRA allows David to accumulate seniority and pension plan benefits during his leave and, upon his return, reinstates his health insurance and provides job skills (re)training (and accommodations if David is disabled). USERRA also protects David from discrimination in employment based upon past, present, or future military service. Although USERRA does not specify how far in advance an employer must receive notice, David should provide as much notice as is reasonable under the circumstances. The Department of Defense strongly recommends that an employee give notice of at least thirty days prior to departure, if it is feasible to do so.

So, David needs to summon up as much courage as it took him to enlist and as it will take him to defend his country and tell Ray that he is going on active duty and his employer must accommodate this request. When David tells Ray, he should bring a copy of the act (or a summary), review his rights, provide as many details as he can as to when he will leave and the projected length of his deployment, and discuss what he can do now to help in the transition before and after deployment.

This situation also provides an opportunity for Ray to exercise moral courage by speaking proactively to his boss, not only to defend David's right to take his military leave without fear of repercussions but also to begin a conversation regarding ways to implement USERRA provisions and protections into their employment practices.

The Fourth Road Bump: Unsafe Workplace

David returns from his military service. Ray and the employer welcome David back and comply fully with the USERRA provisions. David and Elaine settle back into their comfortable suburban life and comment that having no more road bumps would be a good thing. The plant's construction project has been completed. David quickly makes himself indispensable again with his hard work and innovative ideas.

Then, one of David's coworkers, Michael, is injured when he trips and falls on a walkway near the top of the building, almost tumbling off the walkway to the ground, about fifteen feet below. There has never been a railing around this walkway. In response to David's suggestion to install a railing to prevent similar future accidents, Ray barks, "Why spend the money? Michael is an idiot for tripping over his own two feet. Besides, with OSHA [the Occupational Safety and Health Administration] experiencing such tremendous personnel cutbacks, they will never inspect our little shop, and we will never get caught. Get out of my office and do your job!"

About a week after that incident, David receives a notification from the workers' compensation office requesting that he attend the workers' compensation hearing for Michael's claim. David has recognized the danger of this particular walkway since he returned from his military service. He knows he could easily install the railing at minimal cost to the company. David has always been a "team player," but he worries that unless Ray makes these changes to increase workplace safety, the next person who trips on the walkway could fall to his death.

What Are His Morally Courageous Options?

Risk of injury or risk of losing job—is there really a choice for David? David needs to approach Ray to encourage him to make the changes, explaining the practical as well as legal ramifications of the improvements. If Ray refuses to acknowledge the danger of the situation and the need for the changes, David needs to march into the plant manager's office and present the same suggestions. If the plant manager fails to follow up on these suggestions, then filing a complaint with OSHA is the next logical step, morally as well as legally.

What Are the Legal Protections for These Actions?

Workplace safety is everyone's concern. Workers' compensation laws are state-administered programs designed to ensure that employees who are injured or disabled on the job are provided with fixed monetary awards, eliminating the need for litigation. Typically these laws also provide benefits for dependents of those workers who are killed because of work-related accidents or illnesses. Whenever an employee is injured on the job, a report is filed with the appropriate plant officials and then provided to the workers' compensation board. If David fears retribution for his testimony at Michael's hearing, he should review the applicable state workers' compensation statutes to determine the extent of their anti-retaliation protection.

The Occupational Health and Safety Act also provides protection for both Michael (the injured employee) and David by enacting regulations to promote workplace safety.[9] In addition, Section 11(c) of the Act prohibits the employer from discharging or in any manner retaliating against an employee for exercising his or her rights under the act. These rights include complaining to OSHA and seeking an OSHA inspection, participating in an OSHA investigation, and participating or testifying in any proceeding related to an OSHA inspection. If David believes that he is being discriminated against for exercising his rights under the Act, he needs to be mindful that the time for filing a complaint is only thirty days. Because state OSHA laws have different complaint-filing deadlines, David should determine whether state or federal laws are applicable and pay attention to filing dates. Unfortunately for David, the old adage of "you snooze, you lose" applies when dealing with the issue of filing deadlines.

Another Road Bump: Age and Gender Discrimination

Years pass. The kids are now adults and are actively pursuing their own careers. . . . David and Elaine have grown older together and are looking forward to their retirement years. Both have been employed by their respective companies their entire working careers, and both have company pensions, two things that are not typical in today's "job-changing-at-the-drop-of-a-hat" employee mindset. David reaches his milestone forty years with his company, applies for his pension to begin the next month, and watches as his employer processes the paperwork efficiently.

Elaine is a few months short of her forty years with the company, but decides that it is probably time to retire. A few days after she announces her intention to retire in two weeks, Elaine is shocked to receive a very negative annual evaluation. The evaluation attacks her work ethic and output and concludes with a recommendation for termination by the end of the week. Elaine knows that because she lives in an employment-at-will state, her employer can terminate her at any time for any reason or no reason and she has no rights of continued employment in her job. She also knows that under this legal doctrine governing her employment relationship, unless she proves her termination is due to unlawful discrimination, she is heading for the unemployment office. She ducks into the ladies' room right after the evaluation meeting, and her best friend, Joan, comes up to comfort her. Joan comments that everyone in Elaine's section of the HR department group is going to be eliminated by the end of the week. Elaine cannot comprehend why, until she realizes that she and her three coworkers are all approaching the forty-year mark for pension purposes, a milestone that provides a significantly higher pension payout compared with a pension for an employee with fewer than forty years of service. It would be a huge cost savings to the company to get rid of all four employees now, before they reach that forty-year service mark.

While leaving the bathroom, Joan asks Elaine why, for all of these years, Elaine never complained that her salary was $10,000 less than that of Harold, a coworker in HR. Both Harold and Elaine are midlevel managers, each responsible for managing two employees, administering a small budget, performing substantially similar work (Harold is responsible for benefit administration and claims, and Elaine is responsible for employee performance evaluations and training).

At the end of the day, Elaine trudges to her car, slowly drives home, walks into the house, and wonders whether working for the company all of these years was worth it. Could this possibly be another road bump in life?

What Are Her Morally Courageous Options?

Out with the old, in with the new—a familiar line. Elaine can fade silently into the night or stand up and assert her rights to her pension and her salary. For the sake of the "old" in the workplace, Elaine needs to act, because at least three coworkers are facing the same situation, just because of their age. For the sake of the "new" in the workplace, Elaine needs to act because the future generation of women employees may fall into the same pay inequity structure, just because of their gender.

Elaine needs to pin on her badge of courage and walk into the office of the director of the HR department, armed with the facts regarding the salary differential issue as well as examples of the unequal treatment of the employees based upon their age. She needs to focus on the facts, present the information in a logical manner, insist upon an evaluation of her salary, and remind the director of the various laws protecting employees over the age of forty.

What Are the Legal Protections for These Actions?

The Age Discrimination in Employment Act of 1967 (ADEA) protects Elaine and her coworkers, who are all forty years of age or older, from employment discrimination based on age.[10] Firing these four employees simply because of their age is unlawful. It is also unlawful to retaliate against Elaine for opposing employment practices that discriminate based on age or for filing an age-discrimination charge or testifying or participating in any way in an investigation, proceeding, or litigation under the ADEA.

Closely related to age discrimination is discrimination based upon the actual or presumed "cost" relative to a pension plan. The Employee Retirement Income Security Act of 1974 (ERISA) sets minimum standards for most voluntarily established pension and health plans in private industry in order to provide protection for individuals in these plans.[11] ERISA does not require Elaine's employer to establish a pension plan. Nor does ERISA require that plans provide a minimum level of benefits. Rather, ERISA regulates the pension plan operation once it has been established. Section 510 of ERISA prohibits an employer from interfering with the receipt of benefits protected under the act. Terminating Elaine and her three coworkers simply to avoid or reduce pension liability would be unlawful under ERISA.

Three federal laws prohibit Elaine's employer from setting her pay at a rate different from that of a male performing substantially similar work. First, Elaine is protected under Title VII of the Civil Rights Act of 1964. Paying males and females at different rates when they are performing substantially similar work would be a violation of the act. Elaine would have to establish the similarities between her job and Harold's job and then seek the salary differential.

The Equal Pay Act of 1963 also provides protection for Elaine.[12] This act, an amendment to the Fair Labor Standards Act and administered by the EEOC, requires that men and women receive equal pay for equal work in the same company. It is job content, not job titles, that determines whether jobs are substantially equal. Even though HR manager Harold is responsible for benefit administration and claims and HR manager Elaine is responsible for employee performance evaluations and training, the level of skill, effort, and responsibility Harold and Elaine exercise under similar working conditions is substantially equal. Harold's receiving $10,000 more in compensation than Elaine for performing substantially equal work would be a violation of the act, rendering Elaine eligible to pursue compensation for lost wages and attorneys' fees.

The third act providing protection is the Lilly Ledbetter Fair Pay Act of 2009.[13] This act amends the Civil Rights Act of 1964 and specifically states that the previous 180-day statute of limitations for filing an equal-pay lawsuit regarding pay discrimination now resets with each new discriminatory paycheck. Because Elaine is paid once a month, every month that her pay is different from Harold's pay because of gender discrimination constitutes a potential violation of the act. This "rolling clock" provides Elaine with expanded employment protection, reaching even after her employment is terminated or she retires.

Epilogue

David and Elaine are enjoying their retirement. Their grown children have families and are successful in their careers. Their pension monies are flowing into their coffers.

They possessed the moral courage to stand up for their legal rights throughout their working careers. David and Elaine realize that the laws of our country provide clear guidelines for employers to follow and that perhaps a simple nudge to remind the employer of those responsibilities and rights would result in the employer's doing the right thing. If, however, a nudge does not work, the safety net of the laws provides the protection necessary for David and Elaine to complain about unfair treatment without having to fear the aftermath of their complaints. The remedies available for violations of employment laws (back pay, reinstatement, front pay, reasonable accommodation, attorneys' fees, court costs, and protection from retaliatory discharge) have afforded David and Elaine extensive protections.

So, as David and Elaine sit on their back porch, looking at the red hues of the evening sunset, they comment that they fought the good fight, did what was right for them and for society, finished the race—and now have earned the prize. . . . Life is good.

Notes

1. There are many versions of this quote, which is attributed to Pastor Martin Niemöller (see Marcuse 2010). The earliest documented reference to this quote is Mayer (1955), 168–169.
2. Civil Rights Act of 1964, 42 U.S. Code, Vol. 21, secs. 2000 et seq. (1964).
3. Civil Rights Act of 1964, 42 U.S. Code, Vol. 21, sec. 2000e (1991).
4. Civil Rights Act of 1991, 42 U.S. Code, Vol. 21, sec. 2000e-3 (1991).
5. Avenilla, Rosenthal, and Tice (2006).
6. Pregnancy Discrimination Act, 42 U.S. Code, Vol. 21, sec. 701 (k) of the Civil Rights Act of 1964 (1978).
7. Family and Medical Leave Act, 29 U.S. Code Vol. 28 (1993).
8. Uniformed Services Employment and Reemployment Rights Act, 38 U.S. Code, Vol. 43, secs. 4301–33 (1994).
9. Occupational Safety and Health Act, 29 U.S. Code, Vol. 15, secs. 651–678 (1970).
10. Age Discrimination in Employment Act, 29 U.S. Code, Vol. 14, secs. 621–634 (1967).
11. Employee Retirement Income Security Act, 29 U.S. Code, Vol. 18, secs. 1001–1461 (1974).
12. Equal Pay Act, 29 U.S. Code, Vol. 8, sec. 206 et seq. (1963).
13. Lilly Ledbetter Fair Pay Act, 123 U.S. Statutes at Large 5 (2009).

References

Avenilla, F., Rosenthal, E., and Tice, P. 2006. *Fathers of U.S. Children Born in 2001: Findings from the Early Childhood Longitudinal Study, Birth Cohort* (ECLS-B) (NCES 2006–002). U.S. Department of Education, National Center for Education Statistics. Washington, DC: U.S. Government Printing Office.

Marcuse, H. 2010. Martin Niemöller's famous quotation: "First they came for the Communists." www.history.ucsb.edu/faculty/marcuse/niem.htm#discsources (accessed September 28, 2010).

Mayer, M. 1955. *They Thought They Were Free: The Germans, 1933–45.* Chicago: University of Chicago Press.

Part IV

Changing Organizations with Moral Courage

12

Speaking Truth to Power

The Courageous Organizational Dissenter

Bernard F. Matt and Nasrin Shahinpoor

A Few Good Men is about soldiers stationed at the U.S. Marine base at Guantanamo, Cuba.[1] Two young Marines, Lance Corporal Harold W. Dawson and Private First Class Louden Downey, are on trial for killing Private First Class William T. Santiago, a member of their platoon, after receiving an order, a "Code Red," from their superior officer, Colonel Nathan R. Jessep. The Code Red ordered the violent hazing of Santiago, an act that resulted in his death. Why did these two Marines not speak out? Why did they not voice an objection to their orders? Dawson comes to recognize the ethical lapse of his failure to dissent from the order he was given. Near the conclusion of the film, both defendants are read a verdict that exonerates them of the killing but dishonorably discharges them from the Marines. Although Downey cannot grasp what they have done wrong, Dawson explains, in two of the most powerful lines in the film, "We were supposed to fight for the people who couldn't fight for themselves. We were supposed to fight for Willie."

It is temptingly easy to sit in judgment of these characters and righteously condemn them for either their lack of conscience or their lack of courage to speak their conscience or to act upon their convictions. But as an audience we identify with Harold Dawson. What makes this character so compelling and so troubling is his humanity. His actions, or lack of actions, make him representative of us all; we are more like him than not. Few of us face situations or make decisions that are matters of life and death as he did. But newspapers, broadcast news, and office gossip are all rife with examples of men and women, from CEOs to line workers, who do not speak out about ethically egregious actions, policies, and practices.

In trying to analyze the ethical features of cases such as those in this film, some ethicists focus on individual moral failure: Dawson should have known better, must have known better. Dawson lacked the courage of his convictions. He is an exception, one of the "few bad apples." Others, and we are among this group, see the issues as the product of complex social factors: Dawson is enmeshed in a culture whose values are hostile, antithetical, and unsympathetic to individual conscience and action. He was trained to be loyal, to avoid questioning orders and thinking for himself. Thus, to understand Dawson's silence, we must also understand the social context that shaped him. To understand individual action or inaction, we must also understand the organizational circumstances that make speaking out a perilous alternative. Like Dawson, many employees fail to formulate and articulate their dissent or lack the moral courage to act on their dissent because they find themselves overwhelmed by organizational circumstances that make speaking out inconvenient or even dangerous.

The remainder of this chapter consists of four sections. In the first section, we emphasize that many organizations deny voice; that is, they tend to be authoritative, reward conformity, and require individuals to leave their values outside the workplace. Organizations that operate in this way do so at considerable ethical peril, and the individuals who work within them suffer ethical harm. We argue in the second section that one way to counteract this harm is through dissent. Dissent is coming into voice, or discovering one's voice; the dissenter is compelled by conscience to speak out. However, as the third section indicates, most organizational cultures do not value dissent but, instead, punish dissenters. Thus, dissenters face risks and require moral courage. In the fourth section, we make the case that an organization that comes to see the importance of the dissenter can begin to take steps toward ethical improvement.

Denying Voice

In the late 1980s, anthropologist Robert Jackall gained access to several large corporations for the purpose of describing their organizational structure and behavior. What he observed he named "the bureaucratic ethic," intending nothing flattering in the term. In his descriptions of these organizations, he compared their structure and ethos to the feudal system: a vast hierarchy of king and lords and subjects.[2]

The lords (VPs and upper management) feared the king (the CEO), who expected them to be obedient and loyal; and the subjects (middle managers and workers) stood in fear of the lord, who expected them to be obedient and loyal. The fortunes of the middle managers rose and fell in accordance with the fate of their boss and the capriciousness of the market and economic forces. Most important, individual loyalty—rather than allegiance to principles or ideals—was the glue that held the system together. Loyalty to organizational leaders and conformity to their expectations were rewarded with favors and benefits. Beyond a basic level of competence, what really mattered were one's social connections. This organizational culture made "its own internal rules and social context the principal moral gauges for action. Men and women in bureaucracies turned to each other for moral cues for behavior and came to fashion specific situational moralities for specific significant people in their worlds."[3]

Jackall's observations remain salient today. Adult business students report haunting similarities between Jackall's report and their own places of employment. Although few describe their manager or boss as a lord and themselves as subjects, they use such phrases as "the boys' club," the "good ol' boy network," "going along to get along," "keeping your head down," trying to be among those of the "in group," and struggling to "fit in." These are just newer euphemisms that describe the same organizational structure and culture that Jackall observed more than two decades ago. The common thread in these descriptions is that survival and success are defined by and depend on conformity with and loyalty to the values and behaviors of specific persons in power.

Conformity and loyalty are important values insofar as they facilitate organizational efficiency, but the way in which they operate when part of a bureaucratic ethic is problematic. Why? Because under bureaucratic ethics, what matters most is that employees be subservient to the needs of those in power and to the organization. Conformity and unquestioning loyalty to the organization deprive employees of their individuality and integrity and extract an unacceptable ethical price. When organizational leaders actively cultivate dependency and reliance on someone else's judgment, the casualties for employees include the loss of their independence of thought and autonomy. The result is a loss of self because one cannot be a self without the ability to exercise one's free will and conscience. No one has expressed this more pointedly than Alford, who declared that organizations are "the enemy of individual morality."[4]

Another way of describing the core of bureaucratic ethics is that playing the game and successfully navigating the political aspects of organizational life are of paramount importance. Common workplace behaviors thus include acting in a way that is contrary to one's own beliefs and character, looking the other way when one witnesses wrongdoing, parroting the party line, and mimicking successful behavior. Walton concludes, "[E]very adjustment I make to 'fit in' to such an organizational ethos goes against who I am and what I am morally able to do, and to corrode my integrity."[5] Rather than remaining true to themselves, employees carefully subordinate themselves to meet organizational expectations.

Even if one were to think the bureaucratic ethic characterizes organizational life too negatively or too harshly, milder characterizations of organizational life still present many ethical hazards. For example, groupthink is a phenomenon that occurs when a group operates in isolation with limited access to alternative points of view, or when members give too much priority to cohesiveness and agreement. Members can become so preoccupied with considering only the views of their own members or with the success of their group that they risk committing unethical actions. Organizations that restrict critique and creative thinking may find themselves trapped by groupthink, where "unanimous agreement [is put] ahead of reasoned problem solving. Groups suffering from this symptom are both ineffective and unethical."[6] Sticking with the group is regarded more highly than sticking out, and remaining silent garners more rewards than speaking up against the values and decisions of the group. Those who succeed to become managers and leaders in these organizations surround themselves with unquestioning yes-men and yes-women. They are thus "isolated from criticism, or even serious discussion, of [their] thoughts and actions."[7] Within organizations that habitually suppress unwanted information, managers cultivate loyalty to the point where it crowds out honesty, where, to paraphrase Colonel Jessep, "[They] can't handle the truth."[8]

Admittedly, for many people, managing workplace conflicts that result from divergent views or values is difficult and demanding; it can be seductively easy to indulge in the comfort and safety of groupthink and conformity. After all, the workplace is supposed to be a harmonious and pleasant environment. Ciulla describes and critiques a tendency of managers to be "nice" to their subordinates in the workplace. Niceness includes the belief that social harmony and a lack of conflict are positive ways of "accommodating and adjusting to people."[9] Niceness is the product of managerial reform movements of the 1980s and 1990s that promised empowerment to employees, but actually delivered "bogus empowerment."[10] Being nice in Ciulla's sense relies on merely making employees feel as though they have more independence, voice, and autonomy, when, in fact, management retains all the real power. Empowerment is an illusion managers create to manipulate their employees by promising autonomy while actually diminishing it. The managers who maintain this kind of organizational culture are "unauthentic, insincere and disrespectful of others."[11]

At its best, this culture of niceness invites a kind of superficial and insincere pleasantness. And at its worst, it engenders alienation and dehumanization because it relies on layers of dishonesty and inauthenticity. Consider an organization that asserts that it is one big family in which managers genuinely care about and listen to their employees and value, rely upon, and act on employees' issues. An employee, feeling thusly empowered, tells her manager that she has discovered a defect in one of the company's products that makes it unsafe. Her manager smiles pleasantly, thanks her for her concern, and promises to look into the matter. When nothing happens after a few weeks, the employee returns to ask what has happened. Her manager makes the excuse that he needs more time, but assures the employee that the organization will give her concern serious attention. The manager acts cordially, but power sharing is only an illusion. Ultimately, management has the prerogative to ignore any employee-initiated issue that is too inconvenient to address. The next time this employee has a concern, she will be less likely to raise it, having learned that her superior only pretends to value her opinion.

Discovering Voice

Not everyone conforms or remains silent. Some people in the workplace speak out against controlling structures and individuals. We focus on one such voice as possessing a tremendous amount of significance and power: the voice of the conscientious dissenter. Why a "conscientious" dissenter? We use this term to underscore the importance of the dissenter's speaking from conscience, from ethical principles, from deeply held core values. By conscientious dissent, we mean "principled" dissent, as defined by Graham: "*Principled organizational dissent* is the effort by individuals in the workplace to protest and/or to change the organizational status quo because of their conscientious objection to current policy or practice."[12] When dissenters speak from conscience, they are revealing themselves and they are speaking honestly and truthfully. It is important to distinguish conscientious dissent from other forms of disagreement. For example, someone can seem to voice dissent by playing the devil's advocate or being a member of the loyal opposition (e.g., a union) or being a chronic complainer. However, these are not authentic voices, but roles one plays or habits one displays. In contrast, the voice of the dissenter expresses genuine and deeply held principles and values, commitments, and emotions.[13]

What characterizes the dissenter? Conscientious dissenters are similar to whistleblowers. However, whereas some whistleblowers go outside their organization to report wrongdoing, the dissenter remains within the organization and attempts to resolve matters on the inside. Indeed, a defining feature of the principled, conscientious dissenter is intense loyalty to the organization. Hirschman finds that dissenters are loyal persons "who choose . . . to respond to perceived organizational decline by remaining and trying to improve things from within."[14] Unlike an unquestioning loyalty based on simply doing what one is told or conforming to organizational expectation, the dissenter's loyalty is built on a commitment to the vision or mission of an organization, or a dedication to professional values. Rather than ignoring or avoiding a problem by remaining silent or quitting, the dissenter voices the problem within the organization with the aim of fixing it. The dissenter's "concern and labor are directed toward the good of the object of his loyalty, as if it were his own good. . . . Loyalty also leads one to act with frankness and rectitude to improve as much as possible the institutions and communities he serves."[15]

Dissenters are driven by their conscience to speak out, to be honest and truthful—whatever the consequences, silence is often more painful and dreadful. For some, not telling the truth is inconceivable; honesty is a kind of "choiceless choice" they cannot resist.[16] Conscience, commitments, values, and passions compel them to speak the truth to those in authority. Only by speaking out can the dissenter find freedom; that is to say, only by dissenting can the individual live honestly and authentically. The organization is fully aware of the individual who, by speaking out, stands apart from the crowd. Not only are the dissenter's name and face known, but his or her deepest convictions, guiding principles, and core values are laid bare. When one speaks from conscience, one's most intimate and private thoughts are made public. The whole of the dissenter is thus exposed for public scrutiny in an organizational environment we have already described as unsympathetic to individuality and nonconformity.

Acting on Voice

We have shown that the dissenter is honest and loyal, a person of integrity. Voicing dissent is an act of courage above all. Courage involves acting well (or for the good) in the face of fear, anxiety, and risk.[17] The courage to dissent entails doing what is right for the sake of its rightness and fulfilling one's obligation to perform one's duty consistent with one's conscience. The courage required to act on dissent makes conceptual sense only in the context of an organizational culture that has the general characteristics of the bureaucratic ethic. If the organizational culture rewarded internal critique, and if bosses welcomed and supported contrary views, then neither dissent nor courage would be necessary—a view we develop fully in the final section. At this point, however, it is important to note that it takes courage, often considerable courage, to voice one's dissent in an organizational environment that is hostile to criticism and to expressions of divergent points of view.

Let us consider the greatest threats and fears a dissenter might face in this organizational environment. If we take our cue from what happens to whistleblowers, we see that the risks for the dissenter are immense. Not only are whistleblowers at risk of losing their jobs, they may also encounter cruel retaliation by former employers, who may take steps that make it difficult for them to find work in their own industry—even if they are proven to be right. Whistleblowers often lose their families, their careers, and their savings attempting to defend or to exonerate themselves. Organizational behavior at this point is often purely irrational, indeed pathological.[18] Organizations are intent on protecting their public image at all cost.[19] It should not be surprising, then, that a person who brings unpleasant issues to the forefront is often perceived as a traitor.[20] Those who have threatened the internal workings of the organization or who are perceived to have tarnished its public image are in for an especially hard time. "Confront[ing] . . . an organisation that is judged to be in the wrong because it is off course or will not listen, is dangerous conduct which requires firm conviction, strength of purpose and considerable courage."[21]

Let us examine other dangers the dissenter faces. Because conformity, harmony, and "going along to get along" so often dominate organizational life, dissenters who keep their jobs may face the threat of dismissal or may experience ostracism and isolation within the organization. They may suffer social sanctions from "withholding social privileges to outright social isolation and rejection as a deviant."[22] Dissenters are not appreciated for the contributions they bring to the organization. Instead, their bosses and fellow employees pressure, bully, punish, and marginalize them. In organizations dominated by groupthink, dissenters are pushed to conform to the majority opinion and "certain members take it upon themselves to protect the leader and others from dissenting opinions that might disrupt the group's consensus."[23] In this way, dissenters are coerced to remain silent and are made to feel that the expression of contrary ideas would harm the organization or individuals. A dissenter who speaks out in such environments faces considerable risks.

Because many employees are friends with workmates and even with their bosses, espousing a dissenting position may involve jeopardizing relationships, social standing within a group or a team, or prestige and reputation. In organizational contexts that rely on a veneer of "niceness" and friendliness, violations of the comforts of conformity and harmony are sometimes taken as personal betrayals. The dissenter is thus often alienated from or avoided by colleagues and coworkers. Those who continue to associate with the dissenter may feel that they are at risk for being seen as sympathetic to or in agreement with the dissenter. Those collegial associations that do continue tend to lack their former spontaneity and become awkward and uncomfortable. And in organizations where developing one's social network is important, straining relationships often equates to forfeiting opportunities for advancement. Perceptions that the dissenter is no longer a team player, or worse, that he or she is disloyal, have potentially damaging consequences.

As Cavanagh and Moberg point out, "It often takes courage for a subordinate to deliver unfavorable news to a superior."[24] As we have considered, stating one's dissent requires considerable courage, especially in organizations dominated by the bureaucratic ethic. In such organizations, the manager's protecting his or her image is crucial for survival. Anyone who contradicts, confronts, or corrects a manager threatens that manager. In authoritative organizations, where managers are to be obeyed and not questioned, the dissenter's voice is often interpreted as a challenge to the manager's legitimacy. Thus, the response to the dissenter is often defensive, as if the manager or the organization were being attacked. The dissenter becomes the proverbial messenger who is blamed for delivering unwelcome comments or perceptions, no matter how valid or vital those points of view may be. Unfortunately, managers are often more prone to shoot the dissenting messenger than to take to heart his concerns. Thus, the dissenter faces multiple risks and dangers, from being ignored to being vilified to being terminated. Speaking out involves considerable moral courage.

Transforming Voice

Imagine a workplace that welcomed dissent, celebrated and cultivated critical thinking and seeking alternative solutions, thanked those who pointed out flaws in plans, and continuously solicited fresh ideas. In such an organizational culture an opposing point of view would merely be part of the normal way of doing business; it would be an integral component of everyday collegial conversation. No moral courage would be required because dissent would be expected, invited, and rewarded.

How can an organization create such a culture? In this final section we argue that the courageous voice of dissent always holds out the possibility for organizational transformation. In that moment of recognizing the importance of the dissenter, a manager can restore dignity to employees and honesty to their day-to-day interactions within their organization.[25]

For the dissenter's voice to be transformational, organizational leaders must recognize the courageous dissenter for who she truly is and for the qualities that conscientious dissent embodies. Dissenters are often hardworking, highly motivated, competent, respected, and committed professionals.[26] Their willingness to bring new perspectives to bear on the organization demonstrates critical thinking and analytical skills. These are exactly the attributes so many organizations claim they desire and actively seek in their employees. At a minimum, dissenters should be appreciated and rewarded for these competencies.

But more important is the profoundly ethical orientation that the dissenting voices bring to the organization. Dissenters possess vital ethical capacities, including integrity, loyalty, and courage; they seek to promote and protect the good of the organization and the dignity of its members. They have "higher levels of moral reasoning."[27] Although some dissenters may be naïve about the ways organizations often respond to dissent (and are surprised that they are so negatively treated), they are loyal above all. Were they not so loyal, were they not so interested in the good of the organization, they would have kept silent or merely left. But they did not do either of these—they stayed and spoke out.

Responding appropriately to courageous dissent gives leaders the opportunity to transform their organizations into ones that are more humane, open, and transparent. Ethical organizational leaders understand this because they "strive to create ethical environments even when faced with opposition from their superiors and subordinates."[28] They seek to recognize and defuse defensive routines and to build a community in which assumptions can be suspended so that all members can think and learn together.[29] Thus, to renew or to create anew an attitude of dignity within the organization is the most important ethical goal of management. An ethical organizational culture requires daily and regular recognition of the dignity of all who work within the organization: the recognition of the integrity of individual conscience; a dedication to the development of individual talent; and a celebration of individual contributions. This kind of culture is "appropriate to the human condition and fosters human fulfillment."[30] It incorporates four elements:

1. Recognition of the person in his or her dignity, rights, uniqueness, sociability, and capacity for personal growth.
2. Respect for persons and their human rights.
3. Care and service for persons around one.
4. Management towards the common good versus particular interests.[31]

Why might a manager desire to create a more humane organizational culture? From an ethical perspective, treating employees with dignity would create a culture of respect in which managers and employees could develop honest and open relationships. Everyone's sense of self-worth would increase in an organizational culture that assured and safeguarded employees' ability to be themselves and allowed individual talents and professional capacities to flourish. From a business perspective, an organizational culture of genuine respect and empowerment would enhance employee satisfaction. This would boost productivity, reduce turnover, and ultimately yield more profit.

How might a manager begin the transformation to an organizational culture that has a high regard for dissenters? Suppose that a low-ranking member of a human resources department discovers the department's systematic practice not to consider job applicants who have foreign sounding names, on the grounds that these applicants would have communication problems. Because this practice is unfair and unjust and (consciously or unconsciously) reinforces organizational prejudices, the conscientious dissenter feels compelled to report her concerns to management. First, instead of responding defensively to dissent, management must look at the dissent as an opportunity for improvement. For example, a manager could respond by taking a moment to listen calmly and to treat the dissenter as a valuable member of the organization, as an asset and not a threat. Listening is not a guarantee of agreement, but it is a necessary step to ensure that the person and his views will be taken seriously and considered carefully. Respectful and dignified treatment of a dissenting employee begins with recognizing and responding to his loyalty, honesty, and courage. With these simple gestures, a manager acts reciprocally; that is, responds to the authentic, conscientious voice of the dissenter. The manager has begun to take small concrete steps to create a transformed organizational culture.

Second, the manager should nourish this new respectful relationship. The manager could ask the dissenter to provide more information about his concerns, or to generate solutions or suggestions for changes, or to become a member of an investigatory task force. In addition, the manager could assure the dissenter that his concerns will be voiced to the proper authorities even if he chooses anonymity. Such requests and assurances generate the dissenter's trust and create new responsibilities for the manager. By responding authentically to the dissenter, the manager will also develop morally as the dissenter's courage and initiative inspire her to overcome the organizational pressures that typically foster conformity.

To implement a transparent organizational culture, top managers should encourage all employees to report, orally or in writing, any perceived wrongdoing or concern and share instances of dissent throughout the organization. Dissenters should receive praise or even financial rewards. Managers should invite employees to challenge the prevailing perceptions and present unconventional points of view by establishing—and adhering to—a code of ethics and policies that honor and protect dissenters and forbid retaliation against them. Problems should be solved openly, and communication (especially from subordinate to superior) should be supportive and participative so as to build trust, confidence, credibility, and candor. Management must assure employees that dissent works for the common good of the organization and that voicing dissent is the responsibility of every member of the organization. Organizations can promote dissent by creating procedures to investigate and respond publicly to concerns—and monitoring these procedures. Managers need training that develops their capacity to listen compassionately and respond to contrary and divergent points of view and prepares them to hire and promote, for positions at every organizational level, individuals who think critically and make proactive decisions.[32]

Top managers should reinforce and sustain a culture of openness and honesty by incorporating it into vision statements and handbooks, reaffirming it at public meetings, and implementing it as part of performance and promotion evaluations. Employees and managers should be encouraged to include critical conversations in the daily operation of their organization. In this way, top management will not be issuing empty promises but will be demonstrating genuine commitment.

An organization that values dissent and dissenters does not fear, but instead welcomes, genuine and unconstrained dialogue. As more and more organizational members abandon the habit of silencing their different voices, more productive and authentic relationships will develop. These trusting relationships will, in turn, induce those who spot wrongdoing to report it.[33] Members of humane organizations will be free to speak out on matters of conscience, and their organizational leaders will benefit because they will be able to avoid mistakes and anticipate problems. Dissent will become a normal and critical component of candid day-to-day conversations, and members of organizations will no longer need moral courage to speak out.

Our final suggestion is for an organization to demonstrate that it values dissent by promoting divergent opinions. An organization could, for example, establish a forum in which both sides could enter into dialogue. In engaging in this dialogue, both management and the dissenter must understand that their view is not guaranteed to prevail, although it might. Compromise may be necessary, reasonable, and consistent with both conscientious objections and organizational values. And both sides must consider the possibility that open dialogue may mean that they come to see their original positions as wrong. Both sides must be open to listening, engaging in genuine dialogue, remaining transparent, and providing reasons and evidence for their position. There should be a firm commitment to the process of searching for a sound ethical solution. And both sides need humility. Authentic dialogue does not always yield a mutually satisfactory outcome. Nonetheless, organizations will be well served in following a process that is fair and protects the integrity of both parties.

Such a process will go a long way in creating an ethical culture. However, because management is in the position of power, this process cannot begin until the dissenter is recognized as a vital and valued member of the organization.

Notes

1. *A Few Good Men*, 1992.
2. Jackall, 1988, 4; see Gini, chapter 1 of this book, for further discussion of Jackall's observations.
3. Jackall, 2002, 301.
4. Alford, 2001, 35.
5. Walton, 2001, 119.
6. Johnson, 2009, 238.
7. Schwartz, 1991, 256; see Gini, chapter 1 of this book, for further discussion of Schwartz's ideas.
8. *A Few Good Men*, 1992.
9. Ciulla, 1998, 66–67.
10. Ibid., 68.
11. Ibid.
12. Emphasis in original; Graham, 1986, 2.
13. For a more detailed examination of the distinctions between the devil's advocate, the member of the loyal opposition, and the chronic complainer, see Shahinpoor and Matt, 2006.
14. Cited in Graham, 1986; see Comer and Baker, chapter 13 of this book, for a discussion of collective dissenters in organizations.
15. Melé, 2003, 9.
16. Alford, 2001, 40.
17. Harris, 1999.
18. Alford, 2001; see also, Kohn, chapter 5 of this book.
19. Schwartz, 1991.
20. Scarnati, 1999.
21. Jubb, 1999, 81.
22. Cavanagh and Moberg, 1999, 7.
23. Johnson, 2009, 239.
24. Cavanagh and Moberg, 1999, 3.
25. Rothschild and Miethe, 1994.
26. Ibid.
27. Keenan, 2000, 202.
28. Johnson, 2009, 71.
29. Senge, 1999.
30. Melé, 2003, 4.
31. Ibid., 5.
32. For more details about creating open organizations, see O'Toole and Bennis, 2009; and Tourish and Robson, 2006. See also Miceli, Near, and Dworkin, 2009.
33. King, 1999.

References

Alford, C.F. 2001. *Whistleblowers: Broken lives and organizational power.* Ithaca, NY: Cornell University Press.
Cavanagh, G.F., and Moberg, D.J. 1999. The virtue of courage within the organization. In *Research in ethical issues in organizations*, vol. 1, ed. M.L. Pava and P. Primeaux, 1–25. Stamford, CT: JAI Press.

Ciulla, J.B. 1998. Leadership and the problem of bogus empowerment. In *Ethics, the heart of leadership*, ed. J.B. Ciulla, 63–86. Westport, CT: Praeger.

Comer, D.R., and Baker, S.D. 2011. I defy with a little help from my friends: Raising an organization's ethical bar through a morally courageous coalition. In *Moral courage in organizations: Doing the right thing at work*, ed. D.R. Comer and G. Vega, 171–187. Armonk, NY: M.E. Sharpe.

A Few Good Men. 1992. Directed by Rob Reiner. Columbia Pictures.

Gini, A. 2011. A short primer on moral courage. In *Moral courage in organizations: Doing the right thing at work*, ed. D.R. Comer and G. Vega, 3–12. Armonk, NY: M.E. Sharpe.

Graham, J.W. 1986. Principled organizational dissent: A theoretical essay. *Research in Organizational Behavior* 8, 1–52.

Harris, H. 1999. Courage as a management virtue. *Business and Professional Ethics Journal* 19(3 & 4), 27–46.

Jackall, R. 1988. *Moral mazes: The world of corporate managers*. New York: Oxford University Press.

———. 2002. Moral mazes: Bureaucracy and managerial work. In *Ethical issues in business: A philosophical approach*, ed. T. Donaldson, P. Werhane, and M. Cording, 284–301. Upper Saddle River, NJ: Prentice Hall.

Johnson, C.E. 2009. *Meeting the ethical challenges of leadership: Casting light or shadow*. 3d ed. Los Angeles: Sage.

Jubb, P.B. 1999. Whistleblowing: A restrictive definition and interpretation. *Journal of Business Ethics* 21(1), 77–94.

Keenan, J.P. 2000. Blowing the whistle on less serious forms of fraud: A study of executives and managers. *Employee Rights and Responsibilities Journal* 12(4), 199–217.

King, G., III. 1999. The implications of an organization's structure on whistleblowing. *Journal of Business Ethics* 20(4), 315–326.

Kohn, S.M. 2011. For the greater good: The moral courage of whistleblowers. In *Moral courage in organizations: Doing the right thing at work*, ed. D.R. Comer and G. Vega, 60–74. Armonk, NY: M.E. Sharpe.

Melé, D. 2003. Organizational humanizing cultures: Do they generate social capital? *Journal of Business Ethics* 45(1–2), 3–14.

Miceli, M.P., Near, J.P., and Dworkin, T.M. 2009. A word to the wise: How managers and policy-makers can encourage employees to report wrongdoing. *Journal of Business Ethics* 86(3), 379–396.

O'Toole, J., and Bennis, W. 2009. What's needed next: A culture of candor. *Harvard Business Review* 87(6), 54–61.

Rothschild, J., and Miethe, T.D. 1994. Whistleblowing as resistance in modern work organizations: The politics of revealing organizational deception and abuse. In *Resistance and power in organizations*, ed. J.M. Jermier, D. Knights, and W.R. Nord, 252–273. London: Routledge.

Scarnati, J.T. 1999. Beyond technical competence: The art of leadership. *Career Development International* 4(6), 325–335.

Schwartz, H.S. 1991. Narcissism project and corporate decay: The case of General Motors. *Business Ethics Quarterly* 1(3), 249–268.

Senge, P.M. 1999. The leader's new work: Building learning organizations. In *Ethical issues in business: A philosophical approach*, ed. T. Donaldson and P.H. Werhane, 497–518. Upper Saddle River, NJ: Prentice Hall.

Shahinpoor, N., and Matt, B.F. 2006. The power of one: Dissent and organizational life. *Journal of Business Ethics* 74(1), 37–48.

Tourish, D., and Robson, P. 2006. Sensemaking and the distortion of critical upward communication in organizations. *Journal of Management Studies* 43(4), 711–730.

Walton, C. 2001. Character and integrity in organizations: The civilization of the workplace. *Business and Professional Ethics Journal* 20(3 & 4), 105–128.

13

I Defy with a Little Help from My Friends

Raising an Organization's Ethical Bar Through a Morally Courageous Coalition

DEBRA R. COMER AND SUSAN D. BAKER

> *Never doubt that a small group of thoughtful, committed citizens can change the world. Indeed, it is the only thing that ever has.*
>
> —Margaret Mead[1]

> *If engineers agree that they will not submit to pressure to write dishonest reports and then stick with that agreement, employers will not be able to increase the pressure by saying, in effect, "If you don't, I'll get somebody who will." Hence honest engineers will not be penalized. If no such agreement is in force, even an honest engineer may well consider it futile to resist the pressure and therefore not do so.*
>
> —Edwin M. Hartman[2]

Many people lament that an organization without ethical leadership cannot be an ethical place and that any attempt to change the status quo would be pointless. Yet, the pair of quotes above suggests that collective action can promote ethical behavior in an organization. "Moral courage is often lonely courage,"[3] but there is strength in numbers, and people can tackle ethical problems in their organizations by working together. When they recognize that they are not alone, they see the possibility of change and refuse to tolerate morally problematic conduct. In this chapter we explore how a group of right-minded individuals can collaborate to raise their company's ethical bar. We begin by answering this question: How can a few people who would like to do the right thing persuade others in their organization to join them in a morally courageous coalition? After considering how employees often respond to wrongdoing in their organizations, we glean lessons from organizational culture change, social movements, and ethical leaders and role models to offer practical advice for those seeking to effect bottom-up change to make their organization more ethical.

The Response to Wrongdoing in the Workplace

Barbara, a new cashier in a retail store, noticed her supervisor's habit of making bigoted comments about customers from certain demographic groups and treating them rudely. Barbara cringed every time she had to listen to her supervisor, but she could not bring herself to do anything about his remarks.

At shift change in a convenience store, the clerk closing for the evening shift was counting money. As Janelle restocked shelves, she noticed that the clerk was placing only some of the money in the store's safe—and pocketing the rest. Not wanting to believe what she was seeing, Janelle moved to another work area to distance herself from the theft. The next day, when the store manager was upset about the $100 missing from the safe's daily receipts, Janelle reluctantly came forward to describe what she had witnessed.

An electronics retailer employed teenagers after school and during the summers. Whenever monthly sales goals were met, the division manager threw congratulatory parties at which alcohol was served to all employees, even those younger than legal drinking age. Jamal expressed concern to his senior managers, who laughed dismissively and told him, "Loosen up! Everyone gets to celebrate."

Dan, a student working the late shift at a fast-food restaurant, felt uncomfortable because the shift manager, ignoring the sexual harassment policy in the company's handbook, frequently commented on female employees' appearance. Dan's coworkers, Rita and Jasmine, confided in him that they disliked the suggestive remarks, planned on quitting, and were telling their friends not to apply for vacant positions there. After graduation, Dan landed a job at a respected design firm. He noticed that this company's handbook had no sexual harassment policy and worried what would happen should harassment occur, but decided that there was nothing he could do.

All of these situations involve employees who observed unethical behavior at their workplace. At times, as in the example involving Barbara, the new cashier, a person spots wrongdoing but does not report it to anyone. Or, in the case of Janelle, the convenience store employee, a person may report wrongdoing only after someone else is already aware of it. Sometimes, as in the scenario about underage drinking at Jamal's company or the one about sexual harassment at the fast-food restaurant where Dan worked, those in authority see wrongdoing and condone it or are the ones committing the act, leaving a concerned employee wondering what to do. And at other times, as in the case of the design firm that had not drafted a sexual harassment policy, a well-intentioned employee, Dan, wants to protect his company from ethical pitfalls, but ends up doing nothing. Indeed, even though organizations in the private, public, and nonprofit sectors have poured resources into compliance programs and ethics training for employees, alarming numbers of employees still do not report the ethical violations they witness.[4] Why? The two main reasons that employees remain silent about the unethical behavior they observe in the workplace are (1) they do not believe reporting misconduct to their managers would make a difference, and (2) they fear retaliation by management.[5]

Making the Workplace More Ethical Requires Organizational Change

The Challenge of Organizational Change

Can an unethical organization become more ethical? Many employees see no point in reporting or trying by other means to eliminate the unethical behavior entrenched in their organizations. Organizational change requires effort, persistence, follow-through, and follow-up. Inertia, fear, and laziness are common obstacles, as even those in favor of change may resign themselves to living with suboptimal circumstances because of the anticipated difficulty and unknown outcome of doing something new. Even greater resistance comes from those who stand to lose advantages that current conditions confer.[6] Real change requires that people leave their comfort zone and put collective interests before self-interests.[7]

Warren Buffet's leadership at Salomon Brothers in the early 1990s provides a compelling and encouraging account of the possibility of truly transforming an organization's culture to a more ethical one and assures us that "an unethical culture need not be permanent."[8] Buffet cooperated fully with the authorities in the wake of the bond trading scandal involving Salomon's former CEO and chair. In his capacity as new CEO and chair, he restored the company's tarnished reputation by overhauling its leadership, policies, structures, behavior, and beliefs. He behaved ethically himself, focused his employees' attention on the ethical implications of their behavior, rewarded ethical deeds, and fired miscreants. The events that transpired at Salomon Brothers show how the discovery of an organization's transgression can serve as a catalyst for change.[9] When crisis underscores the need to abandon past practices, employees and other stakeholders clamor for rehabilitation. They look for "changes in management, in reward structures, and in codes of conduct . . . [as signs that] the organization is determined to purge negative influences and focus its energy on renewal."[10]

But instead of waiting until their organization crashes, shouldn't employees promote change that would prevent such disgrace? And must these would-be agents of change inhabit the executive suite? What happens when individuals seek to make their organization more ethical by opposing the immoral behavior of their superiors? The mantra of organizational change guru John Kotter is that change will not happen unless the highest echelon of management leads or, at the very least, deeply supports it.[11] Indeed, those seeking to initiate bottom-up change to make their organization more ethical receive sobering advice: they are warned to become marketable—in case they lose their jobs.[12]

Why is organizational change, and bottom-up change in particular, so arduous? Systems and practices persist in organizations not necessarily because they are functional but because they are ingrained.[13] Organizational transformation therefore "requires changing structures, understandings, and beliefs that have long been taken for granted as normal, neutral, and legitimate."[14] Furthermore, those most likely to perceive a need for change are not those most advantaged by existing arrangements.[15] The former need to contend with the latter, who will want to preserve their comfortable position.[16] Ideas and examples from social movements can shed light on how bottom-up change can happen.

Collective Action in Organizations

More than thirty years ago, scholars recognized that the lessons of social movements could inform change within organizations.[17] But there was—and continues to be—a lack of attention to the potential of intra-organizational coalitions. A coalition is a group formed apart from the formal structure of its members' organization in order to achieve a common goal through shared action; "coalitions form because they allow their members to exert more influence than they could as independent individuals."[18] There is strength in unity, and collective action can be an effective path to ethical organizational transformation.[19] Consider the example of the engineers mentioned at the beginning of this chapter: if all the engineers stand together, none of them will have to behave dishonestly; nobody will be penalized; and principled behavior will prevail. If just one or two good apples can envision a more ethical organization and inspire like-minded colleagues to collaborate with them in the quest to achieve that vision, they can change their organization.

Morally Courageous Coalitions

Many people do nothing when they observe misbehavior in their workplaces. They believe that speaking up and taking action would, at best, be useless and, could, at worst, result in retaliation against them. But others *do* step up to try to make a change. Upward dissent in organizations is "one mechanism by which employees can offer corrective feedback about troubling or flawed organizational policies and practices."[20] The "principled organizational dissenter" calls for the organization in which he or she works to put an end to moral improprieties.[21] Typically, this person works alone and does not participate in designing or implementing the desired changes.[22] In contrast, we focus here on principled dissenters who work collectively and aspire not only to draw to attention to, but also to fix, the problems they identify in their organizations. These dissenters unite with others in a morally courageous coalition to strive to change situations. Rather than merely grabbing the bullhorn to report problems, coalition members take the bull by the horns to help solve problems.[23]

Leadership of Morally Courageous Coalitions

How do like-minded dissenters come together in a morally courageous coalition to achieve their common goal? They join forces behind a leader, someone who envisions a better future—and then articulates that vision in a way that arouses others to help implement it.[24] Even in a collective, there is usually one person who forms the group or emerges later as a leader. Key leadership behaviors include "providing motivation, building . . . commitment . . . , and articulating a vision that draws an emotional and enthusiastic response; and . . . plotting a movement strategy and assembling the resources and assigning responsibilities to see that strategy carried out."[25] Because the coalition is attempting to undo inveterate patterns, it must have enough members to accomplish the task.[26] But because quality of membership matters as well as quantity, leaders need to tap into their networks to find members who can provide information, knowledge, and influence to facilitate goal accomplishment.[27] A leader attracts followers by stirring emotions "that may stimulate them to acts of courage."[28] Leaders of coalitions must "establish their credibility to potential followers" in order to convince them that their coalition is worth joining.[29]

- During World War II, German soldiers killed tens of thousands of Jews in western Belorussia and confined others to ghettos. A Jewish resistance group that came to be known as the Bielski partisans chose to reclaim their dignity by refusing either to live in the ghetto or to perish in the death camps; instead, they escaped to the Belorussian forests and encouraged others to join them. Between 1942 and 1944, the entrepreneurial and politically savvy Tuvia Bielski led his brothers and trusted entourage to create a community within the forest that ultimately saved more than 1,200 Jewish lives. Whereas other partisan groups accepted only those who could fight and pull their weight, Bielski welcomed all Jews—including the elderly, young children, and those with no particular survival skills.[30]

- Another charismatic leader was Harvey Milk, the first openly gay man to hold public office in the United States. Famous for opening his speeches with "My name is Harvey Milk, and I'm here to recruit you,"[31] this businessman-turned-grassroots-activist organized the members of the gay community in San Francisco in the mid-1970s by inspiring them to join the fight for their civil rights. In the words of Milk's campaign manager, "What set Harvey apart from you or me was that he was a visionary. He imagined a righteous world inside his head and then he set about to create it for real, for all of us."[32] According to his successor on the San Francisco Board of Supervisors, Harvey Milk gave others the hope "to envision new possibilities . . . and create a different future."[33]
- A third change agent who reshaped her world by building a morally courageous coalition is Liberian Leymah Gbowee. As a parent and a social worker, Gbowee saw the harsh effects of the Liberian civil war on her own children and on the traumatized former boy soldiers exploited by both dictator Charles Taylor and the civilian warlords who fought him for control of Liberia.[34] In 2001, she asked the women at her church to join her in expressing moral outrage through prayer vigils, sit-ins, and peace marches.[35] Within two years, her Christian coalition had enlisted the support of Muslim women in opposition to the war. Her nonviolent coalition attracted international attention and forced Taylor and the warlords to enter into peace negotiations. The coalition's persistence eventually awoke the consciences of many Liberians and drove Taylor into exile in 2003.[36]

Although Bielski, Milk, and Gbowee operated in different times and places, all of them led coalitions by articulating inspirational visions that gained the support and commitment of followers.

Morally Courageous Coalitions in Organizations

Bielski, Milk, and Gbowee led groups that operated outside the powerful systems they opposed. Those seeking to effect change as organizational insiders have unique challenges as they seek to dismantle current policies and practices. To raise their organization's ethical bar, members of a morally courageous coalition must be mindful of the political feasibility of their proposed actions and be sure to secure support for their ideas.[37] Those at the top are likely to resist if "their immediate interests [are] well served by existing power relations and patterns of resource allocation."[38] It is therefore important for coalition members to have an ally who strongly identifies with their goal of change and has a position sufficiently high in the hierarchy. Such an individual is well situated to appeal to the moral values of organizational decision makers whose cooperation is needed to fix the problem.[39]

As we have mentioned, any modification of the status quo that threatens the privileged place of the elite can be a hard sell. Consequently, it is essential to tie the desired change to a goal that appears nonradical—and therefore minimally threatening—to those who would otherwise object.[40] Even if senior managers cannot appreciate the intrinsic value of making their organization more ethical, it may still be possible to convince them of the instrumental benefits by portraying movement toward a more principled organization as a means to help the organization's bottom line.[41] If an organization considers itself progressive or dedicated to continuous improvement, change-seekers can tie their proposal to such avowed commitment. For example, employees who want their company to "go green" to protect the planet may demonstrate that Earth-friendly processes would facilitate the company's achievement of strategic goals.[42] By the same token, a coalition may persuade budget-conscious managers to raise workers' low wages by explaining that fair compensation would reduce the costs of employee theft.[43] Members of a morally courageous coalition can also legitimize their goals to senior management by pointing out that successful industry rivals have already implemented these goals or that achieving the goals would comply with standards set by professional organizations or funding agencies. After Starbucks became a pioneer by offering health insurance to part-time employees, other retailers followed suit.[44] Likewise, an initiative to promote gender equity at the University of Michigan succeeded in large part because it was sponsored and funded by the respected National Science Foundation (NSF), which had spearheaded a similar nationwide program.[45]

Building a Coalition to Implement Ethical Change

There is widespread agreement that leaders in top management positions set the ethical tone for their organization and play a major role in shaping their organization's ethical culture and standards.[46] In contrast, less is known about individuals at lower levels who initiate action to raise their organizations' ethical bar. Yet, employees are more likely to find ethical role models in their immediate supervisors and peers than in their CEOs and top managers.[47] After all, they interact more regularly with supervisors and peers, who influence them informally "below the organizational radar."[48] Lower-level employees whose exemplary behavior earns the respect of their colleagues can orchestrate bottom-up change in their organizations by persuading others to follow their lead. But before those who seek ethical change branch out to connect with like-minded coworkers, they need to do some groundwork by themselves. Then, after careful contemplation, observation, and preparation, they can proceed to recruit others to join them. We now offer you specific steps for building a morally courageous coalition in your organization.[49]

Contemplation, Observation, and Preparation: Getting Your Act Together Before Asking Others to Act with You

Contemplation

First, identify the issue you are facing: Have you observed unethical behavior (your supervisor bullies or harasses others) or practices (salespeople accept expensive gifts or bribes from vendors, customers, or contractors) that you want to eliminate? Is there an unfair policy in your organization that you seek to change (domestic partners are denied health benefits)? Or do you have an idea for a new practice or policy that could enhance your organization's ethical health (the organization could emphasize ethics role-playing in its already existing mentoring program for new employees)?

Next, carefully examine your own feelings about what to do. What possible actions might you take? What would be the ideal outcome? Reviewing the values you learned as a child from your parents, other close family members, guardians, or teachers is a good starting point. But that alone is insufficient because your early-childhood role models may not have modeled workplace behaviors.[50] Consider, then, ethical individuals you have admired in your work environment: what would they advise you to do? As you reflect on this question, you may also want to think about the consequences of *not* acting. If you had to explain to your closest relatives, friends, or colleagues why you had not acted in this situation, could you do so proudly? Would you want others to act as you did in the same circumstances?

Observation

After your initial self-exploration, your next step is an assessment of the likely consequences of your possible actions. To develop a realistic appraisal of your organization's response to your ideal outcome and the challenges you may encounter, pay attention to top managers and supervisors. By observing how they act themselves and how they reward or discipline your coworkers for their ethical or unethical acts, you will learn what is acceptable and unacceptable in your organization.[51]

Preparation

After identifying the issue and desired outcomes, exploring your own ethical feelings and possible actions, and then assessing your organization's ethical culture, your next step is to identify available recourses and resources. Before you can bring others on board, you will have to convince them that your goal is attainable and that you are prepared and not naïvely optimistic. Be sure to check your organization's written code of conduct, the employee handbook, and your industry's professional ethical code. Any or all of these may contain a relevant policy statement or guideline that could validate the change you propose by linking it to sanctioned behavior.[52] But because decision making in organizations depends as much on politics as on logic,[53] it is also important to secure the help of key individuals, such as a sympathetic supervisor in another area of your organization or a senior manager who supports your viewpoint. As noted earlier, it is invaluable to secure the endorsement of like-minded allies whose status within the organizational hierarchy establishes their credibility and gives them access to those with the formal power to change your organization's culture.[54] Other important allies can be external stakeholders whose opinions command the attention of your senior management. In 1994, for example, Exxon Mobil responded to activists' concerns about the social and political risks of its Chad-Cameroon project by asking the World Bank to assess the project's impact on indigenous communities. The World Bank's solutions satisfied Exxon and activists.[55]

After identifying the resources you have, determine what you still need. For example, is there a potential senior ally whom you do not know personally? Make it a priority to recruit a new coalition member who knows this potential ally. Perhaps you have a friend or acquaintance in the organization, someone for whom you have done a favor in the past, who could connect you to this person. Alternatively, recognize that someone in your coalition will have to enlist this senior ally. Then, as a last preparatory step, outline and rehearse your thoughts and practice what you want to say to others you would like to recruit for your coalition. It is not necessary to work out every detail before consulting others; in fact, soliciting the viewpoints of other coalition members as to what to do and how to do it can yield better solutions and increase members' commitment to the coalition and the shared goal.[56]

Enlisting the Support of Others to Build a Coalition

What can you say to persuade coworkers to join you in working toward a more ethical organization? Remember, first, that you are trying to recruit those you know—or suspect may—have concerns similar to your own. Still, in order to spur them to take action, you must frame the issue in a way that pulls them away from the sidelines and into your coalition.[57] You need to direct their attention to a specific problem, guide them to come up with concrete steps for fixing the problem, and motivate them to take part in fixing it. An individual will participate in collective action to the extent that he or she perceives a moral problem, wants to express moral dissatisfaction, and believes that collective action will be effective.[58] Therefore, the content of your discussion needs to be an appeal to prospective members' emotions and values, as well as their sense of reason.[59] Describe the current situation in terms that emphasize the injustice of the status quo and the benefits they would personally reap from changing it. Tell prospective members how they could contribute to the coalition. Assure them that collective effort can succeed to solve the problem by making the proposed change seem less radical and thus more doable,[60] breaking down the proposed change into manageable goals and tasks, and demonstrating your awareness of the organization's political constraints and opportunities.

Strive to anticipate the perspective of each potential coalition member so that you can shape your message to fit that person. Imagine how to align his or her ambitions with your goal. When you approach someone, be sure that you have a private distraction-free setting and block of time. Begin with a quick attention-grabber that focuses the person on what you want to say:[61] a concise statement of what you want to accomplish (along the lines of "I'm Harvey Milk, and I'm here to recruit you!"); an alarming statistic ("Our department's accident rate has increased 25 percent in the past six months!"); a question that requires your colleague to recognize an issue whose seriousness he or she has not yet considered ("How would you feel if the company denied health benefits for your dependents?"); or a picture of the desired results ("Can you imagine how great it would be not to have to worry that someone might find out that our boss is taking kickbacks—and then jump to the conclusion that you and I are doing the same thing?").

Remind your colleague of the long-term benefits that you seek (that is, a more ethical organization) and of any short-term benefits that may accrue,[62] such as the pride of doing the right thing, the personal satisfaction of working with colleagues to achieve a goal, and the political advantage of expanding one's network. Illustrate your ideas with vivid personal experiences or stories. Heed the adage "A picture is worth a thousand words" by developing one striking, easily visualized image that expresses your goal.[63] This shared image creates a common bond and unity of purpose for coalition members—and a shortcut to understanding the end results you all seek.

Build rapport, reinforce your verbal message, and convey hope. Keep your colleague engaged in the discussion by providing your undivided attention, asking for his or her opinions, and listening actively to what he or she would like to accomplish. Check that you understand what your colleague has said by paraphrasing his or her comments.[64] As you try to recruit others into your coalition, be careful not to seem self-righteous. Do not cause others to feel as though you are putting them down for not stepping up to the plate as soon as you have.[65] Instead, welcome them by emphasizing that they, too, can take the higher ground and make a difference. End your conversation by asking for your colleagues' support and agreement to take specific actions, such as identifying and meeting with like-minded colleagues within a week's time or inviting them to a larger discussion.

You have spoken with others about your moral concerns and given them an assessment of your organization's ethical culture and the resources available to help you address these concerns. You have thereby encouraged those who share your feelings, but were reluctant to act on them, to join your coalition and shoulder some of the work. As your coalition grows and you are no longer alone, you can point to the progress you have already made to keep coalition members motivated and maintain the momentum to focus on and achieve long-term goals.

At this point all of the coalition members should collectively fine-tune the plan to address the issue. Tasks should be assigned according to competencies—and you may or may not want to continue your role as leader. Remember that it is essential to arrange to connect with a senior-level person in your organization who supports your goal and to have this person schedule a meeting with organizational decision makers. Because employees who have solid relationships with their superiors feel freer to express risky information,[66] it makes sense for coalition members who are well connected to ("tight with") key members of senior management to be the group's spokespersons. Use the collective strengths of your coalition members to achieve your common goal.

Conclusion

Unethical behavior persists in organizations when employees believe there is nothing they can do about it. Although the endeavors of one individual acting alone may not be enough to undo entrenched workplace misconduct, the collective efforts of the members of a morally courageous coalition can change their organization. In this chapter, we have recommended that coalitions gain political support and legitimacy for their ideas and position their proposed changes in a way that is least threatening to top management. We have also provided concrete suggestions for building a morally courageous coalition. We hope these ideas will inspire and equip you to join with right-minded colleagues to make your organization more ethical.

Notes

1. This quote has been attributed to Margaret Mead.
2. Hartman, 1996, 76.
3. Miller, 2000, 255.
4. Of the well over half of private-sector, nonprofit, and government employees who asserted that they had witnessed misconduct at their workplace within the past year, an average of 30–40 percent did not report the wrongdoing that they observed (private- and nonprofit-sector respondents had 42 and 38 percent nonreport rates, respectively, while government-sector respondents had 30 percent nonreport rates); Ethics Resource Center, 2008a, 2008b, and 2008c.
5. Ethics Resource Center, 2008a and 2008b; see also Kohn, in chapter 5 of this book.
6. Campbell, 2005.
7. Quinn, 2004.
8. Sims, 2000, 75.
9. Sims, 2009, also describes how ethical scandals can prompt corporate leaders to focus on creating a values-driven culture.
10. Pfarrer et al., 2008, 739.
11. Kotter, 1996; Kotter and Rathgeber, 2002.
12. Uhl-Bien and Carsten, 2007.
13. DiMaggio and Powell, 1983; Meyer and Rowan, 1977.
14. Meyerson and Tompkins, 2007, 306.
15. Meyerson and Tompkins, 2007.
16. Misangyi, Weaver, and Elms, 2008.
17. Zald and Berger, 1978. Davis et al., 2005, explored subsequent research on the intersection between social movements and organizations.
18. Stevenson, Pearce, and Porter, 1985, 262. Bruxelles and Kerbrat-Orecchioni, 2004, likewise define a coalition as a temporary group of allies united against another party to achieve their common objective.
19. As Meyerson and Tompkins, 2007, comment: "The possibility of group as institutional change agent suggests intriguing possibilities for the design of change and points to an important topic for future research to address in greater depth" (322). It is telling that the term "change agent," used to denote the person in an organization most responsible for championing and implementing change, appears nearly exclusively as a singular noun. We do not hear or read about "change agents" at an organization. Even though a collective may have a leader, this single individual cannot do everything alone; the power of the group lies in the mutual association of like-minded change-seekers.
20. Kassing, 2009, 434.
21. Graham, 1986; see also Matt and Shahinpoor in chapter 12 of this book.
22. Graham, 1986.
23. Garner, 2009, reported that some organizational dissenters find allies and propose possible solutions to the problems they have identified. Our morally courageous coalitions both initiate and contribute to the implementation of change, as do the institutional entrepreneurs described by Battilana, Leca, and Boxenbaum, 2009.
24. Bass, 1990; Battilana, Leca, and Boxenbaum, 2009; Kouzes and Posner, 2002.
25. Aminzade, Goldstone, and Perry, 2001; also see Campbell, 2005.

26. Having a critical mass ensures that the coalition's collective output will be sufficient, and thus boosts morale by giving members hope that they can succeed. Nelson, 2009, documented the activities of the Red Orchestra (*Rote Kapelle*), a resistance network that tried to thwart Hitler's fascist regime. Tragically, the group was too small, and many members ultimately lost their lives.

27. Gabbay and Leenders, 2001; Knoke, 2009.

28. Jablin, 2006, 107; also see Burns, 1978.

29. Einwohner, 2007, 1310.

30. Tec, 1993.

31. Shilts, 1982.

32. Kronenberg, 2002, 37.

33. Britt, 2002, 80.

34. Tate, 2004, documented the extensive use of child soldiers in the Liberian civil war.

35. Moyers, 2009.

36. Conley, 2008; Moyers, 2009. Also see the documentary, *Pray the Devil Back to Hell.*

37. Campbell, 2005; Misangyi, Weaver, and Elms, 2008.

38. Agócs, 1997, 925.

39. Meyerson and Tompkins, 2007.

40. Scully and Creed, 2005.

41. Thomas, 1991, recognized that few companies would embrace demographic diversity as a moral good, but that many would learn to accept diversity for economic reasons.

42. For a counterpoint on undertaking green management for strategic versus moral reasons, see, respectively, Siegel, 2009, and Marcus and Fremeth, 2009.

43. Alstete, 2006; Niehoff and Paul, 2000.

44. Michelli, 2007; DiMaggio and Powell, 1983, discussed intra-organizational mimicry.

45. Meyerson and Tompkins, 2007.

46. Andreoli and Lefkowitz, 2009; Brown and Treviño, 2006; Schminke, Ambrose, and Neubaum, 2005; Sims and Brinkmann, 2002; Treviño, Brown, and Hartman, 2003.

47. Weaver, Treviño, and Agle, 2005.

48. Ibid., 328.

49. These suggestions draw on current theory and research about organizational culture change, social movements, and ethical leaders and role models, as well as organizational communication.

50. Brown and Treviño, 2006.

51. Brown and Treviño, 2006; Sims and Brinkmann, 2002.

52. Likewise, in chapter 2 of this book, Callahan tells Comer that employees can use professional codes and standards to justify their ethical decisions.

53. Bolman and Deal, 2008.

54. Strang and Jung, 2005, note that change-seekers who cannot obtain institutional support become frustrated and spent.

55. Battilana, Leca, and Boxenbaum, 2009.

56. Maier, 1967; Watson, Michaelsen, and Sharp, 1991.

57. Campbell, 2005.

58. Klandermans, 2003; Misangyi, Weaver, and Elms, 2008. Whereas Gandhi and King encouraged people to do the right thing regardless of the outcome, for the very

reason that it is the right thing, few members of organizations are willing to struggle without decent odds of succeeding.

59. Campbell, 2005; Hornsey et al., 2006; Misangyi, Weaver, and Elms, 2008.

60. Battilana, Leca, and Boxenbaum, 2009.

61. Munter, 2006.

62. Veech, 2002.

63. Ibid.

64. Ober, 2001.

65. Those who display unusually virtuous behavior may incur the resentment of others; see Monin, Sawyer, and Marquez, 2008; and Treviño and Victor, 1992.

66. Botero and Van Dyne, 2009.

References

Agócs, C. 1997. Institutionalized resistance to organizational change: Denial, inaction and repression. *Journal of Business Ethics* 16(9), 917–931.

Alstete, J. 2006. Inside advice on educating managers for preventing employee theft. *International Journal of Retail and Distribution Management* 34(11), 833–844.

Aminzade, R.R., Goldstone, J.A., and Perry, E.J. 2001. Leadership dynamics and dynamics of contention. In *Silence and voice in the study of contentious politics,* ed. R.R. Aminzade, J.A. Goldstone, D. McAdam, E.J. Perry, W.H. Sewell, S. Tarrow, and C. Tilley, 126–154. Cambridge: Cambridge University Press.

Andreoli, N., and Lefkowitz, J. 2009. Individual and organizational antecedents of misconduct in organizations. *Journal of Business Ethics* 85(3), 309–332.

Bass, B.M. 1990. From transactional to transformational leadership: Learning to share the vision. *Organizational Dynamics* 18(3), 19–36.

Battilana, J., Leca, B., and Boxenbaum, E. 2009. How actors change institutions: Towards a theory of institutional entrepreneurship. *Academy of Management Annals* 3(1), 65–107.

Bolman, L.G., and Deal, T.E. 2008. *Reframing organizations: Artistry, choice, and leadership.* New York: John Wiley & Sons.

Botero, I.C., and Van Dyne, L. 2009. Employee voice behavior: Interactive effects of LMX and power distance in the United States and Colombia. *Management Communication Quarterly* 23(1), 84–104.

Britt, H. 2002. Harvey Milk as I knew him. In *Out in the Castro: Desire, promise, activism,* ed. W. Leyland, 78–81. San Francisco, CA: Leyland Publications.

Brown, M.E., and Treviño, L.K. 2006. Ethical leadership: A review and future directions. *Leadership Quarterly* 17(6), 595–616.

Bruxelles, S., and Kerbrat-Orecchioni, C. 2004. Coalitions in polylogues. *Journal of Pragmatics* 36(1), 75–113.

Burns, J.M. 1978. *Leadership.* New York: Harper and Row.

Callahan, D., and Comer, D.R. 2011. "But everybody's doing it": Implications of the cheating culture for moral courage in organizations. In *Moral courage in organizations: Doing the right thing at work,* ed. D.R. Comer and G. Vega, 13–24. Armonk, NY: M.E. Sharpe.

Campbell, J.L. 2005. Where do we stand? Common mechanisms in organizations and social movements research. In *Social movements and organization theory,* ed. G.F. Davis, D. McAdam, W.R. Scott, and M.N. Zald, 41–68. New York: Cambridge University Press.

Conley, K. 2008. The rabble rousers. *O, The Oprah Magazine*, November 18. www.oprah.com/article/omagazine/200812_omag_liberia (accessed Aug. 12, 2009).

Davis, G.F., McAdam, D., Scott, W.R., and Zald, M.N., eds. 2005. *Social movements and organization theory.* New York: Cambridge University Press.

DiMaggio, P.J., and Powell, W.W. 1983. The iron cage revisited: Institutional isomorphism and collective rationality in organizational fields. *American Sociological Review* 48(2), 147–160.

Einwohner, R.L. 2007. Leadership, authority, and collective action. *American Behavioral Scientist* 50(10), 1306–1326.

Ethics Resource Center. 2008a. National Business Ethics Survey®: An inside view of private sector ethics. Arlington, VA: Ethics Resource Center.

———. 2008b. National Government Ethics Survey®: An inside view of public sector ethics. Arlington, VA: Ethics Resource Center.

———. 2008c. National Nonprofit Ethics Survey®: An inside view of nonprofit sector ethics. Arlington, VA: Ethics Resource Center.

Gabbay, S.M., and Leenders, R.T.A.J. 2001. Social capital of organizations: From social structure to the management of corporate social capital. *Research in the Sociology of Organizations* 18, 1–20.

Garner, J.T. 2009. When things go wrong at work: An exploration of organizational dissent messages. *Communication Studies* 60(2), 197–218.

Graham, J.W. 1986. Principled organizational dissent: A theoretical essay. *Research in Organizational Behavior* 8, 1–52.

Hartman, E. 1996. Organizational ethics and the good life. New York: Oxford.

Hornsey, M.J., Mavor, K., Morton, T., O'Brien, A., Paasonen, K-E., Smith, J., and White, K.M. 2006. Why do people engage in collective action? Revisiting the role of perceived effectiveness. *Journal of Applied Social Psychology* 36(7), 1701–1722.

Jablin, F.M. 2006. Courage and courageous communication among leaders and followers in groups, organizations, and communities. *Management Communication Quarterly* 20(1), 94–110.

Kassing, J.W. 2009. "In case you didn't hear me the first time": An examination of repetitious upward dissent. *Management Communication Quarterly* 22(3), 416–436.

Klandermans, B. 2003. Collective political action. In *Oxford handbook of political psychology,* ed. D.O. Sears, L. Huddy, and R. Jervis, 670–709. New York: Oxford University Press.

Knoke, D. 2009. Playing well together: Creating corporate social capital in strategic alliance networks. *American Behavioral Scientist* 52(12), 1690–1708.

Kohn, S.M. 2011. For the greater good: The moral courage of whistleblowers. In *Moral courage in organizations: Doing the right thing at work,* ed. D.R. Comer and G. Vega, 60–74. Armonk, NY: M.E. Sharpe.

Kotter, J.P. 1996. *Leading change.* Boston: Harvard Business School Press.

Kotter, J.P., and Rathgeber, H. 2002. *Our iceberg is melting: Changing and succeeding under any conditions.* New York: St. Martin's Press.

Kouzes, J.M., and Posner, B. Z. 2002. *The leadership challenge* (3d ed.). San Francisco: Jossey-Bass.

Kronenberg, A. 2002. Everybody needed milk. In *Out in the Castro: Desire, promise, activism,* ed. W. Leyland, 37–43. San Francisco: Leyland Publications.

Maier, N.R.F. 1967. Assets and liabilities in group problem solving: The need for an integrative function. *Psychological Review* 74(4), 239–249.

Marcus, A.A., and Fremeth, A.R. 2009. Green management matters regardless. *Academy of Management Perspectives* 23(3), 17–26.

Matt, B.F., and Shahinpoor, N. 2011. Speaking truth to power: The courageous organizational dissenter. In *Moral courage in organizations: Doing the right thing at work*, ed. D.R. Comer and G. Vega, 157–170. Armonk, NY: M.E. Sharpe.

Meyer, J.W., and Rowan, B. 1977. Institutionalized organizations: Formalized structure as myth and ceremony. *American Journal of Sociology* 83(2), 340–363.

Meyerson, D., and Tompkins, M. 2007. Tempered radicals as institutional change agents: The case of advancing gender equity at the University of Michigan. *Harvard Journal of Law and Gender* 30, 303–322.

Michelli, J.A. 2007. *The Starbucks experience: 5 principles for turning ordinary into extraordinary*. New York: McGraw-Hill.

Miller, W.I. 2000. *The mystery of courage*. Cambridge, MA: Harvard University Press.

Misangyi, V.F., Weaver, G.R., and Elms, H. 2008. Ending corruption: The interplay among institutional logics, resources, and institutional entrepreneurs. *Academy of Management Review* 33(3), 750–770.

Monin, B., Sawyer, P.J., and Marquez, M.J. 2008. The rejection of moral rebels: Resenting those who do the right thing. *Journal of Personality and Social Psychology* 95(1), 76–93.

Moyers, B. 2009. Transcript. *Bill Moyers Journal*, June 19. www.pbs.org/moyers/journal/06192009/transcript1.html (accessed August 12, 2009).

Munter, R. 2006. *Guide to managerial communication: Effective business writing and speaking* (7th ed.). Upper Saddle River, NJ: Pearson Prentice Hall.

Nelson, A. 2009. *Red orchestra: The story of the Berlin underground and the circle of friends who resisted Hitler*. New York: Random House.

Niehoff, B.P., and Paul, R.J. 2000. Causes of employee theft and strategies HR managers can use for prevention. *Human Resource Management* 39(1), 51–64.

Ober, S. 2001. *Contemporary business communication*. Boston: Houghton Mifflin.

Pfarrer, M.D., Decelles, K.A., Smith, K.G., and Taylor, M.S. 2008. After the fall: Reintegrating the corrupt organization. *Academy of Management Review* 33(1), 730–749.

Pray the devil back to hell. 2008. Directed by G. Reticker. Fork Films.

Quinn, R.E. 2004. *Building the bridge as you walk on it: A guide for leading change*. San Francisco: Jossey-Bass.

Schminke, M., Ambrose, M.L., and Neubaum , D.O. 2005. The effect of leader moral development on ethical climate and employee attitudes. *Organizational Behavior and Human Decision Processes* 97(2), 135–151.

Scully, M.A., and Creed, W.E.D. 2005. In *Social movements and organization theory*, ed. G.F. Davis, D. McAdam, W.R. Scott, and M.N. Zald, 310–332. New York: Cambridge University Press.

Shilts, R. 1982. *The mayor of Castro Street: The life and times of Harvey Milk*. New York: St. Martin's Press.

Siegel, D.S. 2009. Green management matters only if it yields more green: An economic/strategic perspective. *Academy of Management Perspectives* 23(3), 5–16.

Sims, R.R. 2000. Changing an organization's culture under new leadership. *Journal of Business Ethics* 25(1), 65–78.

Sims, R. Toward a better understanding of organizational efforts to rebuild reputation following an ethical scandal. *Journal of Business Ethics* 90(4), 453–472.

Sims, R.R., and Brinkmann, J. 2002. Leaders as moral role models: The case of John Gutfreund at Salomon Brothers. *Journal of Business Ethics* 35(4), 327–339.

Stevenson, W.B., Pearce, J.L., and Porter, L.W. 1985. The concept of "coalition" in organization theory and research. *Academy of Management Review* 10(2), 256–268.

Strang, D., and Jung, D.-I. 2005. Organizational change as orchestrated social movement: Recruitment to a corporate quality initiative. In *Social movements and organization theory,* ed. G.F. Davis, D. McAdam, W.R. Scott, and M.N. Zald, 280–309. New York: Cambridge University Press.

Tate, T. 2004. How to fight, how to kill: Child soldiers in Liberia. *Human Rights Watch* 16(2) (February). www.hrw.org/reports/2004/liberia0204/liberia0204.pdf (accessed August 29. 2009).

Tec, N. 1993. *Defiance.* New York: Oxford.

Thomas, R.R., Jr. 1991. *Beyond race and gender: Unleashing the power of your total work force by managing diversity.* New York: AMACOM.

Treviño, L.K., Brown, M., and Hartman, L. 2003. A qualitative investigation of perceived executive ethical leadership: Perceptions from inside and outside the executive suite. *Human Relations* 56(1), 5–37.

Treviño, L.K., and Victor, B. 1992. Peer reporting of unethical behavior: A social context perspective. *Academy of Management Journal* 35(1), 38–64.

Uhl-Bien, M., and Carsten, M.K. 2007. Being ethical when the boss is not. *Organizational Dynamics* 36(2), 187–201.

Veech, A. 2002. *Managerial communication strategies: An applied casebook.* Upper Saddle River, NJ: Pearson Prentice Hall.

Watson, W., Michaelsen. L.K., and Sharp, W. 1991. Member competence, group interaction, and group decision making: A longitudinal study. *Journal of Applied Psychology* 76(7), 803–809.

Weaver, G.R., Treviño, L.K., and Agle, B. 2005. "Somebody I look up to": Ethical role models in organizations. *Organizational Dynamics* 34(4), 313–330.

Zald, M.N., and Berger, M.A. 1978. Social movements in organizations: Coup d'etat, insurgency, and mass movements. *American Journal of Sociology* 83(4), 823–861.

14

The Organizational Context of Moral Courage

Creating Environments That Account for Dual-Processing Models of Courageous Behavior

Dennis J. Moberg

Case 1. The Fire Captain

I arrived to discover an ordinary one-story home in a residential area with no immediate signs of fire. My first impression was that this was a perfectly standard building with nothing out of the ordinary. I was told that the fire was in the back in a kitchen area. The lieutenant led the hose crew through the front door to the rear. However, when they sprayed water on the flames, the fire roared back at them. That was a curious effect and one that continued after even more water was sprayed. The hose crew retreated a bit, and I got a strange feeling that things were not right. Even though this was the kind of building I was very familiar with, the fire did not seem right. So I ordered the hose crew out of the building. As soon as everyone was out, the floor where they had been standing collapsed into a basement that none of us suspected even existed. Had they still been inside, the hose crew would have fallen into the flames below.[1]

Case 2. The Ambitious Employee

I was very prepared for my meeting with Ellen, having thought through all of her options and mine. This was a promotion I felt I was ready for and deserved. Ellen began by telling me something I already knew, that Paula was being moved to a senior position working directly for her. And then,

Ellen dropped a bombshell—she was going to *post* Paula's vacated position rather than move me directly into it. While she assured me that I would be the number-one candidate, I knew that this would mean that I would have to go through a risky process to get the position I felt entitled to. I had been working on my relationship with Ellen for two years. I regularly exercised initiative and volunteered to champion any projects she sponsored. I requested feedback from her whenever I could. I read articles about "managing your boss" and took a course in organizational politics to learn how to influence her more effectively.

My relationship with Paula was quite another thing. No matter how much I tried to work with her, we were "oil and water." Nothing I tried seemed to build any sort of trust with Paula, so when Ellen dropped her bombshell, I suspected that Paula was behind it. Under normal circumstances, I would have rolled over and accepted Ellen's decision. However, from everything I had studied, I knew I had a good argument and plan of attack. So I decided to push my case. First, I discussed the calendar with Ellen and pointed out that posting the position would surely delay several projects that were important to her. Second, I pointed out that the last time Ellen faced a similar situation, she did not post the position but filled it immediately with an inside candidate. I reminded her that in this former case, everything had worked out well. I was a bit disappointed that she didn't immediately change her mind, but later that afternoon, she called to tell me that she had reconsidered her decision and that the promotion was mine.[2]

At first glance, neither of these cases seems to be evidence of great courage. The fire captain retreated from danger, and the ambitious employee seemed not to be in great jeopardy. However, courage is implicated in both cases. One element of courage is that it involves choosing rightly when faced with the likelihood of personal harm.[3] The threat the fire captain was facing is obvious, but the ambitious employee faced harm as well. The prospect of months of paperwork and delay would have been personally costly to her, both psychologically and probably financially, and the fact that "speaking truth to power" was involved also made the harm politically consequential.

A second element of courage is that as a moral virtue, it lies on a continuum between two vices—in this case, between the vice of cowardice and the vice of foolhardiness.[4] Depending on the circumstance, courage may demand bold action or it may call for retreat. Even though the ambitious employee and the fire captain acted differently, both chose a manifestation of courage that certainly fit the circumstance. Neither act was cowardly or foolhardy.

A third important element of courage is that it is aimed at a vision of the good.[5] Given the moral priority of human beings over property, there is no question that the fire captain intended to bring about a more moral state of affairs. And the ambitious employee did as well, although in order to be sure, we would have to agree with her view that receiving the promotion without posting was fair and just.

Our two cases actually represent something even more profound about morally courageous behavior: It can result from an impulsive, almost automatic process like the fire captain's. Alternatively, it can follow a more deliberate, reflective process like that of the ambitious employee. Moral psychologists have offered several different accounts of how this dual-processing system of moral cognition operates.[6] There is general agreement, however, that like other moral acts, courage emerges in one of two cognitive processes: an immediate and primarily emotive intuitive process, and a deliberative rational process. Throughout the remainder of this chapter, we will use the terms "hot courage" to refer to the more automatic process and "cool courage" to refer to the more deliberative one.[7]

The goal of this chapter is to identify the features of the work environment that make it easier to express courage. In the first section, we will examine the most promising models offered by contemporary moral psychologists for the hot and cool processes involved in courageous acts. In the second section, we will describe the organizational conditions that managers can establish to foster employees' acts of courage.

Hot Courage Processing

Three of the most significant dual-processing models that ascribe the genesis of most courageous acts to intuition or gut feelings are the Social Intuitionist Model (SIM), the Chronic Accessibility Model (CAM), and the Expert Decision Model (EDM). Each offers a contrasting explanation for how acts of courage come about.

The Social Intuitionist Model

Jonathon Haidt and his colleagues argue that when moral behavior like courage emerges, it most often begins as a preconscious and emotionally charged recognition of some pattern in the situation the person is facing (five such patterns are described below).[8] The person becomes aware of this intuition as a moral judgment—a recognition that some particular thing about this situation is wrong. The origin of this intuition is an interaction of human evolutionary biology selecting for general features necessary for species survival with contemporary definitions of culturally appropriate behavior. Thus, the impulse is evolutionarily ancient, but the action that follows it is generally adapted to the modern conditions. Contemporary humans rarely bash superiors on the head when they sense that something is wrong; rather, they more commonly channel their courage into rational appeals and other forms of assertive behavior.

According to the SIM formulation, therefore, when a situation fits a relevant pattern, gut feelings are triggered suddenly and spontaneously without conscious processes or rational calculations. These feelings that "something is wrong and must be changed" can lead to immediate and unthinking action that can be later called courageous.

When individuals are called to account for their actions, these intuitions are followed by more purposeful deliberation in order to explain to the self and to others how the intuitions fit with accepted norms of ethical behavior.[9] For example, if a salesperson courageously risks displeasing authorities by waiving late fees for a good customer who is facing temporary cash problems, she is much more likely to emphasize the prospect of future sales than the emotional impulse that stirred the courageous action. According to the SIM model, immediate intuition with its strong emotional charge is the driving force for courageous behavior, and reasoning plays an after-the-fact supporting role.

To understand how managers might influence their employees' courageous behavior, it is important to keep in mind the two factors behind courageous intuitions: evolutionary impulses and social facilitation. Typically, humans have the impulse to be courageous when they intuit patterns in situations much like their ancestors faced in earlier evolutionary periods. Haidt and his colleagues have identified five sets of these patterns that they claim are the result of natural selection and are thus species-specific:

- Reaction to the pain and suffering of others, particularly in the young and vulnerable;
- Enforcement of norms of fairness or reciprocity, expressed especially toward people who renege or fail to reciprocate;
- Maintenance of a hierarchical social order, expressed as hostility toward people who do not show proper deference and respect or who use their position coercively;
- Preference for purity or sanctity, explaining why there are so many moral rules governing food, sex, cleanliness, etc.; and
- Defense of boundaries between in-groups and out-groups, resulting in partiality and privilege for in-groups.[10]

Obviously, these patterns are exogenous to managerial action. All employees are likely to react more or less to these patterns.

The precise forms that courage takes for a particular individual are "socially afforded," meaning that a person's sociocultural milieu will indicate how these evolutionary impulses are to be expressed. Indeed, the term "social" in SIM refers to the need to configure evolutionary-based motivation in ways that fit the immediate social context. Commonly, this social affordance takes place as the result of conversation and socialization; it is this conversational interaction that promises the most managerial leverage. Among firefighters, for example, thanks to professional training, courage is more likely to be expressed to protect others from pain and suffering than to address some problem of inequity or lack of reciprocity. Firefighters are taught to rescue all persons in danger whether or not they have paid their taxes or been nice to their neighbors. In summary, then, SIM defines a "hot" process based on evolutionary impulses as shaped by sociocultural forces. "Cool" processes may follow in order to rationalize to oneself and others the courageous action taken, but these are incidental to the SIM formulation.

A classic case of SIM and courage is the case of Jackie Robinson, the first African American to play major league baseball. Baseball executive Branch Rickey signed Robinson to a professional contract in 1946 and promoted him to the Brooklyn Dodger major league team in 1947. As racism was rampant at the time and a serious backlash to his playing was expected, Rickey discussed with Robinson how he should act in the face of threats. Jackie Robinson obviously felt the need to defend himself courageously as an outcast (in-group/out-group evolutionary tensions). In the game of baseball, courage in the face of an insult is usually repaid in kind—you insult me, I kick dirt on you; you throw at my head, I charge the mound to pound you. However, Rickey got Robinson to agree not to fight back but instead use his aggressive energy to play harder. In retrospect, this social affordance that redefined courage in baseball worked out very well, for in spite of tremendous harassment, Robinson had a successful first season, winning the league's Rookie of the Year award.[11]

The Chronic Accessibility Model

A different mechanism governing impulsive and deliberative processes has been proposed by Darcia Narvaez and her colleagues.[12] Their CAM model asserts that some knowledge schemas (i.e., prototypes, scripts, episodes, constructs about the self, goals, beliefs, expectations) become chronically accessible through priming, experience, and repetition, and these influence how courageous decisions are made spontaneously with a minimum of conscious thought. One type of schema concerns self-constructs of courageous character (e.g., heroes are modest; Gandhi is my role model), and if these are chronically accessible, the person is prone to act consistently with these knowledge schemas.[13] The other relevant type of schema concerns the situational context in which courageous behavior might be enacted (courage should not place the unwilling in jeopardy; courage may involve bending but seldom breaking rules). If self and situational schema like these are primed and repeated sufficiently so that they become chronically accessible, courageous acts are more likely to emerge. Imagine, for example, the inner-city high school teacher who must make several decisions per day about how to create a favorable learning environment in a climate where there is little respect for authority. Not all inner-city teachers are equally concerned with exercising courage for this purpose. Sadly, some may be more concerned with promoting the school's reputation or protecting its internal political order. However, a teacher whose background leads her automatically to call up schemas of brave acts or courageous role models is likely to act in accord with these concepts and prototypes. Relevant situational schema might include how and when to be courageous, and which students are likely to respond favorably to her actions.

For a historical example of CAM at work, consider the extraordinarily brave people who rescued Jews during the Nazi occupation of Western Europe. The following quote is from one rescuer describing his motivation: "I could not stand idly by and observe the daily misery that was occurring."[14] The phrase "not stand idly by" is a clear marker of courage as a chronically accessible character attribute. A different rescuer evidences a chronically accessible model of the situation facing the Jews such that the outcomes of his own inaction were clear: "I knew they were taking them and they wouldn't come back. I didn't think I could live with that, knowing I could have done something."[15] So, what we find among rescuers is a combination of chronically accessible notions of courage and chronically accessible notions of the situations in which courage is morally obligatory.

Thus, while the SIM claims that sensitivity to certain situations is built into a human's genetic makeup but may be subject to managerial influence in terms of how it is expressed, the CAM suggests a more straightforward mechanism. If managers make salient images of courageous people and courageous acts (together with the situations in which they arise), courage is more likely to be the result. Both involve "hot" gut feelings, but CAM provides a way for managers to program rather than merely to shape the intuitions themselves.

The Expert Decision Model

Neither the SIM nor the CAM requires the employee to have any experience with the situation in which courage is called for. The SIM assumes that evolutionary history drives the impulse, and the CAM gives a more prominent role to the concepts and scripts that have been "programmed into" the person. Thus, courage is as likely to arise from a novice accountant as from someone who has been practicing for twenty years. Obviously, novice courage is less likely to be as aesthetic, nuanced, or effective as expert courage, and that is where the EDM comes in.

Psychologists and other students of expertise have examined the cognitive processes of people who have attained very high levels of performance in such activities as chess,[16] sports,[17] medical diagnostics,[18] and computer programming.[19] As a result, they have identified several common elements of expertise.[20] These apply also to different types of moral behavior.[21]

One element of expertise is pattern recognition in which exposure to certain chunks of data triggers particular action sequences that are well adapted to the situation. As part of this process, the expert mentally simulates the action sequence based upon the mental models of the situation derived from experience.[22] These mental models are the result of "deliberate practice" in which the individual accumulates experience by facing typical situations in a progressively more complicated sequence.[23] Throughout the process, the expert acquires "tacit knowledge" about the task. This term derives from the work of Michael Polanyi, who contended that "we know more than we can tell."[24] Thus, although experts draw on their knowledge when they make decisions, they may not be able to explain accurately why they have acted or to educate another person to make the same decisions in the same circumstances.

Once again, expert behavior is triggered by intuitions or "gut feelings" that a particular action sequence evokes. Thus, when our fire captain "got a strange feeling that things were not right," that was typical of the hot processing associated with expert behavior.[25] In fact, EDM is common in occupations where courageous acts are frequently called for. Klein reports that firefighters use EDM in 80 percent of their toughest cases, army officers use it in 96 percent of their planning decisions, and officers in the navy use EDM in 95 percent of their decisions.[26] Klein notes similar results with commercial air crews and managers of offshore oil platforms.[27] Although not all of these decisions involve courage, many do, so the EDM is at work in many situations where bravery is required.

Repeated exposure to danger through deliberate practice significantly affects how experts experience the risks involved in courageous acts. Expert bomb-disposal specialists, for example, seem able to endure incredible terror without the elevated heart rates that typically accompany acute stress.[28] Similarly, although paratroopers are fearful in their first attempts, most experience a significant decrease in fear after five jumps.[29] Indeed, experienced stuntmen perceive their job more as *challenging* than dangerous.[30]

Among the most dazzling displays of courage attributable to EDM was by US Airways pilot Chesley B. Sullenberger III in New York City on January 15, 2009. Shortly after taking off, Sullenberger's plane hit a large flock of birds that disabled both engines. He briefly discussed with air traffic control the possibility of an emergency airport landing. However, he quickly determined that was impossible and decided instead to ditch in the Hudson River. Captain Sullenberger warned the passengers to "brace for impact," then guided the plane to a smooth water landing in the river. Miraculously, all passengers and crew survived.[31] It is noteworthy that Sullenberger's expertise had been recognized long before the "Miracle on the Hudson." He was a graduate of the Air Force Academy, where he received the Outstanding Cadet in Airmanship Award, which is given to the top flier in each graduating class. And that was before he accumulated nearly thirty years as a commercial pilot.

It may not always be clear to the employee experiencing hot courage whether it has phylogenetic, cognitive, or experiential origins. What is important is that it is driven by a quick, mindless process in which the person acts in spite of danger or threat. The result may not be pretty or even effective, but it will thrust the individual headlong into acting courageously. Sadly, some firefighters perish following their evolutionary urge to save lives, some rescuers of Jews died even though their chronically accessible images led them to intervene against the Nazis, and some airline pilots, even expert ones, fail in response to situations with which they are unfamiliar.

Cool Courage Processing

Courage can also emerge not as the result of impulse or intuition but after a series of conscious mental calculations made about the situation one is facing.[32] For example, a person can estimate his or her readiness to endure the specific hazards involved and one's strength of commitment to the goal in question. Take a customs officer who wonders if a particular person suspected of carrying contraband will react violently if detained. Some of the things the officer may consider include the physical size of the alleged smuggler, the social value of confiscating the contraband in question, and how to use the element of surprise in consummating the arrest. Such factors are part of the training that customs officers receive, and a particular officer may learn other considerations through experience. The point is that cool processing involves a rational process whereby information is brought to bear on the decisions whether and how to be courageous. In almost every instance, cool processing of this kind includes weighing alternatives according to five criteria: goal importance, risk/return, capability assessment, timing, and contingency plans.

Goal Importance

Genuine courage requires a moral goal. It is not courageous to drive too fast to deliver a pizza or to blow the whistle without verifiable proof of wrongdoing.

Most situations calling for courage involve clear moral goals, but occasionally, conflicts between goals exist. For example, a manager may struggle with the decision to be totally candid with a customer about the pending release of a secret new product that might offer better value than the product the customer is about to purchase. Divulging this information may require courage, for it puts the welfare of the company in jeopardy on account of a deferred sale. And not divulging the information may require courage in that the customer may feel betrayed by the salesperson if he learns of the release after committing to the earlier product. Wrestling with moral dilemmas of this kind lends itself to the mental work involved in cool processing.[33] Ultimately, the person must decide whether the goals involved in the contemplated courageous action are sufficiently important from a moral standpoint.

Although cool processes are often linear, they need not be. Sometimes, an act that involved no courage at all blossoms into an act of astonishing valor. In such a case, we might say that an opportunity preceded a goal. Many Medal of Honor stories entail sequences of events in which openings presented themselves and goals were created instantaneously. In one of the most famous of these, then Corporal Alvin C. York of Tennessee, a former conscientious objector, was part of a contingent of troops ordered to take control of a hill in the Argonne during World War I. Because a map was misread, the group found itself behind enemy lines under machine-gun attack. At that point, the group abandoned its original goal, and, amidst the fog of war, more than a hundred German soldiers surrendered to a small band of troops including York, who was credited with eliminating the last machine-gun nest that threatened to annihilate the Americans.[34] Thus, cool processing may not begin with a thorough consideration of the importance of the goals involved; instead, opportunities invite goal improvisation.[35]

Risk/Return

Courageous action is always risky, and a second factor involved in conscious deliberation about courage is whether the expected results warrant the risks incurred.

> Lieutenant General Claudia J. Kennedy, the first female three-star general in the U.S. Army, went through a difficult risk-benefit assessment before reporting a fellow officer who had plagiarized a research paper at a professional army school. Kennedy weighed the negatives (discomfort and embarrassment for "snitching" on a fellow officer) against the positives (allegiance to the army's high standards for its future leaders, and adherence to her own ethics). The decision was difficult: an instinct for self-protection, loyalty to

her colleagues and to the institution, and her personal integrity all contended within her. She considered speaking privately to the officer, but realized that he would react angrily and that, after all, it was not her job to manage him. In the end, she decided that her loyalty to army standards was paramount: "I . . . recognized that overlooking an ethical lapse was tantamount to participating in the event," she writes in her book *Generally Speaking*. She discreetly reported the incident; her reputation remained intact, and her career thrived.[36]

Capability Assessment

Every situation that potentially calls upon courage is different, but a key consideration is whether the individual has adequate physical, economic, social, psychological, and temporal resources to implement the contemplated course of action. It makes little sense to dive in after a drowning man if you cannot swim. Similarly, acting courageously within an organization often requires a dispassionate assessment of one's own social power relative to others involved in the courageous act.[37] Dissenting against a powerful adversary is prudent only if one has the ability to defend oneself from the predictable backlash. Some options call for not just a single act of courage, but rather for a persistent series of actions. In such cases, the person must decide whether he or she has the capability to sustain such a campaign.[38] It requires a great deal of energy to persevere in the face of adversity, so candidates for positions like Peace Corps volunteer must carefully assess their own physical and psychological resources before making the commitment. Within organizations, a common reaction to one's first courageous move is nonconcurrence, that is, the complete absence of any kind of reaction at all. Unless one can sustain the motivation that drove the first initiative, nothing will have been gained.[39] Whether or not a person has persistence, then, is an important part of a realistic self-assessment of his or her readiness for courage.

Another psychological capability that may prepare people well for courage is mental toughness.[40] Studies of mentally tough individuals show that they have overall psychological health,[41] are optimistic,[42] and believe themselves to be competent.[43] Research on the context within which mental toughness is most likely to occur shows that fearlessness is enhanced when it is supported by a small, tightly integrated, familiar group of people.[44] Thus, it is not surprising that combatants during World War II gave the reason for their courage as not wanting to let their comrades down.[45]

Timing

Although courage is often associated with emergency situations, some of the bravest acts require patience while a situation develops. Internal auditors often have to resist acting precipitously until all of the evidence supports a "finding." Nongovernmental organization fund-raisers often require patience, as they frequently have to call on a prospective donor many times as they build up to a well-timed "ask." Patience was required of FAA inspector Bobby Boutris, who in 2003 began to complain to his superiors that Southwest Airlines was flying aircraft out of compliance with inspection schedules. In spite of being "blown off" by his boss, he patiently kept filing his reports until he ultimately went to the press with his complaints.[46]

Timing was an all-important factor in many of the courageous decisions that were made by the ground crew and astronauts aboard Apollo 13.[47] Two days into a lunar mission, an explosion damaged oxygen tanks and curtailed electrical power, resulting in an insufficient supply of lithium hydroxide for removing carbon dioxide on board the spacecraft. Under significant time pressure, minutes before the crew would have perished, the ground crew heroically improvised a way to use materials available on board to adapt incompatible canisters to the air system.

Contingency Plans

Cool processing does not end when a decision on how to act is made. The courageous person should create backup plans in case the initial effort goes awry. Experienced decision makers often use mental simulations to think through their options, occasionally involving "premortems" that imagine what could go wrong with each.[48] In Case 2, in the beginning of this chapter, the ambitious employee claimed to have thought through alternative moves carefully before pressing her boss not to post the position to which she felt entitled.

When Rachel Hubka started Rachel's Bus Company in the late 1980s to provide transportation services to the Chicago public school system, she took out a loan against her home to found the company. She had experience in the busing business and wanted to start a company with a social mission: "I wanted to give inner city people an opportunity to come in and work, where they may not have had opportunities in the past."[49] Accordingly, she chose to locate her offices in one of the most impoverished areas in the city and expected to draw from the local neighborhood for drivers and other employees. Unfortunately, the area was so depressed that few qualified drivers applied, and Rachel faced her first setback. Luckily, she had a contingency plan that included transporting workers to her facility and offering them training in the jobs she needed to fill. Her enterprise has been lauded for its social responsibility, and she is widely acknowledged for her courage.[50]

Hot Courage or Cool?

Thirty years ago, most decision experts agreed that cool, analytical decision making was superior to hot, intuitive decision making. Janis and Mann argued in 1977, for example, that analytical methods minimize post-decision regret. In moral decisions about whether or not to act courageously, such regret would take the form of guilt or perhaps even shame.[51]

Today, decision scholars are more sanguine about hot processes, particularly when situations seem to warrant it. When an expert decision maker has a highly complex decision and time pressure, a hot, intuitive process is justified.[52] In contrast, when decision situations require careful explanation, a cooler process is in order.[53] Thus, a contingency approach has been advanced, in which the best process depends on the situation. However, there is evidence that decision makers may not be entirely flexible with respect to a choice between hot and cool processes. Being in a positive mood makes one more likely to engage in intuition, while a sad mood is associated with analysis.[54] Similarly, a personality characterized by "need for cognition" disposes one toward cool processes.[55] In all, then, a host of factors in an individual case may influence whether courage arises through a hot or a cool process.

Some researchers have offered evidence, however, that a choice between hot and cold processes is really illusory; hot processes in fact predominate.[56] If analysis occurs, it usually happens only after the person has an inclination provided by gut feelings.[57] Analysis, according to this view, is thus the servant to intuition, at best rationalizing and justifying the hot intuitions and gut reactions. This does not mean that courage is always primitive and instinctive. Indeed, people can be taught how to act upon their gut reactions so that courage takes on a form that is socially and institutionally appropriate. Yet, intuitions are often the driving force for courageous acts.

If there is time, and if the individual is likely to be asked to explain or justify courageous acts, there is probably no substitute for cooler processes. Accordingly, managers who want to foster courage among their subordinates must account for whether or not both processes are fully determinative.

Work Environments Conducive to Courage

The diverse views about the social and psychological mechanisms that give rise to courageous acts point to a variety of work environments that facilitate employee courage. Managers can be more effective if they recognize the importance of courage and understand how to direct it to the achievement of organizational goals.

Taming the Courage Beast

The Social Intuitionist Model claims that courage has evolutionary origins that can potentially animate a form of courage that is not adapted to the social situation at hand. Although one's biologically based gut feelings might call for courageous expression of anger toward an aggressive customer, such an action would certainly not fit a contemporary retail environment. Similarly, although an employee might be tempted to courageously defend his departmental colleagues from being blamed for a mistake they did not commit, such a defense might not be politically wise.

According to proponents of the SIM, the best way to "tame" the evolutionary beast that can result in socially inappropriate forms of courage is social influence. Compared to other species shaped by their own evolutionary history, "only human beings cooperate widely and intensely with nonkin, and we do it in part through a set of social psychological adaptations that make us extremely sensitive to and influenceable by what other people think and feel."[58] Taming the evolutionary beast occurs naturally when people converse about the precursors, shape, and aftermath of courageous acts. This is accomplished regularly in incident-debriefing sessions among military professionals to ensure that instances of physical courage fall within the bounds of social/professional acceptability. Talk about courage among other kinds of jobholders, however, is less typical.[59] In extreme cases, supervisors are expected to "tone down" overly enthusiastic displays of courage or to encourage meek employees to "speak up" where their job responsibilities require levels of courage they are not manifesting. For the most part, though, "courage counseling" is certainly not part of the normal supervisor-subordinate interaction.

Mentors can make up for this lack of systematic attention to courage as a supervisory issue.[60] In some cases, mentors may have more experience with certain forms of courage than supervisors, and they may be in a more independent position to advise employees whether to escalate issues up the chain of command.

Priming the Courage Pump

Proponents of the Chronic Accessibility Model argue that people act courageously at work when the environment makes concepts and images of courage salient. This suggests that organizational cultures should regularly expose members to narratives of their courageous predecessors. Consider, for example, the heroes whose stories midshipmen at the U.S. Naval Academy repeatedly hear: "The young lieutenant on Guadalcanal who asked his loved ones always to pray, not that he came back, but that he would have the courage to do his duty. The chaplain on a sinking ship who gave his life preserver to a young sailor, telling him, take it lad, you need it more than I do. The admirals of the greatest sea battles in history who faced enormous decisions that had to be made on gossamers of information, with thousands of lives and indeed a nation in the balance."[61] Other professional schools incorporate first-person testimonies of people who have risen above significant challenges. Cynthia Cooper, for example, the accountant who blew the whistle at WorldCom, is a regular speaker at schools of business.

Making salient those situations in which courageous behaviors are appropriate is typically the province of professional and organizational training and development. Training protocols often employ rehearsals and simulations as a means to assist trainees in adapting to unfamiliar and potentially threatening situations. In this way, their fear levels can be better adapted to and managed.[62] Consider, for example, the training that managers and other officials receive concerning what to do in case of workplace violence. Typically, their training involves recognizing hazardous situations and practicing protocols that minimize escalation.[63] For example, schools commonly train teachers to follow emergency procedures, know who is in charge, and look out for someone else when confronted by an instance of violent behavior.

Enabling the Courage Expert

Recall that "hot" courage can result from having so much experience with a particular phenomenon that a person masters how to deal with it. Organizations can enable this process of expertise development in several ways.[64] First, they must value experience over mere credentialing. Rapid turnover is obviously an enemy to experience, as is a policy of frequent job rotation. Standardization and the enforcement of work procedures are also problematic. Developing procedures makes it easier for new workers to adapt to their responsibilities, but "can make it even harder to build up intuitions if the procedures eliminate the need for judgment calls."[65]

To facilitate the accumulation of expertise, tasks must provide feedback conducive to learning. Jobholders must receive feedback about their performance that is unambiguous, accurate, and immediate.[66] Physicians must have sustained contact with patients and learn to listen to them, as should salespeople with customers, and sculptors with art patrons.

Since expertise involves the accumulation of tacit knowledge, it is unlikely to be transmitted from one person to another in a normal educational setting. However, because tacit knowledge is conveyed more effectively in narrative,[67] environments that encourage storytelling about courageous events will facilitate the socialization of expert understanding about how and when to be courageous. Postmortems of actual episodes may aid this process. An effective debriefing session will help others identify important patterns of cues (for example, when was the problem first recognized? And were there earlier signs that were ignored?). As a practical matter, however, debriefing sessions frequently become derailed by side issues. Employees may argue over the facts and details of the situation, or discussions can turn from what happened to who is to blame.

A more effective debriefing procedure is described by Atul Gawande in his book on surgery and surgeons.[68] Once a week at the Morbidity and Mortality Conference in U.S. academic hospitals, surgeons discuss the mistakes and deaths of the prior week and figure out what to do differently the next time. The sessions involve the entire surgery contingent and are closed to outsiders. The purpose of this cultural ritual is to improve performance and promote better patient outcomes in the future.

Developing Deliberative Courage

Organizational environments that facilitate the development of cool courage processes must encourage employees to slow down, be less impulsive, and use deliberative judgment before acting. Insisting that employees follow procedures inhibits tapping into people's expertise, but it can promote deliberative courage. Having people consider potential ethical situations and anticipate possible personal responses and associated outcomes will help them be prepared when they actually do need to exercise courage. For example, ethicists typically require prospective whistleblowers to be certain that:

- Their intent is to prevent serious and unnecessary harm to others;
- They have exhausted all available internal procedures for rectifying the problematic behavior before public disclosure;
- Their evidence of wrongdoing is persuasive to "a reasonable person";
- Their action must have a reasonable chance for success;
- The act of blowing the whistle itself does not violate any other serious ethical principle besides those associated with one's loyalty to the organization.[69]

Training an organization's members to act according to these criteria and holding them responsible for following these criteria will slow them down and open their thinking to other cool considerations regarding the appropriate way to act courageously.

We have previously discussed the usefulness of debriefing sessions in the context of hot processes. In order to encourage deliberative processes, these should culminate in some sort of determination that the courageous acts were justified and honorable. This is the process used in the military with the granting of decorations and citations. Commendations can convey and reinforce cool courage criteria if they tie the courageous acts to specific deliberative considerations such as contingency plans and risk analysis.

Training employees to use the criteria associated with cool courage processes (goal importance, risk/return, capability assessment, timing, and contingency plans) will build cool courage skills. This training must be tailored to the particular situations that employees are likely to face, since the dilemmas encountered by a courageous nurse are certainly different from those of a Homeland Security official. Training should also involve simulation, case studies, and role playing, to reinforce the use of calculative consideration in more complicated situations. One challenge found in almost every organizational context is the so-called "tough conversation," and many organizations help employees prepare for and execute these difficult encounters following essentially the same factors in the cool courage process.[70]

Fire Captains, Ambitious Employees, and Context

Courage takes diverse forms in modern organizations and, as we have seen, arises from several different psychological processes. Sometimes, as with our fire captain, courage occurs so spontaneously and enigmatically that it appears to defy the design of mechanisms to encourage or facilitate it. On closer view, however, it seems possible to design environments that are capable of doing just that. With cool courage, the design of favorable contexts is more straightforward; indeed, one scholar who has fashioned a cool model termed courage "a skill."[71] Whether it is an impulse or a skill, genuine courage rarely fails to impress. Nurturing it requires an environment that encourages employees to aspire to function "at their best." Given the many paths to that noble end, there is no one best way to enable it.

Notes

The author wishes to thank Brooke Hamilton for help in preparing this chapter.
1. Adapted from a case cited in Klein, 1998.
2. Adapted from a case submitted by an MBA student.
3. Cavanagh and Moberg, 1999.
4. Aristotle, 2002.
5. Ibid.; cf. Woodward and Pury, 2007.
6. Lapsley and Hill, 2008.
7. Greene et al., 2001.
8. Haidt, 2007, 2008; Haidt and Joseph, 2004.
9. Haidt, 2001.

10. Haidt and Bjorklund, 2008.
11. Rampersad, 1997.
12. Narvaez, 2008a and 2008b; Narvaez and Gleason, 2007; Narvaez et al., 2006.
13. Narvaez et al., 2006.
14. Oliner, 2004, 44.
15. Ibid.
16. Chase and Simon, 1973.
17. Allard and Starks, 1980.
18. Elstein, Shulman, and Sprafka, 1990.
19. Adelson and Soloway, 1985.
20. Ericsson and Charness, 1994.
21. Dreyfus and Dreyfus, 1991.
22. Klein, 2004.
23. Ericsson and Charness, 1994.
24. Polanyi, 1966, 4.
25. Sternberg et al., 1995.
26. Klein, 2004.
27. Ibid.
28. Cox et al., 1983.
29. McMillan and Rachman, 1987.
30. Piet, 1987.
31. Rivera, 2009.
32. Gould, 2005; Reardon, 2007; Sekerka and Bagozzi, 2007.
33. Moore, Clark, and Kane, 2008.
34. Lee, 2002.
35. Klein, 2004.
36. Reardon, 2007, 62.
37. Meyerson, 2008.
38. Ghoshal and Bruch, 2003.
39. Dalton, 2009.
40. See, for example, Maddi, 2007.
41. Rachman, 1990.
42. Seligman, 1988.
43. Bandura, 1977.
44. Rachman, 1990.
45. Stouffer et al., 1949.
46. Hilkevitch, 2008.
47. Lovell and Kluger, 1994.
48. Klein, 2004.
49. Bollier, 1996, 83.
50. See, for example, Clinton, 1996; Spreitzer and Sonnenshein, 2004.
51. Janis and Mann, 1977.
52. Dijksterhuis, 2004; Klein, 2004.
53. Beach and Mitchell, 1978.
54. de Vries, Holland, and Witteman, 2008.
55. Epstein et al., 1996; Witteman et al., 2009.
56. Bargh and Chartrand, 1999; Wilson, 2002.
57. Haidt, 2001.

58. Haidt and Bjorklund, 2008, 192.
59. Bird and Waters, 1989.
60. Moberg, 2008.
61. Webb, 1996, 1.
62. Rachman, 1990.
63. OSHA, 2007.
64. Klein, 2004.
65. Ibid., 34.
66. Horvath, 2001.
67. Linde, 2001.
68. Gawande, 2002.
69. Bowie, 1999; Duska, 2008.
70. Weeks, 2001.
71. Reardon, 2007.

References

Adelson, B., and Soloway, E. 1985. The role of domain expertise in software design. *IEEE Transactions in Software Engineering* 11, 1351–1360.

Allard, F., and Starks, J.L. 1980. Perception in sport: Volleyball. *Journal of Sport Psychology* 2(1), 14–21.

Aristotle. 2002. *Nicomachean ethics*, trans. C. Rowe. New York: Oxford University Press.

Bandura, A. 1977. Self-efficacy: Toward a unifying theory of behavioral change. *Psychological Review* 84, 191–215.

Bargh, J.A., and Chartrand, T.L. 1999. The unbearable automaticity of being. *American Psychologist* 54, 462–479.

Beach, L.R., and Mitchell, T.R. 1978. A contingency model for the selection of decision strategies. *Academy of Management Review* 3, 439–449.

Bird, F.B., and Waters, J.A. 1989. The moral muteness of managers. *California Management Review* 32(1), 73–88.

Bollier, D. 1996. *Aiming higher: 25 stories of how companies prosper by combining sound management and social vision.* New York: AMACOM.

Bowie, N.E. 1999. *Business ethics: A Kantian perspective.* New York: Wiley Blackwell.

Cavanagh, G.F., and Moberg, D.J. 1999. The virtue of courage within the organization. In *Research in ethical issues in organizations*, vol. 1, ed. M.L. Pava and P. Primeaux, 1–25. Greenwich, CT: JAI.

Chase, W.G., and Simon, H.A. 1973. Perception in chess. *Cognitive Psychology* 4(1), 55–81.

Clinton, H.R. 1996. *It takes a village.* New York: Simon and Schuster.

Cox, D., Hallam, R., O'Connor, K., and Rachman, S. 1983. An experimental analysis of fearlessness and courage. *British Journal of Psychology* 74, 107–117.

Dalton, C.M. 2009. The power of one. *Business Horizons* 52(1), 3–5.

de Vries, M., Holland, R.W., and Witteman, C.L. 2008. Fitting decisions: Mood and intuitive versus deliberative decision strategies. *Cognition and Emotion* 22(5), 931–943.

Dijksterhuis, A. 2004. Think different: The merits of unconscious thought in preference development and decision-making. *Journal of Personality and Social Psychology* 87, 586–598.

Dreyfus, H., and Dreyfus, S. 1991. Towards a phenomenology of moral expertise. *Human Studies* 14(4), 229–250.

Duska, R. 2008. Whistleblowing and employee loyalty. In *Ethical theory and business,* ed. T. Beauchamp, N. Bowie, and D. Arnold, 335–349. Upper Saddle River, NJ: Prentice Hall.

Elstein, A.S., Shulman, L.S., and Sprafka, S.A. 1990. Medical problem solving: A ten year retrospective. *Evaluation and the Health Professions* 13, 5–36.

Epstein, S., Pacini, R., Denes-Raj, V., and Heier, H. 1996. Individual differences in intuitive-experiential and analytical-rational thinking styles. *Journal of Personality and Social Psychology* 71, 390–405.

Ericsson, K.A., and Charness, N. 1994. Expert performance: Its structure and acquisition. *American Psychologist* 49(8), 725–747.

Gawande, A. 2002. *Complications: A surgeon's notes on an imperfect science.* New York: Henry Holt.

Ghoshal, S., and Bruch, H. 2003. Going beyond motivation to the power of volition. *Sloan Management Review* 44(3), 51–57.

Gould, N.H. 2005. Courage: Its nature and development. *Journal of Humanistic Counseling, Education and Development* 44, 102–116.

Greene, J.D., Sommerville, R.B., Nystrom, L.E., Darley, J.M., and Cohen, J.D. 2001. An fMRI investigation of emotional engagement in moral judgment. *Science* 293, 2105–2108.

Haidt, J. 2001. The emotional dog and its rational tail: A social intuitionist approach to moral judgment. *Psychological Bulletin* 108(4), 814–834.

———. 2007. The new synthesis in moral psychology. *Science* 316(5827), 998–1002.

———. 2008. Morality. *Perspectives on Psychological Science* 3(1), 65–72.

Haidt, J., and Bjorklund, F. 2008. Social intuitionists answer six questions about moral psychology. In *Moral psychology,* vol. 2: The cognitive science of intuition and diversity, ed. W. Sinnott-Armstrong, 181–218. Cambridge, MA: MIT Press.

Haidt, J., and Joseph, C. 2004. Intuitive ethics: How innately prepared intuitions generate culturally variable virtues. *Daedalus* 133(4), 55–66.

Hilkevitch, J. 2008. FAA whistle blowers describe lapses in airline safety. *Chicago Tribune,* April 3, 1.

Horvath, R.M. 2001. *Educating intuition.* Chicago: University of Chicago Press.

Janis, I.L., and Mann, L. 1977. *Decision making: A psychological analysis of conflict, choice, and commitment.* New York: Free Press.

Klein, G. 1998. *Sources of power: How people make decisions.* Cambridge, MA: MIT Press.

———. 2004. *The power of intuition.* New York: Currency.

Lapsley, D.K., and Hill, P.L. 2008. On dual processing and heuristic approaches to moral cognition. *Journal of Moral Education* 37(3), 313–332.

Lee, D.D. 2002. *Sergeant York: An American hero.* Lexington, KY: University of Kentucky Press.

Linde, C. 2001. Narrative and social tacit knowledge. *Journal of Knowledge Management* 5, 160–171.

Lovell, J., and Kluger, J. 1994. *Lost moon: The perilous voyage of Apollo 13.* New York: Houghton Mifflin.

Maddi, S. 2007. Relevance of hardiness assessment and training to the military context. *Military Psychology* 19(1), 61–70.

McMillan, T.M., and Rachman, S.J. 1987. Fearlessness and courage in paratroopers undergoing training. *Personality and Individual Differences* 9, 373–378.

Meyerson, D. 2008. *Rocking the boat*. Boston: Harvard Business School Press.

Moberg, D.J. 2008. Mentoring for protégé character development. *Mentoring and Tutoring: Partnership in Learning* 16(1), 91–103.

Moore, A.B., Clark, B.A., and Kane, M.J. 2008. Who shalt not kill? Individual differences in working memory capacity, executive control, and moral judgment. *Psychological Science* 19(6), 549–557.

Narvaez, D. 2008a. Triune ethics: The neurobiological roots of our multiple moralities. *New Ideas in Psychology* 26, 95–119.

————. 2008b. Human flourishing and moral development: Cognitive science and neurobiological perspectives on virtue development. In *Handbook of moral and character education*, ed. L. Nucci and D. Narvaez, 310–327. Mahwah, NJ: Erlbaum.

Narvaez, D., and Gleason, T. 2007. The influence of moral judgment development and moral experience on comprehension of moral narratives and expository texts. *Journal of Genetic Psychology* 168(3), 251–276.

Narvaez, D., Lapsley, D.K., Hagele, S., and Laskey, B. 2006. Moral chronicity and social information-processing: Tests of a social cognitive approach to moral personality. *Journal of Research in Personality* 40(6), 966–985.

Occupational Safety and Health Administration, U.S. Department of Labor (OSHA). 2007. Training and reference materials library: Workplace violence. www.osha. gov/dte/library/wp-violence (accessed October 7, 2010).

Oliner, S.P. 2004. *Do unto others: Extraordinary acts of ordinary people*. New York: Basic Books.

Piet, S. 1987. What motivates stunt men? *Motivation and Emotion* 11, 195–213.

Polanyi, M. 1966. *The tacit dimension*. Garden City, NY: Basic Books.

Rachman, S.J. 1990. *Fear and courage*. New York: W.H. Freeman.

Rampersad, A. 1997. *Jackie Robinson: A biography*. New York: Knopf.

Reardon, K. 2007. Courage as a skill. *Harvard Business Review* 85(1), 58–64.

Rivera, R. 2009. A pilot becomes a hero years in the making. *New York Times,* January 16. www.nytimes.com/2009/01/17/nyregion/17pilot.html?_r=2 (accessed may 26, 2009).

Sekerka, L.E., and Bagozzi, R. 2007. Moral courage in the workplace: Moving to and from the desire and decision to act. *Business Ethics: A European Review* 16(2), 132–149.

Seligman, M.E. 1988. Competing theories of panic. In *Panic: Psychological perspectives*, ed. S. Rachman and J.D. Maser, 23–39. Hillsdale, NJ: Erlbaum.

Spreitzer, G.M., and Sonnenshein, S. 2004. Toward the construct definition of positive deviance. *American Behavioral Scientist* 47(6), 828–847.

Sternberg, R.J., Wagner, R.K., Williams, W.M., and Horvath, J.A. 1995. Testing common sense. *American Psychologist* 50, 912–927.

Stouffer, S.A., Lumsdaine, A.A., Lumsdaine, M.H., Williams, R.M., Jr., Smith, M.B., Janis, I.L., Star, S.A., and Cottrell, L.S., Jr. 1949. *Studies in Social Psychology in World War II*. Vol. 2, *The American soldier: Combat and its aftermath*. Princeton, NJ: Princeton University Press.

Webb, J. 1996. Defending the navy's culture. Speech at the Naval Institute's 122nd Annual Meeting and Sixth Annapolis Seminar, April 25. www.pbs.org/wgbh/pages/ frontline/shows/navy/readings/jwebbspeech.html (accessed 5/5/09).

Weeks, H. 2001. Taking the stress out of stressful conversations. *Harvard Business Review* 79(7), 112–119.

Wilson, T.D. 2002. *Strangers to ourselves: Discovering the adaptive unconscious.* Cambridge: Belknap Press.

Witteman, C., van den Bercken, J., Claes, L., and Godoy, A. 2009. Assessing rational and intuitive thinking styles. *European Journal of Psychological Assessment* 25(1), 39–47.

Woodward, C.R., and Pury, C.L. 2007. The construct of courage: Categorization and measurement. *Consulting Psychology Journal: Practice and Research* 59(2), 135–147.

Part V

Integration

15

What Have We Learned About Moral Courage in Organizations?

GINA VEGA AND DEBRA R. COMER

A Brief Reprise

Most books approach the topic of business ethics by focusing on the negatives—what is evil, wrong, bad, or unfair in our world and in our behavior. In December 2009, members of the Organizational Behavior Teaching Society participated in a rich discussion on their listserv (obts-1@bucknell.edu) about teaching business ethics. Many decried the negative approach taken by several mainstream business ethics textbooks and sought more positive ways to instruct and inform their students, preparing them to confront the kinds of issues that abound in the workplace.

The authors and contributors to this book share the frustration of this group of instructors. We have a more hopeful premise—that it is possible for members of organizations to do the right thing . . . if they act with moral courage. We identified in our introductory chapter the need to incorporate moral courage, the missing ingredient in business ethics instruction, into our courses, our training programs, and our personal actions.

You have learned why moral courage matters in the workplace. You have read a short primer on moral courage; an introduction to the ways in which the cheating culture steers people to act unethically at work; and a discussion of the Personal Ethical Threshold, which alerts us to the likelihood of our violating our moral principles because of organizational and institutional pressures.

You have read about people who have and have not acted with moral courage, ranging from infamous modern moral failures to whistleblowers, those who act with (and without) faithful conviction in the workplace, social entrepreneurs, and human rights leaders.

You have learned methods to give voice to your values and have seen how leaders can develop professional moral courage in themselves and their followers. You have also gained information about the legal protections that we have in the United States for those who act with moral courage in their places of employment.

You have been given some guidelines to help change organizations so that they can promote moral courage and have read anecdotes about dissenting in organizations, building morally courageous coalitions, and creating supportive organizational environments.

Now is the time to back up and take a macro view of these more than a dozen microelements in order to tie these disparate pieces together.

Fourteen Lessons

Lesson 1: Consider Others

Al Gini tells us that, heroes and cowards alike, we live our lives fearing death. In so doing, we direct our behaviors with a series of mental gymnastics meant to distract us from the end of life by redirecting our thoughts to the here and now. But moral behavior requires that we forfeit the luxury of nonengagement in favor of focusing on selflessness. We need moral courage to look beyond ourselves and our own self-interests to do the right thing.

Lesson 2: Question Norms and Institute Reforms

According to David Callahan, as discussed with Debra R. Comer, materialism and inequality foster cheating, as does an ever-increasing focus on the "bottom line." This bottom-line mentality suggests that we are tempted to live by two different sets of ethical standards—our private standards and our business standards. An ugly "get-them-before-they-get-me" approach starts at the top and permeates organizational life. The antidote begins by recognizing the destructive patterns in our institutions and taking steps toward professional and industrial regulation.

Lesson 3: Recognize Your Weak Spots

Debra R. Comer and Gina Vega present the concept of the Personal Ethical Threshold, PET, as a means for self-evaluation. Decent people can slip easily into flawed moral decisions despite their good intentions. In acknowledging that being human means being imperfect, it can be helpful to identify both the kinds of circumstances that are most likely to disorient our moral compass and the rationalizations we tend to use to excuse our inadequate behavior, in order to prepare responses to these obstacles to right action.

Lesson 4: Your Values Guide Your Actions

Gina Vega shows how risk, reward, and moral hazard work together to create an environment that is antithetical to moral courage and conducive to moral failure. The financial scam that Bernard Madoff perpetrated, the mortgage meltdown that affected property values across the United States and the subprime loans that devalued the mortgages themselves, the shady deals and illegal activities at many respected U.S. firms, and the plain-vanilla swindles, cons, and rip-offs provide ample evidence of the downhill run that appears when we forget to engage our values in our actions.

Lesson 5: Moral Courage Triggers Change

Stephen M. Kohn illustrates the important role whistleblowers play in the fight against fraud and organizational corruption. Using the case of FBI supervisory special agent Frederic Whitehurst, who blew the whistle on forensic fraud in the FBI crime lab after the 1993 World Trade Center bombing, he argues that the moral courage of whistleblowers themselves can change corporate and governmental ethics oversight and increase whistleblower protections.

Lesson 6: Personal Convictions Spur Moral Courage

Religious or spiritual faith can make business decisions easier to formulate. According to G. Jeffrey MacDonald, people of faith frequently find a way to exhibit their principles in their daily lives, regardless of what faith tradition they practice. Morally courageous employees often call on the strength their faith gives them to face the ethical challenges of daily organizational life. The stakes are not just personal; they are transcendent.

Lesson 7: Moral Courage Can Build Communities

Social entrepreneurship—sustained efforts at community development— exemplifies a sense of moral courage in those who lead their businesses in this direction. Roland Kidwell provides examples from one small city in Wyoming of what social entrepreneurs can do to improve life for others when they have the moral courage to tackle social problems. He shares three examples of courageous social entrepreneurship that inspire us in our own efforts.

Lesson 8: Moral Courage Requires Personal Sacrifice

Judith White takes us to Southeast Asia to epitomize moral courage in a repressive military dictatorship. The moral courage she discusses is tightly coupled with physical courage, as the NGO leaders undertaking the battle for human rights in Burma live with chronic risk and sacrifice, putting themselves in harm's way and enduring hardships as they strive for a principled vision and a greater good.

Lesson 9: Prepare for the Opportunity to Voice Your Values

Mary C. Gentile supports those who want to act with moral courage by providing a series of guiding steps to undergird good intentions. Her emphasis is on reframing both situations and actions to keep us from feeling cornered by ethical problems in favor of being prepared to confront them with practiced strategies. By building on our personal strengths, we can develop the confidence and willingness to voice our values.

Lesson 10: Leaders Must Model Moral Courage

Proactive concern about ethics led the U.S. Navy to explore what promotes right action. From their interviews with military officers, Leslie E. Sekerka, Justin D. McCarthy, and Richard P. Bagozzi shed light on moral courage in civilian organizations. They identify personal governance practices, or components, of professional moral courage and emphasize that it is up to leaders to set the example for others to follow and to create an atmosphere that cultivates ethical action.

Lesson 11: Stand Up for Your Rights and Those of Your Coworkers

Doing what is right becomes a little easier when we realize that we have the weight of the law behind us. Judy Spain discusses the legal scaffolding that protects those who exercise moral courage as they undertake risky action on their own behalf or on the behalf of others. Title VII, the Family Medical Leave Act, the Occupational Health and Safety Act, and other, perhaps less familiar, pieces of legislation offer a measure of protection to those who choose to call upon them.

Lesson 12: Loyalty Can Drive Moral Courage

Speaking out is not a simple matter, Bernard F. Matt and Nasrin Shahinpoor remind us. Most organizations expect loyalty and conformity from their members and penalize those who express different viewpoints. But those who have the moral courage to dissent bring to light important perspectives that could benefit the organizations to which they are loyal. Organizations therefore need to recognize and encourage dissenters' truth telling.

Lesson 13: A Morally Courageous Coalition Can Move Mountains

Applying lessons from social movements, Debra R. Comer and Susan D. Baker underscore how collective action can make organizations more ethical. Although it may be difficult for individuals working independently to effect ethical change in organizations, we would do well to persuade others to collaborate with us in a morally courageous coalition. Together we can raise the ethical bar in our organizations.

Lesson 14: Create Contexts That Promote Courage

Dennis J. Moberg teaches us that how courage plays out varies with the challenges of a given situation and that both emotive intuitive ("hot") processes and deliberative rational ("cool") ones contribute to moral decisions. Our impulsive tendencies may take charge when urgent reaction is demanded. When we have more time to process cognitively, we may opt for analytical evaluation. Moberg urges managers to create organizational contexts that support employees' appropriate expressions of both "hot" and "cool" courage.

Where Do We Go from Here?

Lesson 1:   Consider others.
Lesson 2:   Question norms and institute reforms.
Lesson 3:   Recognize your weak spots.
Lesson 4:   Your values guide your actions.
Lesson 5:   Moral courage triggers change.
Lesson 6:   Personal convictions spur moral courage.
Lesson 7:   Moral courage can build communities.
Lesson 8:   Moral courage requires personal sacrifice.
Lesson 9:   Prepare for the opportunity to voice your values.
Lesson 10:   Leaders must model moral courage.
Lesson 11:   Stand up for your rights and those of your coworkers.
Lesson 12:   Loyalty can drive moral courage.
Lesson 13:   A morally courageous coalition can move mountains.
Lesson 14:   Create contexts that promote courage.

If we consider these fourteen lessons as a single unit, we find that we cannot reduce them much further. Moral courage demands vigilance, commitment, and frequent testing. Our best defense against personal failure seems to lie in preparation, in "offensive" rather than "defensive" action. It is not easy to take the initiative against temptation, conflict, and danger. It is not easy to forgo personal comfort for the greater good. It is not easy to put others before self.

We designed the four sections of this book to lead naturally into one another. We began by defining moral courage (as the resolve to do the right thing despite potentially negative consequences to ourselves) and explaining its importance in organizational contexts. Next we provided examples of people who have and have not exhibited moral courage. Then we offered guidelines for gaining the skills and knowledge that facilitate morally courageous action. We concluded with ways to change organizations to promote moral courage.

It is possible, it is doable, and it is critically important to act on our values consistently and deliberately. The last story we share with you is of someone who has put his principles into action, despite great personal sacrifice. Robert Lappin, one of the victims of Bernard Madoff's Ponzi scheme, is a Boston business owner and philanthropist whose personal worth was approximately $20 million as of December 2008. Mr. Lappin had $83 million invested in funds with Madoff, receiving annual returns of between 10 and 21 percent. These funds included the 401(k) plan for his employees, two plans for his charitable foundations, and two for limited partnership funds that held his and his children's money. After the discovery of the Ponzi scheme, all the money from the employee fund and the charitable foundations was gone, as was most of the money from his and his children's personal accounts. In order to ensure part of the retirement funds for his employees, Mr. Lappin and his children restored more than $5 million to the 401(k) plan from their own funds. This reduced Mr. Lappin's personal wealth to $2 million, one-tenth of what it had been just one year before. Mr. Lappin made his unexpected decision without the approval of his attorneys, but with the support of his children. Mr. Lappin is pleased about their response and about having passed "a test of moral character."[1]

We would not dream of proposing to tell people how to behave. Nor would we mandate that people lose all self-respect upon giving in to overwhelming circumstances—or even, occasionally, to the temptation of convenience. After all, each of us must live with the consequences of our actions. We would suggest, however, that people could do far worse than to emulate Robert Lappin, Nang Charm Tong, Joey Puettman, Frederic Whitehurst, Frank Serpico, or Elaine and David and to practice, prepare, and remain aware of their own potential for moral courage in the organizations in which they work and live.

Note

1. Swidey, 2009, 29.

Reference

Swidey, N. 2009. The good boss. *Boston Globe Magazine*, December 20, 28–29.

About the Editors and Contributors

Richard P. Bagozzi is a professor of behavioral science in management at the Ross School of Business and professor of clinical, social, and administrative sciences in the College of Pharmacy at the University of Michigan. A PhD graduate of Northwestern University, he also holds BSEE, MS, MBA, and MA degrees. Currently, he is doing research in ethics, knowledge sharing, and communities in organizations, among other areas.

Susan D. Baker is an assistant professor of management in the Earl G. Graves School of Business and Management at Morgan State University. She received her BA in English from Clark University, her MBA from the University of Baltimore, and her PhD in organizational behavior from George Washington University. Her research interests include business ethics, leadership, and followership, particularly the effect of follower behaviors on organizational outcomes.

David Callahan, a cofounder of Demos, now leads its International Program. His research and writing focus on global affairs and issues of values and ethics. He has authored several books, including *The Cheating Culture: Why More Americans Are Doing Wrong to Do Well* (Harcourt, 2004) and *The Moral Center: How We Can Reclaim Our Country from Die-Hard Extremists, Rogue Corporations, Hollywood Hacks, and Pretend Patriots* (Harcourt, 2006). He received his BA at Hampshire College and his PhD in politics at Princeton University.

Debra R. Comer is a professor of management in the Zarb School of Business at Hofstra University. She received her BA with honors in psychology from Swarthmore College and her MA, M Phil, and PhD in organizational behavior from Yale University. Her current research interests include ethical behavior in organizations, on-line learning, crisis management, and the use of popular culture in management education.

Mary C. Gentile is director of Giving Voice to Values (www.givingvoic-etovalues.org) and senior research scholar and lecturer at Babson College. She received her BA in English from the College of William and Mary and her MA and PhD in literature and film from the State University of New York at Buffalo. Her current work focuses on the development of an innovative global pedagogy for values-driven leadership behavior.

Al Gini is professor of business ethics and chair of the Department of Management in the School of Business Administration at Loyola University–Chicago. He is also the cofounder and associate editor of *Business Ethics Quarterly*, the journal of the Society for Business Ethics. His most recent books include *Why It's Hard to Be Good* (Routledge, 2006), *The Seven Deadly Sins Sampler: An Anthology* (Great Books Foundation, 2007), and *Even Deadlier: A Sequel* (Great Books Foundation, 2009).

Roland E. Kidwell is associate professor of management in the College of Business at the University of Wyoming, where he teaches courses in new ventures and entrepreneurial management. He has a PhD in business administration from Louisiana State University, an MBA from Radford University, and a BS in journalism from the University of Maryland. His research focuses on deviant behavior in various organizational contexts, including franchising and family businesses; human resource management in new ventures; and social entrepreneurship and business ethics.

Stephen M. Kohn, the executive director of the National Whistleblower Center (www.whistleblowers.org), has represented whistleblowers since 1984. He has authored seven books on whistleblowing, including the forthcoming *The Whistleblower's Handbook: A Step-by-Step Guide to Doing What's Right and Protecting Yourself* (Lyons Press, 2011). Mr. Kohn graduated magna cum laude from Boston University in 1979 and has an MA degree in political science from Brown University and a JD from Northeastern University.

G. Jeffrey MacDonald is an award-winning journalist and an ordained minister in the United Church of Christ. His reporting has appeared in four other books and several major national publications. His in-depth coverage of religion has earned six awards from the Religion Newswriters Association and the American Academy of Religion. A graduate of Yale Divinity School, he is the author of *Thieves in the Temple: The Christian Church and the Selling of the American Soul* (Basic Books, 2010).

Bernard F. Matt is a professor of English and of religion and philosophy, and director of liberal studies at Wilmington College–Blue Ash Branch. He received his BA in English and in theology, and his MA in English from Georgetown University, and his PhD in literature and religion from the Institute for the Liberal Arts at Emory University. His research interests include business ethics and corporate social responsibility.

Vice Admiral **Justin D. McCarthy**, SC, USN (ret.), is a retired 38-year navy veteran and independent defense consultant. He received a BS in engineering from Oakland University and an MS in management (with distinction) from the Naval Postgraduate School. He is currently a visiting executive lecturer and member of the Corporate Advisory Board of the Darden Graduate School of Business Administration. He also lectures in executive education programs at the Kenan-Flagler Business School and the Naval Postgraduate School.

Dennis J. Moberg is the Gerald and Bonita A. Wilkinson Professor of Management at Santa Clara University. He received a doctor of business administration degree from the University of Southern California. He is a past president of the Society for Business Ethics. His research interests include moral imagination, organizational virtues, and poverty alleviation.

Moses L. Pava is the Alvin H. Einbender Professor of Business Ethics and professor of accounting at Yeshiva University's Sy Sims School of Business. He received his BA from Brandeis University and his PhD from New York University. His research interests include business ethics, financial accounting, corporate social responsibility, and the interface between religion and business. He serves as editor of the *Research in Ethical Issues in Organizations* series (Emerald) and is on the editorial board of the *Journal of Business Ethics*.

Leslie E. Sekerka is an associate professor of organizational behavior in the Management and Psychology Departments at Menlo College, where she directs the Ethics in Action Research and Education Center. She is also an academic member of the Business and Organizational Ethics Partnership at Santa Clara University. She received her MA in communication theory from Cleveland State University and her PhD in organizational behavior from Case Western Reserve University. Her research focuses on adult moral development and strengths in the workplace.

Nasrin Shahinpoor is associate professor of economics and international studies at Hanover College. She received her BS in economics and banking sciences from the Institute of Banking Sciences, her MA in international affairs from Ohio University, and an MA and PhD in economics from the University of Cincinnati. Her current research interests include ethics and corporate social responsibility, poverty and discrimination, and microfinance.

Judith W. Spain is university counsel and professor of management at Eastern Kentucky University, where she formerly served as interim assistant dean for business and director of the MBA program in the College of Business and Technology. She teaches business law and business ethics, and her current research interests include ethics and employment law. She received her JD degree from Capital University Law School.

Gina Vega is professor of management and director of the Center for Entrepreneurial Activity in the Bertolon School of Business at Salem State University. She received her BA in romance languages and MA in urban studies from Queens College/CUNY and her PhD in entrepreneurship and organizational behavior from the Union Institute and Graduate School. She conducts her research in three complementary streams revolving around organizational structure: entrepreneurship and business transitions, ethics, and the evolving world of work.

Judith White teaches at the Leavey School of Business at Santa Clara University. She has a BA in social anthropology and an MS in rehabilitation counseling from San Francisco State University, an MA in interdisciplinary social sciences from Stanford, and a PhD in organizational behavior from Case Western Reserve University. Her research interests include Burma's democracy and human rights movement and the teaching and learning of business ethics.

Name Index

Subject Index